GEORGE MICHAEL

All The Top 40 Hits

Craig Halstead

First Edition

for Aaron

BY THE SAME AUTHOR ...

Christmas Number Ones

This book details the Christmas No.1 singles in the UK from 1940 to date, and also reveals the Christmas No.2 single and Christmas No.1 album. The book also features the Christmas No.1s in five other countries, namely Australia, Germany, Ireland, the Netherlands and the United States, and is up-dated annually in January.

The '*All The Top 40 Hits*' Series

This series documents, in chronological order, all the Top 40 Hit Singles and Albums by the featured artist:

ABBA
Annie Lennox
Bee Gees
Blondie
Boney M.
Boy George & Culture Club
Carpenters
Chi-Lites & Stylistics
Donna Summer
Janet Jackson
Kate Bush
Kim Wilde
Marvin Gaye
Michael Jackson
The Jacksons
(Jackson 5 / Jacksons / Jermaine / La Toya / Rebbie / 3T)
Olivia Newton-John
Sam Cooke & Otis Redding
Dame Shirley Bassey
Spice Girls
Tina Turner
Whitney Houston

The '*For The Record*' Series

The books in this series are more comprehensive than the 'All The Top 40 Hits' volumes, and typically include: The Songs (released & unreleased), The Albums, The Home Videos, The TV Shows/Films, The Concerts, Chartography & USA/UK Chart Runs, USA Discography & UK Discography.

Donna Summer
Janet Jackson
Michael Jackson
Whitney Houston

Fiction

The James Harris Trilogy

The Secret Library
Shadow Of Death
Twist Of Fate

Cataclysm

Book 1: The First 73 Days
Book 2: A New Year

Stand Alone Novel

Tyranny

THE FACE No. 64

AUGUST 1985 85p US $2.75

THE FACE

SWEAT

The grilling of
GEORGE MICHAEL
TONY PARSONS WARMS TO WHAM

The secret life of
MAX HEADROOM

FINE YOUNG CANNIBALS/DAVID OWEN/PAUL SMITH
LOOSE ENDS/THERESA RUSSELL/EUSTON FILMS
CHRISTOPHER LAMBERT/AMANDA LEAR/THOMAS DOLBY

ACKNOWLEDGEMENTS

I would like to thank Chris Cadman, my former writing partner, for helping to make my writing dreams come true. It's incredible to think how far we have come, since we got together to compile 'The Complete Michael Jackson Discography 1972-1990', for Adrian Grant's *Off the Wall* fan magazine in 1990. Good luck with your future projects, Chris ~ I will look forward to reading them!

Chris Kimberley, it's hard to believe we have been corresponding and exchanging chart action for 30+ years! A big thank you, I will always value your friendship.

I would like to thank the online music community, who so readily share and exchange information at: Chartbusters (chartbusters.forumfree.it), ukmix (ukmix.org/forums), Haven (fatherandy2.proboards.com) & Buzzjack (buzzjack.com/forums). In particular, I would like to thank:

- 'BrainDamagell' for posting current Canadian and USA charts on ukmix;
- 'chartwatcherdl' & 'wranglerjeans' for posting UK chart breakers on ukmix;
- 'flatdeejay' & 'ChartFreaky' for posting German chart action, and 'Indi' for answering my queries regarding Germany, on ukmix;
- 'grendizer' for posting Japan chart action on ukmix;
- 'Davidalic' for posting Spanish chart action on ukmix;
- 'Shakyfan', 'CZB', 'beatlened' & 'trebor' for posting Irish charts on ukmix;
- 'Hanboo' for posting and up-dating on request full UK & USA chart runs on ukmix. R.I.P., Hanboo, your posts on ukmix are sadly missed;

If you can fill any of the gaps in the chart information in this book, or have chart runs from a country not already featured in the book, I would love to hear from you. You can contact me via email at: **craig.halstead2@ntlworld.com** ~ thank you!

CONTENTS

BLITZ

VERY NICE

THE GOLDEN WORLD OF
GEORGE
MICHAEL

PLUS HOSTAGE TAKING
– NO WAY OUT
ROMEO GIGLI
JACKIE COLLINS
THE BISHOP OF DURHAM
NEAL ASCHERSON
RED ACTION

FILM, MUSIC, MEDIA & PRINT REVIEWED

INTRODUCTION

George Michael ~ as Georgios Kyriacos Panayiotou ~ was born on 25th June 1963 in East Finchley, Middlesex, England. His father Kyriacos 'Jack' Panayiotou was a Greek Cypriot restaurateur who had emigrated to England in the 1950s, and his English mother Lesley Angold (formerly Harrison) was a dancer. George had two older sisters, Yioda and Melanie.

When he appeared as a guest on the BBC's popular *Desert Island Discs* radio show, George revealed he first developed an interest in music as a young boy, following a head injury.

'At the age of about eight I had a head injury,' he said, 'and I know it sounds bizarre and unlikely, but it was quite a bad bang, and I had to get stitched up and stuff, but all my interests changed.'

Previously, George had been obsessed with insects and creepy crawlies.

'I used to get up at five o'clock in the morning,' he said, 'and go out into this field behind our garden and collect insects before everyone else got up and, suddenly, all I wanted to know about was music. It just seemed a very, very strange thing.'

A few years later, when he was in his early teens, George's family moved to Radlett, Hertfordshire, where he attended Bushey Meads School. It was here he first met Andrew Ridgeley, who shared George's ambition to become a musician.

George began his music career by working as a DJ at local schools and clubs, and by busking on the London Underground. Briefly, he formed a band called The Executive with Andrew Ridgeley, Andrew's brother Paul, Andrew Leaven, David Mortimer and Jamie Gould.

After The Executive split in 1981, George and Andrew Ridgeley decided to form a duo, and after much thought they agreed to call themselves Wham! According to Andrew, they were looking for 'something that captured the essence of what set us apart ~ our energy and our friendship ~ and then it came to us: Wham! Wham! was snappy, immediate, fun and boisterous, too'. Adding the exclamation mark to the duo's name was credited to the British graphic design studio, Stylorouge.

Keen to secure a record deal, George and Andrew borrowed a Fostex 4-track Portastudio, to record a demo tape of four songs they had written themselves, *Wham Rap!*, *Club Tropicana*, *Come On* and *Careless Whisper*. Andrew happened to frequent *The Three Crowns* pub in Hertfordshire, which is where Mark Dean from Inner Vision Records also liked to drink, so Andrew took a chance and handed him a demo tape. Mark Dean was sufficiently impressed to arrange a meeting with George and Andrew in February 1982, to offer them a deal.

'I'm going to offer Wham! a deal with my new label Inner Vision,' Mark Dean told George and Andrew. 'It's not a huge thing, I'm taking a punt. I'd like you to have a crack at recording a single or two, and we'll see what happens from there.'

Wham Rap!, the duo's debut single, was released on 16th June 1982 in the UK. The single wasn't playlisted by the BBC's Radio 1, not least because the Unsocial Mix of the song featured bad language, but the single was a very minor hit ~ it spent three weeks on the Top 100, but could only manage two non-consecutive weeks at no.99 and a week at no.100 before dropping off the chart.

The duo's second single, *Young Guns (Go For It!)*, was issued in October 1982. It fared better, but it was charting outside the all-important Top 40 when Wham! got a lucky break. At the time, the UK's premier music show *Top Of The Pops* normally only featured acts with Top 40 hits, but when one act cancelled at short notice, Wham! were offered their slot and readily accepted. The following week, *Young Guns (Go For It!)*, broke into the Top 40, and it went on to give Wham! a Top 3 smash.

As a follow-up, *Wham Rap!* was reissued, and this time it gave George and Andrew a Top 10 hit. The hits kept on coming, and Wham! released two hugely successful albums, *FANTASTIC* and *MAKE IT BIG*. However, George especially was increasingly keen to move away from the duo's primarily teenage girls audience, and make music aimed at a more mature, adult audience.

In early 1986, George and Andrew formally announced they were breaking up, with George commenting, 'I think it should be the most amicable split in pop history.' Before going their separate ways, the duo released one final single, *The Edge Of Heaven*, and a greatest hits album, *THE FINAL*. Wham! also played one farewell concert, also titled 'The Final', staged at London's Wembley Arena on 28th June 1986, which was attended by 72,000 people including Elton John, who joined George and Andrew on stage to perform *Candle In The Wind*. And, as an encore, Wham! were joined by Elton John and Duran Duran's Simon Le Bon, to sing *I'm Your Man*.

George released his debut solo album, *FAITH*, in 1987 ~ it was the first of only five studio albums he recorded, the most recent of which *PATIENCE* was issued in 2004. He released a live album, *SYMPHONICA*, in 2014, plus two greatest hits albums, *LADIES & GENTLEMEN – THE BEST OF GEORGE MICHAEL* in 1998 and *TWENTY FIVE* in 2006.

George won numerous awards over the years, including four BRIT Awards, one of them with Wham!:

- 1985 ~ Best British Group
- 1988 & 1997 ~ Best British Male
- 1991 ~ British Album of the Year: *LISTEN WITHOUT PREJUDICE VOL.1*

George won two Grammy Awards:

- 1988 ~ Best R&B Performance by a Duo or Group with Vocals: *I Knew You Were Waiting (For Me)*
- 1989 ~ Album of the Year: *FAITH*

George's authorised biography *Bare* was published in 1990, and he was inducted into the Songwriters Hall of Fame in 2017.

Tragically, George Michael was found dead in his bed at his Goring-on-Thames home on the morning of 25th December 2016 by his partner, Fadi Fawaz ~ he was aged just 53 years. His passing was eventually ruled as being due to natural causes, including heart failure and fatty liver. George was buried next to his mother in north London's Highgate Cemetery in a private ceremony on 29th March 2017.

Three years to the day after George's passing, his sister Melanie died. She was buried on the other side of her brother in Highgate Cemetery.

All The Top 40 Hits

For the purposes of this book, to qualify as a Top 40 hit, a single or album must have entered the Top 40 singles/albums chart in at least one of the following countries: Australia, Austria, Belgium, Canada, Finland, France, Germany, Ireland, Italy, Japan, the Netherlands, New Zealand, Norway, South Africa, Spain, Sweden, Switzerland, the United Kingdom, the United States of America and Zimbabwe.

The Top 40 singles and albums are detailed chronologically, according to the date they first entered the chart in one or more of the featured countries. Each Top 40 single and album is illustrated and the catalogue numbers and release dates are detailed, for the UK, followed by the chart action in each featured country, including any chart re-entries. Where full chart runs are unavailable, peak position and weeks on the chart are given.

For both singles, the main listing is followed by 'The Almost Top 40 Singles', which gives an honourable mention to singles that peaked between no.41 and no.50 in one or more countries (no albums were 'Almost Top 40 Albums'). There is also a points-based list of George's Top 40 Singles and Top 10 Albums, plus a fascinating 'Trivia' section at the end of each section which looks at the most successful singles and albums in each of the featured countries.

The Charts

The charts from an increasing number of countries are now freely available online, and for many countries it is possible to research weekly chart runs. Although this book focuses on Top 50 hits, longer charts runs are included where available, up to the Top 100 for countries where a Top 100 or longer is published.

Nowadays, charts are compiled and published on a weekly basis – in the past, however, some countries published charts on a bi-weekly or monthly basis, and most charts listed far fewer titles than they do today. There follows a summary of the current charts from each country featured in this book, together with relevant online resources and chart books.

Australia
Current charts: Top 100 Singles & Top 100 Albums.
Online resources: current weekly Top 50 Singles & Albums, but no archive, at **ariacharts.com.au**; archive of complete weekly charts dating back to 2001 at **pandora.nla.gov.au/tep/23790**; searchable archive of Top 50 Singles & Albums dating back to 1988 at **australian-charts.com**.
Books: 'Australian Chart Book 1940-1969', 'Australian Chart Book 1970-1992' & 'Australian Chart Book 1993-2009' by David Kent.

Austria
Current charts: Top 75 Singles & Top 75 Albums.
Online resources: current weekly charts and a searchable archive dating back to 1965 for singles and 1973 for albums at **austriancharts.at**.

Belgium
Current charts: Top 50 Singles & Top 200 Albums for two different regions, Flanders (the Dutch speaking north of the country) and Wallonia (the French speaking south).
Online resources: current weekly charts and a searchable archive dating back to 1956 for singles and 1995 for albums at **ultratop.be**.
Book: '*Het Belgisch Hitboek – 40 Jaar Hits In Vlaanderen*' by Robert Collin.
Note: the information in this book for Belgium relates to the Flanders region.

Canada
Current charts: Hot 100 Singles & Top 100 Albums.
Online resources: weekly charts and a searchable archive of weekly charts from the Nielsen SoundScan era at **billboard.com/biz** (subscription only); incomplete archive of weekly RPM charts dating back to 1964 for singles and 1967 for albums at **https://www.bac-lac.gc.ca/eng/Pages/home.aspx** (search 'RPM charts'). Scans of RPM Weekly magazine can be viewed at **https://3345.ca/rpm-magazine/** and **https://worldradiohistory.com/RPM.htm** (RPM folded in 2000).
Book: 'The Canadian Singles Chart Book 1975-1996' by Nanda Lwin.

Finland

Current charts: Top 20 Singles & Top 50 Albums.

Online resources: current weekly charts and a searchable archive dating back to 1995 at **finnishcharts.com**.

Book: '*Sisältää Hitin*' by Timo Pennanen.

France

Current charts: Top 200 Singles & Top 200 Albums.

Online resources: current weekly and archive charts dating back to 2001 can be found at **snepmusique.com**; a searchable archive dating back to 1984 for singles and 1997 for albums is at **lescharts.com**; searchable archive for earlier/other charts at **infodisc.fr**.

Book: '*Hit Parades 1950-1998*' by Daniel Lesueur.

Note: Compilation albums were excluded from the main chart until 2008, when a Top 200 Comprehensive chart was launched.

Germany

Current charts: Top 100 Singles & Top 100 Albums.

Online resources: current weekly and searchable archive charts dating back to 1977 can be found at **offiziellecharts.de/charts**.

Books: '*Deutsche Chart Singles 1956-1980*', '*Deutsche Chart Singles 1981-90*' & '*Deutsche Chart Singles 1991-1995*' published by Taurus Press.

Ireland

Current charts: Top 100 Singles & Top 100 Albums.

Online resources: current weekly charts are published at IRMA (**irma.ie**); there is a searchable archive for Top 30 singles (entry date, peak position and week on chart only) at **irishcharts.ie**; an annual Irish Chart Thread has been published annually from 2007 to date, plus singles charts from 1967 to 1999 and album charts for 1993, 1995-6 and 1999, have been published at ukmix (**ukmix.org**); weekly album charts from March 2003 to date can be found at **acharts.us/ireland_albums_top_75**.

Note: the information presented in this book is for singles only.

Italy

Current charts: Top 100 Singles & Top 100 Albums.

Online resources: weekly charts and a weekly chart archive dating back to 2005 at **fimi.it**; a searchable archive of Top 20 charts dating back to 2000 at **italiancharts.com**; pre-2000 information has been posted at ukmix (**ukmix.org**).

Books: *Musica e Dischi Borsa Singoli 1960-2019* & *Musica e Dischi Borsa Album 1964-2019* by Guido Racca.

Note: as the FIMI-Neilsen charts didn't start until 1995, the information detailed in this book before this date is from the Musica & Dischi chart.

Japan

Current charts: Top 200 Singles & Top 300 Albums.

Online resources: current weekly charts (in Japanese) at **oricon.co.jp/rank**; selected information is available on the Japanese Chart/The Newest Charts and Japanese Chart/The Archives threads at **ukmix.org**.

Netherlands
Current charts: Top 100 Singles & Top 100 Albums.
Online resources: current weekly charts and a searchable archive dating back to 1956 for singles and 1969 for albums at **dutchcharts.nl**.

New Zealand
Current charts: Top 40 Singles & Top 40 Albums.
Online resources: current weekly charts and a searchable archive dating back to 1975 at **nztop40.co.nz**.
Book: 'The Complete New Zealand Music Charts 1966-2006' by Dean Scapolo.

Norway
Current charts: Top 20 Singles & Top 40 Albums.
Online resources: current weekly charts and a searchable archive dating back to 1958 for singles and 1967 for albums at **norwegiancharts.com**.

South Africa
Current charts: no official charts.
Online resources: none known.
Book: 'South Africa Chart Book' by Christopher Kimberley.
Notes: the singles chart was discontinued in early 1989, as singles were no longer being manufactured in significant numbers. The albums chart only commenced in December 1981, and was discontinued in 1995, following re-structuring of the South African Broadcasting Corporation.

Spain
Current charts: Top 50 Singles & Top 100 Albums.
Online resources: current weekly charts and a searchable archive dating back to 2005 at **spanishcharts.com**.
Book: *'Sólo éxitos 1959-2002 Año a Año'* by Fernando Salaverri.

Sweden
Current charts: Top 60 Singles & Top 100 Albums.
Online resources: current weekly charts and a searchable archive dating back to 1975 at **swedishcharts.com**.

Switzerland
Current charts: Top 75 Singles & Top 100 Albums.
Online resources: current weekly charts and a searchable archive dating back to 1968 for singles and 1983 for albums at **hitparade.ch**.

UK

Current Charts: Top 100 Singles & Top 200 Albums.

Online resources: current weekly and archive charts dating back to 1960 at **officialcharts.com**; weekly charts are posted on a number of music forums, including ukmix (**ukmix.org**), Haven (**fatherandy2.proboards.com**) and Buzzjack (**buzzjack.com**).

Note: weekly Top 200 album charts are only available via subscription from UK ChartsPlus (**ukchartsplus.co.uk**).

USA

Current charts: Hot 100 Singles & Billboard 200 Albums.

Online resources: current and archive weekly charts are available at **billboard.com** (some archive charts via subscription only); weekly charts are also posted on a number of music forums, including ukmix (**ukmix.org**), Haven (**fatherandy2.proboards.com**) and Buzzjack (**buzzjack.com**).

Note: older 'catalog' albums (i.e. albums older than two years) were excluded from the Billboard 200 before December 2009, so the chart didn't accurately reflect the country's best-selling albums. Therefore, in this book Billboard's Top Comprehensive Albums chart has been used from December 2003 to December 2009, as this did include all albums. In December 2009 the Top Comprehensive Albums chart became the Billboard 200, and Billboard launched a new Top Current Albums chart – effectively, the old Billboard 200.

Zimbabwe

Current charts: no official charts.

Online resources: none known.

Books: 'Zimbabwe Singles Chart Book' & 'Zimbabwe Albums Chart Book' by Christopher Kimberley.

Note: In the past, there was often one or more weeks over Christmas and New Year when no new album chart was published in some countries. In such cases, the previous week's chart has been used to complete a chart run. Similarly, where a bi-weekly or monthly chart was in place, for chart runs these are counted at two and four weeks, respectively.

All The Top 40 Singles

August 20, 1983   40p

Soft Cell — is this the end?

RECORD MIRROR

Big Country, OMD dates!

WHAM!

Galaxy

Whitesnake

H$_2$O

Chopper **H**arris

Isley **B**rothers

STAR SONGS

Limahl

We style **Paul Young's** new look

Paul Young pic by Jill Furmanovsky

Wham! pic by Scope Features

1 ~ Young Guns (Go For It)

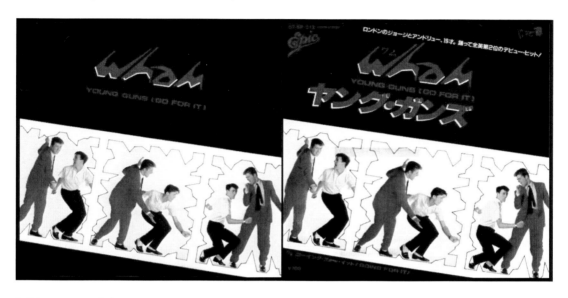

UK: Inner Vision IVL A2766 (1982).
  B-side: *Going For It!*

16.10.82: 72-48-52-42-24-10-4-**3**-4-8-13-13-14-18-29-41-66

Australia
17.01.83: peaked at no.**4**, charted for 18 weeks

Belgium
25.12.82: 33-31-24-14-**8-8**-9-14-18

Finland
01.83: peaked at no.**13**, charted for 4 weeks

Germany
24.01.83: 53-48-43-43-46-21-**20**-26-26-34-37-51-51-63-57-72

Ireland
28.11.82: 12-6-**3**-12-12-12

Netherlands
18.12.82: 42-15-12-**9**-11-11-**9**-16-17-31-50

New Zealand
20.03.83: 11-6-6-**4**-5-6-11-10-16-20-29-31

Norway
12.03.83: **10**

Sweden
22.02.83: 8-4-**1**-3-5-7-17 (bi-weekly)

#	LW		Artist Title	Label Company	Prefix Suffix	W
			SVERIGETOPPLISTAN - SINGLES TOP 100 ← 1983-03-22 → 1983 ⌄ 22.03.1983 ⌄ Show			
1	4	^	**Wham!** Young Guns (Go For It)	CBS CBS	CBS 2766	3
2	1	⌄	**F-R David** Words	Carrere EMI	CARS 49963	8
3	3	›	**Joe Cocker & Jennifer Warnes** Up Where We Belong	Island GDC/Sonet	WIP 6830	8

Zimbabwe
21.05.83: peaked at no.**9**, charted for 15 weeks

George wrote *Young Guns (Go For It!)*, and he and Andrew Ridgeley recorded it for Wham!'s debut album, *FANTASTIC*, which was released in 1983. The song was recorded at London's Maison Rouge Studio, and featured backing vocals by the American singer Lynda Hayes.

The theme of the song was a teenage boy, who is concerned his best friend is becoming too committed to his girlfriend, when the teenage boy thinks he should be enjoying himself instead.

Young Guns (Go For It!) was issued as Wham!'s second single, after *Wham Rap!*, but it was the first to achieve Top 40 status anywhere ~ thanks in part to a lucky break.

At the time, it was rare for acts with singles outside the Top 40 to be invited to appear on the UK's premier music show, *Top Of The Pops*. But when an act pulled out at short notice, having leapt from no.52 to no.42 with *Young Guns (Go For It!)*, Wham! were invited to fill the vacant slot, and readily accepted. They were joined on the show by backing singers Dee C. Lee and Shirlie Holliman.

As a result of Wham!'s *Top Of The Pops* appearance, *Young Guns (Go For It!)* entered the all important Top 40 at no.24, and peaked at no.3 three weeks later. Elsewhere, the single hit no.1 in Sweden, and achieved no.3 in Ireland, no.4 in Australia and New Zealand, no.8 in Belgium, no.9 in the Netherlands and Zimbabwe, no.10 in Norway, no.13 in Finland and no.20 in Germany.

2 ~ Wham Rap! (Enjoy What You Do)

UK: Inner Vision IVL A2442 (1982 & 1983).
  B-side: *Wham Rap! (Club Mix)* (1982), *Wham Rap! (Enjoy What You Do) (Special Club Re-Mix)* (1983).

17.07.82: 99-100-99
8.01.83: 87-63-41-34-11-9-**8**-10-14-23-39-54

Australia
18.04.83: peaked at no.**9**, charted for 18 weeks

Belgium
19.03.83: 37-**12-12**-16-16-20-32

Germany
11.04.83: 54-47-41-**17**-33-34-44-40-62-64-x-75

Ireland
6.01.83: 21-14-**13**-24

Netherlands
5.03.83: 29-11-11-**9**-18-21-31-49

New Zealand
22.05.83: 32-26-**18**-26-34-28

Wham Rap!, as it was originally titled, was the first song George and Andrew Ridgeley wrote together, after their band The Executive split. In part, the lyrics were inspired by George being given an ultimatum by his father: Get yourself a job or get out of this house.

'When we began working on it and putting the whole thing down on tape,' said George, 'we could see from the way it was working out that it was more than just a straightforward song. The lyrics and the entire structure of the thing presented its way to us in the format of a small playlet.'

George and Andrew recorded a rough demo of *Wham Rap!*, along with *Club Tropicana, Come On* and *Careless Whisper*, in February 1982. The following month, after hearing the demo tape, Inner Vision paid for George and Andrew to record a proper demo of the song, which they did at Holloway's Halligan Band Centre.

Wham Rap! was released as Wham!'s debut single on 16th June 1982 in the UK. At the time, George was calling himself George Panos, so the songwriting credit on the record label was 'Panos/Ridgeley'.

George was sitting in songwriter David Austin's living room when he said, 'I like your dad's name, Michael Mortimer. I really like Michael and my dad's brother is called Michael. Also, I had a friend at school, a Greek kid whose name was Michael. So … what about Michael? I thought it was a nice name. It rolled off the tongue and I didn't have to give up on the Greekness totally.'

Wham Rap! gave George and Andrew their first Top 100 chart entry, but during a three week chart run the single spent two non-consecutive weeks at no.99, but climbed no higher.

The single's chances weren't helped when on the 12" single, the Unsocial Mix of *Wham Rap!*, which featured bad language throughout, was mistakenly released as the A-side, with the actual A-side ~ the Social Mix ~ as the B-side.

Following the success of *Young Guns (Go For It!)*, Inner Vision tried again, by reissuing *Wham Rap!* as *Wham Rap! (Enjoy What You Do) (Special U.S. Remix)*. This time, George and Andrew promoted the single with a music video, which was filmed in February 1983. In it, George and Andrew appeared as two unemployed teenagers wearing leather jackets, as they roamed the streets of London.

Wham Rap! (Enjoy What You Do) gave Wham! their second Top 10 hit in the UK, where it peaked at no.8. Elsewhere, the single charted at no.9 in Australia and the Netherlands, no.12 in Belgium, no.13 in Ireland, no.17 in Germany and no.18 in New Zealand.

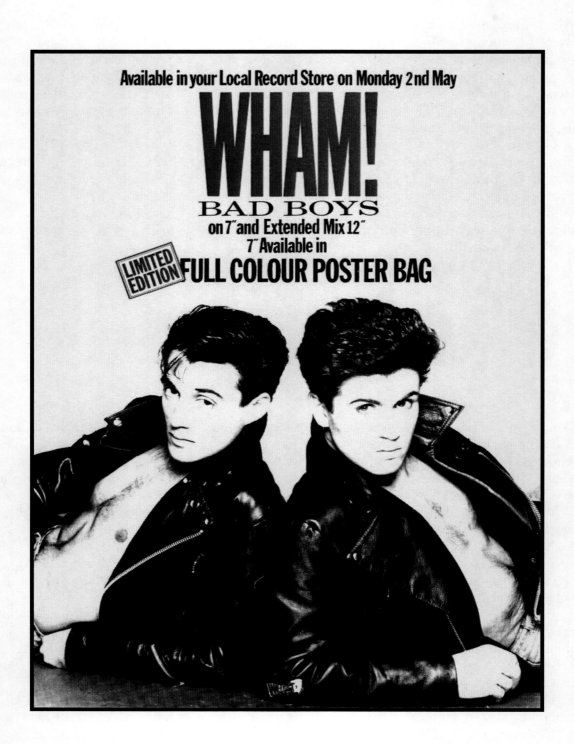

3 ~ Bad Boys

UK: Inner Vision A3143 (1983).
  B-side: *Bad Boys (Instrumental)*.

14.05.83: 37-12-5-**2-2**-3-5-9-16-24-36-45-54-75-x-95

Pos	LW		Title, Artist		Peak Pos	WoC
1	7 ↑		EVERY BREATH YOU TAKE THE POLICE	A&M	1	2
2	5 ↑		BAD BOYS WHAM!	INNERVISION	2	4
3	1 ↓		CANDY GIRL NEW EDITION	LONDON	1	8

Australia
11.07.83: peaked at no.**9**, charted for 13 weeks

Belgium
9.07.83: 35-25-20-15-**8**-22-38

Finland
06.83: peaked at no.**5**, charted for 8 weeks

Germany
6.06.83: 58-45-30-17-15-14-**12-12**-13-14-16-23-32-44-46-58-70

Ireland
22.05.83: 19-8-**3-3**-6-9-23

Japan
21.12.83: peaked at no.**64**, charted for 17 weeks

Netherlands
25.06.83: 42-28-28-27-**26**-33-45

New Zealand
31.07.83: 41-21-18-13-13-**10**-11-12-14-21-29-37-50

Norway
28.05.83: **8**
23.07.83: 10

Sweden
31.05.83: 16-**11**-14-17-15 (bi-weekly)

Switzerland
10.07.83: 14-7-**6**-8-12

USA
20.08.83: 90-80-69-62-**60-60**-73-77-97

George wrote *Bad Boys*, and he recorded the song with Andrew Ridgeley at London's Maison Rouge Studios, for Wham!'s debut album, *FANTASTIC*. George was only 19 when he wrote the song, and he penned the lyrics from the point of view of a rebellious teenager whose parents are always having a go at him.

Bad Boys was released as Wham!'s third single, and George and Andrew promoted it with a music video directed by Mike Brady. In it, George's father was played by 18 year old Anthony Souter, who was made up to look much older.

'We look like a pair of wankers in it,' George later reflected. 'How can anybody look at those two people on screen doing what we were doing and think it's good?'

Bad Boys gave Wham! their biggest hit to date in the UK ~ the single spent two weeks at no.2, but was kept off the top spot by The Police with *Every Breathe You Take*.

Around the world, *Bad Boys* achieved no.3 in Ireland, no.5 in Finland, no.6 in Switzerland, no.8 in Belgium and Norway, no.9 in Australia, no.10 in New Zealand, no.11 in Sweden, no.12 in Germany and no.26 in the Netherlands. The single was also a minor hit ~ Wham!'s first ~ in Japan and the United States, peaking at no.64 and no.60, respectively. In the United States, initial pressings of *Bad Boys* were credited to Wham! U.K..

Despite its success, George quickly came to hate *Bad Boys* ~ he once dismissed it as 'an albatross round my neck', and he deliberately left it off Wham's 1997 compilation, *THE BEST OF WHAM!*

4 ~ Club Tropicana

UK: Inner Vision A3613 (1983).
  B-side: *Blue*.

30.07.83: 27-10-5-**4**-5-6-11-18-25-42-59

Australia
31.10.83: peaked at no.**60**, charted for 11 weeks

Belgium
29.10.83: 39-27-27-27-**23**-27

Germany
5.09.83: 20-18-**13**-15-15-18-25-34-52-47-57-69

Ireland
31.07.83: 30-16-5-**4**-10-14-24

Japan
21.09.83: peaked at no.**62**, charted for 8 weeks

Netherlands
1.10.83: 28-**14-14**-16-15-23-41-48

New Zealand
30.10.83: 27-27-28-26-27-29-**25-25-25-25-25**-44-45

Norway
3.09.83: **10**

South Africa
10.12.83: peaked at no.**9**, charted for 10 weeks

Club Tropicana was the second song George and Andrew Ridgeley wrote together, after *Wham Rap!*, and like *Wham Rap!* it was one of the songs the duo recorded a rough demo of, before they signed with Inner Vision and became Wham!

The song was largely written in Andrew's living room, and unlike the duo's previous singles it had a light, summery feel to it, and was inspired by the Club 18-30 package holidays that were so popular at the time. George and Andrew recorded *Club Tropicana* at London's Maison Rouge Studios, for their *FANTASTIC* album.

Club Tropicana was issued as the fourth single from the album. George and Andrew promoted the release with a music video that explored the song's theme, and was filmed at Pikes Hotel in Ibiza, Spain. The promo was directed by Duncan Gibbins, and co-starred Pepsi & Shirlie (*aka* Helen DeMacque & Shirlie Holliman).

It was while in Ibiza that George had his first sexual encounter with another man, but at the time he was unsure if he was bisexual or gay. He confided in Shirlie first, then told Andrew, and they were both fine with it ~ however, it would be many years before George came out publically.

Club Tropicana continued Wham!'s run of Top 10 hits in the UK, where it peaked at no.4, sales boosted by the issue of a 7" picture disc single.

Club Tropicana was also a no.4 hit in Ireland, and charted at no.9 in South Africa, no.10 in Norway, no.13 in Germany, no.14 in the Netherlands, no.23 in Belgium and no.25 in New Zealand. The single was also a minor hit in Australia and Japan, where it achieved no.60 and no.62, respectively.

5 ~ Club Fantastic Megamix

UK: Inner Vision A3586 (1983).
  B-side: *A Ray Of Sunshine (Instrumental Mix)*.

3.12.83: 30-18-**15**-21-21-25-27-71

Germany
2.01.84: **56**-73-74-62

Ireland
11.12.83: 21-**16-16-16**

Netherlands
7.01.84: **44**-49

Legal issues with their recording contract meant George and Andrew Ridgeley were battling their record company, wanting to be released from their contract, when Inner Vision released this medley of three songs from Wham!'s *FANTASTIC* album as a single. The three songs, mixed together by Alan Couthard with Inner Vision's Mike Dean's approval, were *A Ray Of Sunshine*, *Love Machine* and *Come On*. George and Andrew publically denounced the release, and urged their fans not to buy it.

    Club Fantastic Megamix was the first Wham! single, excluding the original release of *Wham Rap!*, to miss the Top 10 in the UK, where it peaked at no.15. Elsewhere, the single achieved no.16 in Ireland, no.44 in the Netherlands and no.56 in Germany, but it failed to chart in many countries.

6 ~ Wake Me Up Before You Go-Go

UK: Epic A 4440 (1984).
  B-side: *Wake Me Up Before You Go-Go (Instrumental).*

26.05.84: 4-**1**-**1**-2-2-5-9-18-22-28-30-36-46-46-62-69

Pos	LW	Title, Artist			Peak Pos	WoC
1	4 ↑		WAKE ME UP BEFORE YOU GO GO WHAM!	EPIC	1	2
2	3 ↑		LET'S HEAR IT FOR THE BOY DENIECE WILLIAMS	CBS	2	6
3	1 ↓		THE REFLEX DURAN DURAN	EMI	1	6

Australia
25.06.84: peaked at no.**1** (7), charted for 24 weeks

Austria
15.07.84: 14-**6**-9-9-16-20 (bi-weekly)

Finland
06.84: peaked at no.**3**, charted for 16 weeks

Belgium
9.06.84: 36-33-30-15-2-2-**1-1-1-1**-2-3-4-8-16-27

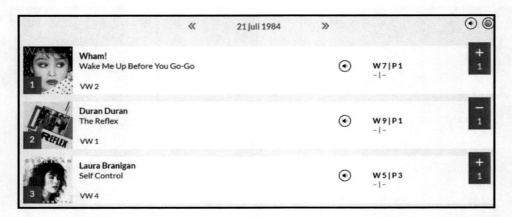

Canada
25.08.84: 97-69-59-41-27-20-16-14-9-5-2-**1-1-1-1**-3-4-5-5-7-12-14-19-23-31-34-38-47-
54-57-60-73

France
3.11.84: 31-27-29-**17**-21-19-20-20-23-23-23-19-31-31-34-32-32-x-48
31.12.16: 27-46

Germany
18.06.84: 58-11-5-4-**2-2**-3-5-6-9-11-14-19-29-33-44-51

Ireland
3.06.84: 7-**1-1**-2-7-17

Italy
29.09.84: peaked at no.**24**, charted for 4 weeks

Netherlands
9.06.84: 44-43-28-10-5-3-2-2-**1**-2-4-7-9-26-38-46

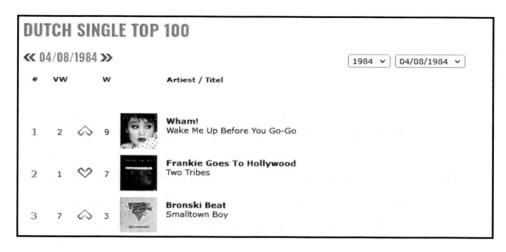

New Zealand
22.07.84: 45-13-6-4-**2**-3-3-5-10-12-33-39-50-x-45

Norway
23.06.84: 6-6-2-2-**1-1-1-1-1-1-1-1-1**-5-8-7

South Africa
22.09.84: peaked at no.**9**, charted for 17 weeks

Spain
29.10.84: peaked at no.**15**, charted for 16 weeks

Switzerland
17.06.84: 16-x-5-4-3-3-**2**-3-**2**-5-5-10-11-12-21-29

WHAM! MAKES IT BIG!

WHAM!'s "WAKE ME UP BEFORE YOU GO-GO" IS #1 IN AMERICA!

Thank you radio and retail everywhere for giving Wham! their first American number one single. And congratulations George and Andrew!

Columbia Records.

Sweden
26.06.84: 12-2-**1**-2-3-6-8-14 (bi-weekly)

USA
8.09.84: 80-59-48-41-32-26-13-6-5-4-**1-1-1**-2-8-11-11-27-41-55-69-77-92-98

Zimbabwe
11.08.84: peaked at no.**5**, charted for 7 weeks

After settling out-of-court with Inner Vision, George and Andrew Ridgeley signed with Epic Records internationally, and with Epic's sister company Columbia Records in North America.

George was inspired to write *Wake Me Up Before You Go-Go* by a scribbled note Andrew left for his parents, which was supposed to read 'Wake me up before you go'. However, when he noticed he'd accidentally written 'up' twice, Andrew deliberately finished the note with a second 'go', making the note read 'Wake me up up before you go go'.

George wrote and produced *Wake Me Up Before You Go-Go*, and Wham! recorded it for their second album, *MAKE IT BIG*, which was released in November 1984. The song was recorded at London's Sarm West Studio 2 with a live rhythm section, and George confirmed the song was completed in one take, with no overdubs or anything added later.

'I just wanted to make a really energetic pop record that had all the best elements of Fifties and Sixties records,' he said, 'combined with our attitude and our approach, which is obviously more uptempo and a lot younger than some of those records … I'd done a demo at home that just had a bass line and a vocal on it. Usually, I write the record in my head. I know what all the parts are going to be and I sing them to all our musicians, and it was great. We actually did it as a rehearsal. We used a LinnDrum because the drummer was late, and it was such a good track that we kept it.'

Wake Me Up Before You Go-Go was chosen as the lead single from *MAKE IT BIG*, and George and Andrew promoted its release with a music video directed by Andy Morahan, which also featured Pepsi & Shirlie. The promo was filmed at London's Brixton Academy before an audience of mostly older teenagers, and in it George and Andrew wore Katharine Hamnett T-shirts with 'CHOOSE LIFE' and 'GO GO' logos.

'It's a bit different, isn't it?' said George. 'It's more of a club record than the last few. Hopefully, it should get us back some of our older fans. It's more us. It's more … more about sex.'

Wake Me Up Before You Go-Go made its chart debut in the UK at no.4, and the following week it gave Wham! their first no.1, deposing Duran Duran's *The Reflex*. The single was equally successful around the world, and hit no.1 in Australia, Belgium, Canada, Ireland, the Netherlands, Norway, Sweden and the United States.

Elsewhere, *Wake Me Up Before You Go-Go* achieved no.2 in Germany, New Zealand and Switzerland, no.3 in Finland, no.5 in Zimbabwe, no.6 in Austria, no.9 in South Africa, no.15 in Spain, no.17 in France and no.24 in Italy.

7 ~ Careless Whisper

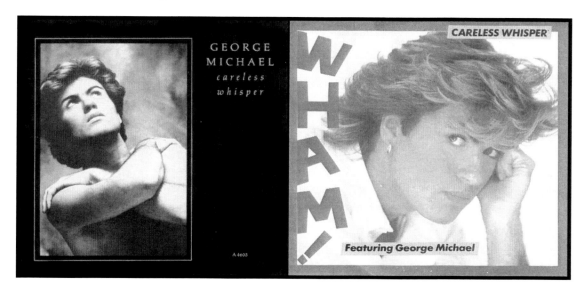

UK: Epic A 4603 (1984).
  B-side: *Careless Whisper (Instrumental)*.

4.08.84: 12-2-**1-1-1**-2-2-3-5-11-18-20-26-34-38-52-60-x-x-x-89-92-86-x-x-100

Pos	LW		Title, Artist		Peak Pos	WoC
1	2 ↑		CARELESS WHISPER GEORGE MICHAEL	EPIC	1	3
2	4 ↑		AGADOO BLACK LACE	FLAIR	2	13
3	1 ↓		TWO TRIBES FRANKIE GOES TO HOLLYWOOD	ZTT	1	10

5.01.17: 44-55

Australia
3.09.84: peaked at no.**1** (4), charted for 28 weeks

Austria
15.10.84: 6-**2-2**-7-12-23-30 (bi-weekly)

Belgium
1.09.84: 33-13-4-**2-2-2-2-2-2-2**-5-10-12-30

Canada
1.12.84: 88-73-59-43-43-28-14-7-**1-1**-2-3-3-4-4-4-5-7-9-10-23-24-24-33-48-62-74-82-87

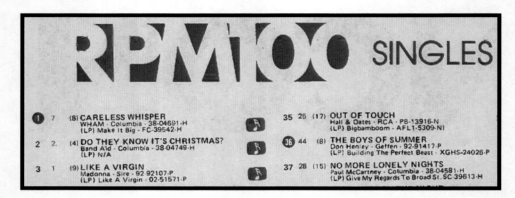

14.01.17: 36

Finland
08.84: Peaked at no.**2**, charted for 16 weeks

France
10.11.84: 43-31-25-13-10-4-6-5-5-4-4-4-4-**3-3**-4-7-14-15-19-18-20-22-37-43
31.12.16: 7-21-53-75

Germany
10.09.84: 59-17-11-5-5-4-**3-3**-4-6-9-11-17-25-32-46-52-53-57-70

Ireland
12.08.84: 6-**1-1-1**-2-2-3-9-11-19
29.12.16: 73-91

Italy
27.10.84: peaked at no.**1** (9), charted for 26 weeks
29.12.16: 39

Japan
25.08.84: peaked at no.**12**, charted for 26 weeks

New Zealand
23.09.84: 35-16-5-**3-3-3-3-3-3-3**-5-7-9-9-9-9-9-32-33-22-30-43-46-47

Norway
18.08.84: 10-4-4-4-3-**2-2-2-2-2-2**-3-4-4-6-9

Netherlands
25.08.84: 23-**1-1-1-1-1-1-1**-3-3-5-11-10-27-31-37

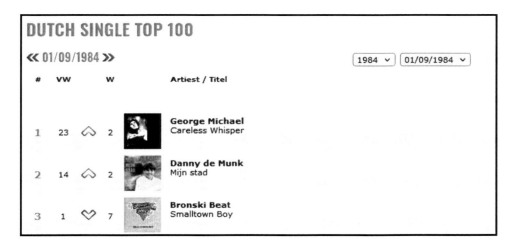

31.12.16: 73

South Africa
2.11.84: peaked at no.**1** (3), charted for 21 weeks

Spain
24.12.84: peaked at no.**11**, charted for 11 weeks

Sweden
14.09.84: 16-4-3-3-3-**2-2**-3-6-9 (bi-weekly)

Switzerland
16.09.84: 6-2-**1-1-1-1**-2-2-3-5-4-12-16-12-23-27

1.01.17: 28-77

USA
22.12.84: 37-37-23-20-10-5-3-3-**1-1-1**-2-7-12-17-27-35-53-68-70-95

The Hot 100				WEEK OF FEBRUARY 16, 1985			
THIS WEEK				AWARD	LAST WEEK	PEAK POS.	WKS ON CHART
1		**Careless Whisper** Wham! Featuring George Michael	+		**3**	**1**	**9**
2		**I Want To Know What Love Is** Foreigner	+		1	1	11
3		**Easy Lover** Philip Bailey With Phil Collins	+		2	2	13

Zimbabwe
13.10.84: peaked at no.**3**, charted for 15 weeks

Careless Whisper, along with *Wham Rap!*, *Come On* and *Club Tropicana*, was a song George and Andrew Ridgeley recorded a rough demo of in Andrew's living room, when they were looking to secure a recording contract.

'I was on my way to DJ at the Bel Air (a restaurant near Bushey, Hertfordshire) when I wrote *Careless Whisper*,' said George. 'I have always written on buses, trains and in cars. It always happens on journeys … With *Careless Whisper*, I remember exactly where it first came to me, where I came up with the sax line. I remember I was handing the money over to the guy on the bus and I got this line, the sax line. I wrote it totally in my head. I worked on it for about three months in my head.'

George and Andrew's first demo of *Careless Whisper* was rushed, as they spent most of the session working on *Wham Rap!* Having attracted the attention of Inner Vision's Mark Dean, they recorded a second demo of the song on 24th March 1982 at Halligan Band Centre in Holloway, London. Later the same day, the duo signed their first recording contract.

'One of the most incredible moments of my life was hearing *Careless Whisper* demoed properly,' George later recalled, 'with a band, a sax and everything. It was ironic that we signed the contract with Mark (Dean) that day, the day I finally believed we had number one material. That same day we signed it all away …'

After working on *Careless Whisper* with Jerry Wexler at the Muscle Shoals Sound Studio in Sheffield, Alabama, George returned to London, and re-recorded the song with a live rhythm section at London's Sarm West Studio 2, with 'loads of stuff bunged on later'.

'Jerry Wexler did one recording of *Careless Whisper* with me,' George confirmed. 'Then we remixed that, which meant re-shooting the video, and then we completely re-did the track about four weeks before it was due to be released.'

Andrew Ridgeley was credited with co-writing *Careless Whisper*, but on record his only contribution was playing acoustic guitar ~ all the vocals, lead and backing, were by George alone. Thus, when it was chosen as the follow-up to *Wake Me Up Before You Go-Go*, it was decided the artist credit should be George Michael, rather than Wham! However, in a few countries ~ including Canada and the United States ~ the single was credited to Wham! featuring George Michael.

The music video for *Careless Whisper* was originally filmed on location in Miama, Florida, with George playing a man who is having an affair. His partner was played by Lisa Stahl, while the woman he's having an affair with was played by Madeline Andrews-Hodge. The promo was directed by Duncan Gibbins, and featured a cameo appearance by Andrew Ridgeley.

However, the video shoot didn't go well ~ some footage was lost, for example, and had to be re-shot. As a result, back in England further footage of George singing *Careless Whisper* was shot at London's Lyceum Theatre, and this footage was spliced with scenes from the original video, to make the final version.

Careless Whisper proved even more popular than *Wake Me Up Before You Go-Go* with the record buying public, and the single hit no.1 in Australia, Canada, Ireland, Italy, the Netherlands, South Africa, Switzerland, the UK and the United States. The single also achieved no.2 in Austria, Belgium, Finland, Norway and Sweden, no.3 in France, Germany, New Zealand and Zimbabwe, no.11 in Spain and no.12 in Japan.

'*Careless Whisper* was written when I was seventeen' said George, 'and I had not really experienced anything that strong in my life, so it was a bit precocious. Yet it really seemed to connect with people, which is a wonderful thing and a marvellous coincidence, you know, but basically I see that song as a bunch of images which I threw together to represent the fact that at the time I was seeing one girl and then I started seeing another, and it was just the guilt in between those two periods.'

There have been numerous cover versions of *Careless Whisper* over the years, including three hit versions:

- Sarah Washington took a dance version to no.45 in the UK in 1993.

- 2Play took their cover to no.29 in the UK in 2004.

- Seether, an alternative rock band from South Africa, took their rock version to no.63 on the Hot 100 in the United States in 2007.

For all its success, George was never overly fond of *Careless Whisper*, and in 1991 he stated the song wasn't an integral part of his emotional development.

'It disappoints me that you can write a lyric very flippantly,' he said, 'and not a particularly good lyrics, and it can mean so much to so many people ~ that's disillusioning for a writer.'

8 ~ Freedom

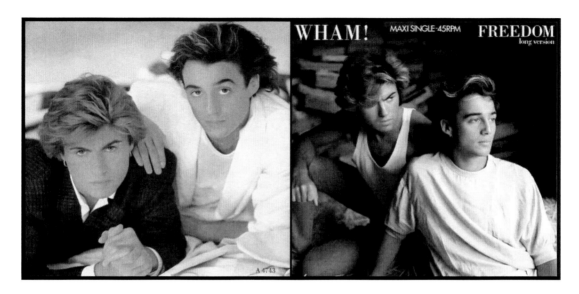

UK: Epic A 4743 (1984).
  B-side: *Freedom (Instrumental)*.

13.10.84: 3-**1**-**1**-**1**-2-4-9-20-25-36-41-39-35-51

Pos	LW	Title, Artist		Peak Pos	WoC
1	3 ↑	**FREEDOM** WHAM!	EPIC	1	2
2	1 ↓	**I JUST CALLED TO SAY I LOVE YOU** STEVIE WONDER	MOTOWN	1	9
3	2 ↓	**THE WAR SONG** CULTURE CLUB	VIRGIN	2	3

Australia
5.11.84: peaked at no.**3**, charted for 20 weeks

Austria
1.01.85: 29-**23** (bi-weekly)

Belgium
20.10.84: 26-11-5-3-3-**2**-3-3-3-11-24

Canada
27.07.85: 94-75-55-44-36-27-19-14-11-**10**-15-17-28-34-51-61-72-77-100

Finland
10.84: peaked at no.**4**, charted for 8 weeks

France
26.01.85: 36-27-31-21-**16**-23-21-20-18-26-26-37-41-47-x-x-47

Germany
22.10.84: 60-26-17-19-17-**14**-15-19-18-29-34-39-65-66-62

Ireland
14.10.84: 13-3-**1-1-1**-6-12-28

Italy
8.12.84: peaked at no.**5**, charted for 11 weeks

Japan
8.12.84: peaked at no.**29**, charted for 13 weeks

Netherlands
20.10.84: 10-4-**3**-4-**3**-**3**-4-5-6-12-15-27-21-29-48

New Zealand
18.11.84: 23-10-9-**8**-10-15-15-15-15-15-18-9-17-36-48-47

Norway
13.10.84: 9-4-3-2-2-**1**-2-4-10-6

South Africa
29.12.84: peaked at no.**8**, charted for 12 weeks

Sweden
26.10.84: 16-11-10-**9**-14 (bi-weekly)

Switzerland
4.11.84: 15-14-8-**5**-**5**-7-10-13-13-15-21-23-28

USA
27.07.85: 43-37-32-27-19-14-12-8-6-**3**-7-14-25-41-60-76-83-96

Zimbabwe
8.12.84: peaked at no.**5**, charted for 11 weeks

Freedom was written by George, and the song was recorded by Wham! for their *MAKE IT BIG* album.

   Freedom was released as the follow-up to *Wake Me Up Before You Go-Go*, or to *Careless Whisper* in countries where it was credited Wham! featuring George Michael, and made its chart debut in the UK at no.3. The following week it hit no.1, a position it held for three weeks, with sales boosted by the issue of square-shaped 7" and 12" picture disc singles.

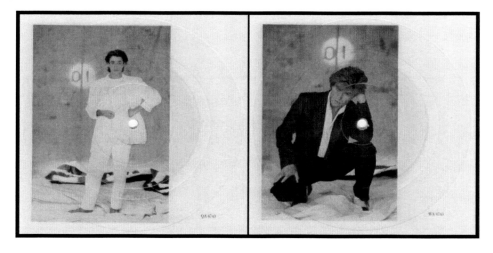

Freedom also went to no.1 in Ireland and Norway, and charted at no.2 in Belgium, no.3 in Australia, the Netherlands and the United States, no.4 in Finland, no.5 in Italy, Switzerland and Zimbabwe, no.8 in New Zealand and South Africa, no.9 in Sweden, no.10 in Canada, no.14 in Germany, no.16 in France, no.23 in Austria and no.29 in Japan.

Do They Know It's Christmas?

UK: Mercury/Phonogram FEED 1 (1984).
  B-side: *Feed The World*.

15.12.84: **1-1-1-1-1**-2-9-17-30-38-57-71

Pos	LW	Title, Artist			Peak Pos	WoC
1	New		**DO THEY KNOW IT'S CHRISTMAS?** BAND AID	MERCURY	1	1
2	New		**LAST CHRISTMAS/EVERYTHING SHE WANTS** WHAM!	EPIC	2	1
3	1 ↓		**THE POWER OF LOVE** FRANKIE GOES TO HOLLYWOOD	ZTT	1	3

7.12.85: 24-6-3-3-4-13-47-x-91
20.12.86: 99-88-86
15.12.07: 38-27-24-57
13.12.08: 64-54-58-72
12.12.09: 65-53-61-50
11.12.10: 62-54-58-58
10.12.11: 62-34-42-41
8.12.12: 82-37-42-51
14.12.13: 62-57-63
29.11.14: 61-88-59-61-60-56

17.12.15: 71-59-38-86
15.12.16: 41-43-35-29
7.12.17: 85-16-12-12-7
6.12.18: 88-26-15-13-6
5.12.19: 77-23-15-17-7
26.11.20: 86-38-15-8-7-9-7
2.12.21: 66-23-14-13-14-12

Australia
24.12.84: peaked at no.**1** (4), charted for 23 weeks
3.01.21: 19-34
20.12.21: 59-25-14

Austria
15.01.85: **1**-8-13-17 (bi-weekly)

10.12.10: 43-55-45-59
9.12.11: 49-57-63
14.12.12: 57-61-74
13.12.13: 56-49-55
12.12.14: 62-61-54
25.12.15: 57-73
6.01.17: 58
15.12.17: 71-54-38
14.12.18: 45-37-22
13.12.19: 43-37-14
4.12.20: 55-13-11-13-10
3.12.21: 52-14-12-17-13

Finland
12.84: peaked at no.**4**, charted for 4 weeks (monthly)
29.12.18: 11

Belgium
22.12.84: 7-**1-1-1-1**-3-5-21-28

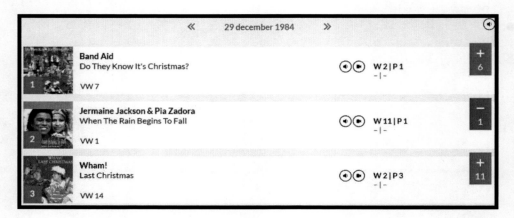

Canada
5.01.85: **1-1**-2-2-7-9-14-21-42-48-56-58-68-83

18.12.21: 44-42-29-33

Denmark
29.11.19: 26-12-13-11-8
27.11.20: 25-10-9-8-**7**
4.12.21: 39-17-15-15-16-13

France
9.02.85: 42-**34**-48

Germany
24.12.84: 6-**1-1**-2-3-7-10-15-35-56-69

9.12.11: 74-79-72-51-73
14.12.12: 72-62-64-63
13.12.13: 83-60-59-57
28.11.14: 95-67-64-61-60-43
11.12.15: 97-100-37
9.12.16: 87-x-82-42
8.12.17: 82-67-62-29
7.12.18: 57-51-38-21
6.12.19: 81-68-51-17
4.12.20: 28-11-18-12-10
3.12.21: 40-29-29-23-19

Netherlands
22.12.84: **1-1-1-1**-2-2-8-18-40

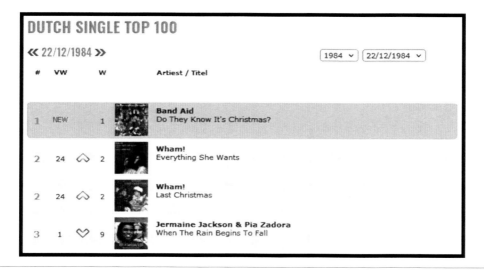

4.01.86: 49-49
20.12.08: 37-27-45
19.12.09: 52-53-60
11.12.10: 90-58-62-68
17.12.11: 91-85-69
29.12.12: 76
21.12.13: 72-49
20.12.14: 42-29-78
12.12.15: 99-49-39-28
12.12.16: 81-64-29
16.12.17: 25-28-9
15.12.18: 30-23-11
14.12.19: 47-42-11
5.12.20: 76-33-19-14-9
11.12.21: 49-35-29-12

Italy
5.01.85: peaked at no.**1** (2), charted for 15 weeks
9.12.21: 70-x-76-40

New Zealand
20.01.85: **1-1-1-1**-6-10-16-27-28-42-45-39-47-13-13-10-17-21-28-35

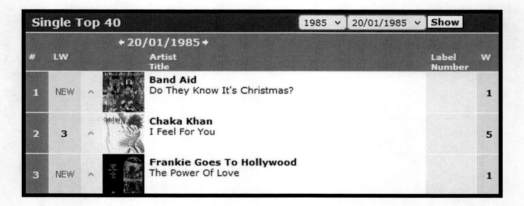

2.01.17: 38
1.01.18: 15
12.12.18: 37-22-4
30.12.19: 6
28.12.20: 14
20.12.21: 38-21-12

South Africa
2.02.85: peaked at no.**13**, charted for 5 weeks

Norway
29.12.84: 3-3-3-3-**1-1-1**-2-2-4-6-5-8

30.12.89: 4-4-4-6-8-9

Spain
25.03.85: peaked at no.**22**, charted for 6 weeks

Sweden
21.12.84: 9-**1**-2-2-2-3-9-16-19 (bi-weekly)

13.12.07: 60-52-23
18.12.08: 39-35-53
11.12.09: 57-41-37-47
24.12.10: 57-49
16.12.11: 53-42-23
7.12.12: 52-36-31-15
13.12.13: 41-38-21
5.12.14: 58-44-34-16-42
4.12.15: 43-31-21-16
2.12.16: 36-31-26-18-10

1.12.17: 59-20-18-11-7
30.11.18: 33-11-10-99
29.11.19: 92-37-39-29-15
27.11.20: 79-19-18-20-13-97
3.12.21: 40-33-30-28-25

Switzerland
23.12.84: 7-**1-1**-3-2-4-6-11-18

30.12.07: 71-96
21.12.08: 70-44
3.01.10: 60
1.01.17: 98
24.12.17: 75-54
16.12.18: 87-58-26
15.12.19: 97-62-19
6.12.20: 58-36-30-28-25
5.12.21: 84-52-45-37-26

USA
22.12.84: 65-65-20-15-**13**-17-49-64-81

Zimbabwe
9.02.85: peaked at no.**3**, charted for 15 weeks

Bob Geldof (Boomtown Rats) and Midge Ure (Ultravox) wrote *Do They Know It's Christmas?* in response to harrowing TV reports about the famine in Ethiopia at the time.

'I was lucky in a way,' said Geldof, 'because I had already written this song, which I provisionally called 'It's My World', and I knew it would be suitable if I just changed the words a bit and called it *Do They Know It's Christmas?* Midge, reliable as ever, sent down this tune which is the sort of Christmassy bit at the end, and we married the two together.'

To record *Do They Know It's Christmas?* Bob Geldof brought together a supergroup of mostly British and Irish acts, and the song was recorded at London's Sarm Studios on 25th November 1984.

George was one of the lead vocalists on *Do They Know It's Christmas?*, along with Paul Young (who opened the song), Boy George (Culture Club), Simon Le Bon (Duran Duran), Paul Weller (Jam), Tony Hadley (Spandau Ballet), Sting (The Police) and Bono (U2).

Other members of the above bands formed part of the all-star chorus, as did Bananarama, Jody Watley, Kool & The Gang, Marilyn and Status Quo. Phil Collins played drums on the recording.

Do They Know It's Christmas? quickly became the fastest selling single in the history of the UK charts. It made its chart debut at no.1, ahead of Wham!'s *Last Christmas*, and held the top spot for five weeks. The single went on to outsell *Mull Of Kintyre* by Wings, thus becoming the UK's No.1 best-selling single of all-time. It was an accolade the song held until 1997, when it was outsold by Elton John's tribute to Diana, Princess of Wales, *Candle In The Wind 1997*.

Do They Know It's Christmas? hit no.1 in numerous countries around the world, including Australia, Austria, Belgium, Canada, Germany, Italy, the Netherlands, New Zealand, Norway, Sweden and Switzerland. Elsewhere, the single achieved no.3 in Zimbabwe, no.4 in Finland, no.13 in South Africa and the United States, no.22 in Spain and no.34 in France.

Bob Geldof hoped the single would raise £70,000 ~ it actually raised, in just the first twelve months, in the region of £8 million, to aid famine relief in Ethiopia.

Towards the end of 1984, Culture Club played five dates at London's Wembley Arena. The final night, as an encore, they performed *Do They Know It's Christmas?* ~ and were joined on stage by George, Bob Geldof, Elton John and Paul Young.

The digital age saw *Do They Know It's Christmas?* re-entering charts in several countries on an annual basis, albeit not terribly highly. This changed with the advent of streaming, and the inclusion of streaming 'sales' and *Do They Know It's Christmas?* on most festive streaming playlists, means the single regularly makes an annual appearance in the Top 10 in several countries every December.

New versions of *Do They Know It's Christmas?* were recorded in 1989, 2004 and 2014, but none featured George.

9 ~ Last Christmas

UK: Epic GA 4949 (1984).
  Double A-side: *Everything She Wants*.

15.12.84: 2-2-2-2-2-3-8-11-21-33-38-51-67 (b/w *Everything She Wants*)
14.12.85: 32-10-6-6-14-36-68 (b/w *Everything She Wants*)
13.12.86: 85-63-47-45-71 (b/w *Everything She Wants*)
8.12.07: 50-23-14-16-40
6.12.08: 67-36-26-27-45
12.12.09: 53-39-41-34
11.12.10: 57-53-56-61
10.12.11: 55-26-28-34
8.12.12: 55-34-41-35-87
7.12.13: 91-44-40-36-68
6.12.14: 86-39-36-35-28
10.12.15: 65-27-24-18-54
8.12.16: 75-19-20-16-7
30.11.17: 81-29-6-3-3-2
6.12.18: 52-14-7-7-3
28.11.19: 80-43-13-7-5-3
19.11.20: 76-44-20-3-2-2-3-**1**

Pos	LW		Title, Artist		Peak Pos	WoC
1	3 ↑		**LAST CHRISTMAS** WHAM	RCA	1	72
2	2		**ALL I WANT FOR CHRISTMAS IS YOU** MARIAH CAREY	COLUMBIA	1	107
3	4 ↑		**THIS CHRISTMAS** JESS GLYNNE	ATLANTIC	3	6

18.11.21: 85-54-28-4-3-3-3-2

Australia
17.12.84: peaked at no.3, charted for 18 weeks
28.12.97: 46
8.01.17: 23
31.12.17: 37-11
16.12.18: 47-34-18-5
15.12.19: 38-30-23-3
13.12.20: 40-24-15-**2**-9
12.12.21: 41-18-12-9-**2**

Austria
14.12.97: 18-14-9-17-39
20.12.98: 34-x-x-20
14.12.03: 64-49-46
12.12.04: 26-23-26-35
9.12.05: 28-24-19-21
1.12.06: 69-55-21-19-18
23.11.07: 65-36-10-7-4-6-68
28.11.08: 57-40-19-17-17-55
27.11.09: 52-27-10-10-9-20
26.11.10: 57-45-11-16-19-33
2.12.11: 40-17-23-23-30
7.12.12: 36-16-18-25
29.11.13: 75-45-28-25-31
5.12.14: 53-19-23-25
11.12.15: 15-19-22-24
9.12.16: 19-14-18-10
1.12.17: 55-22-7-9-5
30.11.18: 48-23-6-5-3
22.11.19: 74-40-16-6-6-2
27.11.20: 26-5-2-2-2-2

26.11.21: 31-7-2-2-2-**1**

AUSTRIA TOP 40 - SINGLES
« **04.01.2022**   2021 ⌄   24.12.2021 ⌄

#	VW			Interpret / Titel	Label / Vertrieb / Physisch	W
1	2	∧		**Wham!** Last Christmas	EPC SONY MUSIC SONY MUSIC	102
2	1	∨		**Mariah Carey** All I Want For Christmas Is You	COLUMBIA SONY MUSIC	75
3	4	∧		**Chris Rea** Driving Home For Christmas	RHINO WARNER MUSIC WARNER MUSIC	49

Belgium
22.12.84: 14-3-**2-2-2**-5-11-20-25

Canada
24.12.16: 40-44-24-17
23.12.17: 36-23-19-15
22.12.18: 19-16-10
14.12.19: 19-18-7-**3**
28.11.20: 36-18-10-4-5-**3**-14
4.12.21: 43-16-10-9-4-6

Finland
12.84: peaked at no.5, charted for 4 weeks (b/w *Everything She Wants*)
18.12.99: 20
15.12.07: 20-16
20.12.08: 10-3-9
19.12.09: 16-9-9
25.12.10: 17
17.12.11: 17-19
28.12.13: 15
24.12.16: 14
30.12.17: 14
15.12.18: 15-8-**2**
21.12.19: 18-**2**
5.12.20: 13-5-5-3
27.11.21: 17-6-6-4-4

France
3.01.15: 91

26.12.15: 65
24.12.16: 64-8-47-97
30.12.17: 66
29.12.18: 19
14.12.19: 87-12
5.12.20: 55-57-13-67
10.12.21: 87-82-42-**7**

Ireland
16.12.84: **2-2-2-2-2-2**-3-22 (b/w *Everything She Wants* from 5th week)
22.12.85: 11-5
21.12.86: 24-24
10.12.09: 37-36-45
1.12.16: 84-34-24-16-9
24.11.17: 90-39-12-7-4-5
29.11.18: 58-26-15-11-7
21.11.19: 80-48-26-15-13-4
12.11.20: 78-40-29-13-6-9-4-6
12.11.21: 99-67-36-13-6-5-3-**2**

Germany
24.12.84: 54-18-13-11-7
6.01.97: 54
8.12.97: 97-60-45-39
7.12.98: 71-43-25-22-64
6.12.99: 99-63-40-33-69
11.12.00: 87-56-41-37-83
3.12.01: 98-78-47-35-26-73
9.12.02: 71-46-33-32-57
1.12.03: 24-25-20-19-18-34-90
6.12.04: 59-37-16-21-20-55-69-93
2.12.05: 88-24-15-13-10-16-57-83
1.12.06: 43-19-14-13-14-69-85
30.11.07: 66-44-19-9-4-64
28.11.08: 73-42-20-20-16-16-65
27.11.09: 85-55-24-18-14-14-57
3.12.10: 57-23-28-29-27-42
2.12.11: 53-31-33-30-25-35
7.12.12: 57-26-27-37-34
6.12.13: 70-32-30-31-37
5.12.14: 72-31-34-28-19
4.12.15: 32-31-26-15-95
2.12.16: 48-14-27-18-7
1.12.17: 52-14-10-11-4

30.11.18: 32-10-5-5-3
22.11.19: 83-37-10-10-6-2
20.11.20: 86-14-2-2-2-2-2
19.11.21: 65-19-2-2-2-**1-1-1**

Italy
12.01.85: peaked at no.**1** (3), charted for 27 weeks
18.12.08: 14-18-14
17.12.09: 19-15-14
26.12.13: 11
29.12.16: 9
28.12.17: 10
27.12.18: 6
26.12.19: 5
10.12.20: 19-x-8-17
2.12.21: 86-17-46-22-14

Japan
15.12.84: peaked at no.**12**, charted for 49 weeks

Netherlands
15.12.84: 24-**2-2-2-2**-6-6-9-16-22-39-48 (b/w *Everything She Wants*)
10.12.88: 87-59-39-28-52-100
16.12.89: 90-70-67
6.12.97: 85-53-39-22-28-40
8.01.00: 69-81
16.12.00: 95-84-x-71-80
20.12.03: 86-64-63-70
25.12.04: 74-73
16.12.06: 54-16-6-25
15.12.07: 41-19-6-5
13.12.08: 89-29-12-19

12.12.09: 55-21-19-32
11.12.10: 57-41-32-53
10.12.11: 85-51-52-52
8.1.12: 98-67-66-47
14.12.13: 68-43-22
13.12.14: 39-24-17-60
12.12.15: 44-16-11-12
10.12.16: 57-21-15-4
2.12.17: 88-37-6-9-5
1.12.18: 64-38-8-9-4
23.11.19: 82-58-27-8-9-**2**
21.11.20: 91-61-35-12-**2-2-2-2**
20.11.21: 80-62-35-13-7-4-**2**

New Zealand
20.01.85: 17-25-24-33-25-41
21.12.86: 34
2.01.17: 14
25.12.17: 31-11
17.12.18: 24-15-**2**
9.12.19: 36-25-17-**2**
14.12.20: 20-10-3
13.12.21: 17-9-6-3

Norway
22.12.84: **2-2-2-2-2**-4
2.12.06: 13-9-10-8-20
15.12.07: 11-8-6-16
13.12.08: 10-6-8-15
12.12.09: 11-10-12-13
10.12.11: 19-14-10
22.12.12: 19-16
14.12.13: 18-13-10-14
13.12.14: 16-17-13-14
3.12.16: 21-20-14-10
2.12.17: 28-5-4-5-3
1.12.18: 20-5-3-3-3
30.11.19: 22-**2**-3-**2-2**
28.11.20: 12-**2**-3-3-**2**-17
27.11.21: 8-4-6-5-4

Spain
20.12.09: 36-**9**
19.12.10: 35-42

18.12.11: 49-26-40
23.12.12: 11-23
15.12.13: 37-37-45
14.12.14: 42-28-23
27.12.15: 61-76
25.12.16: 98-43
24.12.17: 80-45
23.12.18: 81-29
15.12.19: 76-71-21
13.12.20: 57-75-18-35
12.12.21: 58-65-33-19

Sweden
21.12.84: 13-7 (bi-weekly)
25.01.85: 7-5-3-**2**-5-18 (bi-weekly) (b/w *Everything She Wants*)
7.12.06: 47-x-33-40
13.12.07: 42-29-14-48
4.12.08: 42-31-25-10-22
4.12.09: 42-22-19-16-11
3.12.10: 42-36-29-20-17
2.12.11: 40-23-17-10-4
7.12.12: 40-23-17-4
6.12.13: 31-19-14-3
5.12.14: 22-14-11-6-12
27.11.15: 71-17-16-14-8-66
25.11.16: 77-17-14-13-9-3
24.11.17: 47-23-4-5-5-**1**

SVERIGETOPPLISTAN - SINGLES TOP 100 ◆ 2017-12-29 ◆			Artist Title	Label Company	Prefix Suffix	W
#	LW					
1	5	^	**Wham!** Last Christmas	Epic / Sony Music SME	GBBBM8400019	60
2	2	>	**Ed Sheeran** Perfect	Atlantic Records Uk / Warner WMS	GBAHS1701196	42
3	1	v	**Eminem feat. Ed Sheeran** River	Aftermath / Universal UNI	USUM71712944	2

23.11.18: 69-17-3-2-2-**1**
15.11.19: 93-53-20-3-5-3-**1**
20.11.20: 50-10-3-2-35
19.11.21: 99-34-2-2-2-**1-1**

Switzerland
13.01.85: 8-13-8-6-11-15-17-27
4.01.04: 87-85
5.12.04: 99-82-88-86-84
18.12.05: 86-85-19-29
12.11.06: 93-66-54-62-39-18-16-14-12-82
25.11.07: 81-66-45-33-22-10
16.12.07: 33-22-10-15
7.12.08: 63-43-26-12-52
13.12.09: 36-20-14
12.12.10: 41-34-27-34
11.12.11: 52-38-43-34
16.12.12: 25-24-31
15.1.13: 57-40-37-57
7.12.14: 58-33-31-12
13.12.15: 58-49-19-66
4.12.16: 79-45-43-18-4
3.12.17: 62-20-16-16-6
2.12.18: 68-20-12-5-3
24.11.19: 74-44-12-10-4-3
22.11.20: 98-36-3-3-3-4-3
21.11.21: 97-38-9-6-4-**2-2**

USA
7.01.17: 50-41
30.12.17: 44-43
8.12.18: 43-34-31-27-27
7.12.19: 46-27-26-17-11
5.12.20: 42-21-11-14-9
4.12.21: 40-15-13-9-**7**-11

George wrote *Last Christmas* in early 1984 in his childhood bedroom, but he didn't record the song until August, at London's Advision Studios. Although credited to Wham! the single was all George ~ he not only sang the song, he played every instrument and produced the recording himself. The recording was scheduled to be released as a non-album single, backed with *Everything She Wants* in the UK and a few other countries, a ploy designed to extend the single's chart life beyond the festive season.

'As far as I was concerned it was a number one.' said George. 'Then, as Christmas approached, there weren't any novelty records out or anything, and I was thinking, "I can't believe it, there's no real competition around!" … And then I heard about the Band Aid record and wanted to get involved. At the time, it didn't seem a very big deal.'

George quickly changed his mind when he turned up for the *Do They Know It's Christmas?* recording session.

'I think most people that turned up that day were really surprised when they saw all the cameras and everything ~ I was,' he admitted. 'I thought it was like a few people getting together to do this record, and it wasn't until I actually got there that I realised what was really going on, so I was totally shocked by the whole thing.'

Then, when he heard *Do They Know It's Christmas?*, George realised Wham! didn't stand much of a chance of going to no.1 with *Last Christmas*. Even so, this didn't stop him from setting a sales target for *Last Christmas*.

'There's no doubt we're incredibly ambitious,' he said. 'What must it feel like to be Michael Jackson? His album (*THRILLER*) is in more homes than any other record in the world. That's an achievement. As an artist, you want to reach as many people as possible. My aim is for our Christmas single to sell a million and a half.'

The music video for *Last Christmas*, which was directed by Andy Morahan, did feature Andrew Ridgeley as well as George. The promo, which also featured Wham!'s backing singers Pepsi & Shirlie, was filmed at an alpine ski resort in Saas-Fee, Switzerland. In it, the model Kathy Hill play's Andrew's girlfriend, who was previously in a relationship with George ~ hence the song is aimed at her.

George wasn't too surprised, when *Last Christmas* made its chart debut in the UK at no.2, behind Band Aid's *Do They Know It's Christmas?*. This meant, of course, George was a vocalist on the two best selling singles that week and the four weeks that followed, as *Last Christmas* held the runner-up spot for five straight weeks, kept off the top spot by Band Aid.

Last Christmas did hit no.1 in Italy, and it also achieved no.2 in Belgium, Ireland, the Netherlands, Norway and Sweden, no.3 in Australia, no.5 in Finland, no.6 in Switzerland, no.7 in Germany, no.12 in Japan and no.17 in New Zealand.

The aim of *Do They Know It's Christmas?* was to raise funds to aid famine relief in Ethiopia, and it did so more spectacularly than Bob Geldof or anyone else imagined it would. What isn't so well know is that George decided to donate all his proceeds from *Last Christmas* to the same cause.

'Band Aid was great,' he said, 'but it was only one day out of everyone's lives. I don't think that's enough, and you can't not have a conscience about these things when you're making a ridiculous amount of money. I tried to get the record company, CBS, to give their share, too, but they didn't want to set a precedent ~ but I hope some other people in the Christmas top ten will do the same.'

Last Christmas has been reissued many times, in many different formats, over the years. In the digital age, the song often charted in December in several countries, albeit not very highly. This changed with the coming of the streaming age, which has seen the popularity of *Last Christmas* really take off, and the song now re-enters the charts annually in most countries.

Last Christmas finally topped the UK chart at the end of the 2020 festive season ~ 36 years after the single was released, making it the single with the slowest ever climb to the top spot. Twelve months on, the single finally hit no.1 in Germany as well, having spent four weeks at no.2 the previous year, and accumulated well over 100 weeks on the chart.

Elsewhere during the streaming era, *Last Christmas* has peaked at no.1 in Austria and Sweden, no.2 in Australia, Finland, Ireland, the Netherlands, New Zealand, Norway and

Switzerland, no.3 in Canada, no.5 in Italy, no.7 in France and the United States, and no.19 in Spain.

Last Christmas has sold over two million copies in the UK alone, and a similar amount in the United States, despite the single never having being commercially released in North America.

Last Christmas has been covered by numerous artists over the years, with several versions gaining Top 40 status in one or more countries:

- Whigfield ~ no.6 in Denmark, no.12 in Finland, no.21 in the UK and no.24 in Ireland in 1995.

- Crazy Frog ~ no.16 in Ireland and the UK, no.19 in Belgium, France and New Zealand, no.30 in Australia in 2006.

- Cast of 'The Only Way Is Essex' ~ no.33 in the UK in 2011.

Other artists who have covered *Last Christmas* include Ariana Grande, Billie Piper, Carly Rae Jepsen, Cascada, Glee Cast, JLS, Joe McElderry, Rita Ora and Taylor Swift.

10 ~ Everything She Wants

UK: Epic GA 4949 (1984).
  Double A-side: *Last Christmas*.

15.12.84: **2-2-2-2-2**-3-8-11-21-33-38-51-67 (b/w *Last Christmas*)

Pos	LW		Title, Artist		Peak Pos	WoC
1	New		DO THEY KNOW IT'S CHRISTMAS? BAND AID	MERCURY	1	1
2	New		LAST CHRISTMAS/EVERYTHING SHE WANTS WHAM!	EPIC	2	1
3	1 ↓		THE POWER OF LOVE FRANKIE GOES TO HOLLYWOOD	ZTT	1	3

14.12.85: 32-10-6-6-14-36-68 (b/w *Last Christmas*)
13.12.86: 85-63-47-45-71 (b/w *Last Christmas*)

Australia
11.02.85: peaked at no.**7**, charted for 12 weeks

Austria
1.02.85: 6-6-**5**-15-15-27 (bi-weekly)

Canada
6.04.85: 72-53-39-22-15-12-10-10-5-3-**1-1**-12-21-21-42-50-65-74-75-80-93

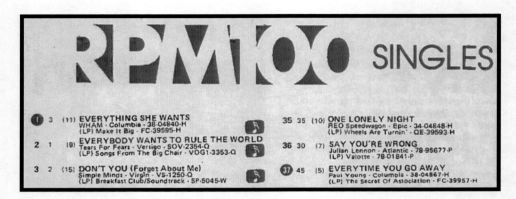

Belgium
19.01.85: 31-16-14-**9**-11-18-30-31-33

Finland
12.84: peaked at no.**5**, charted for 4 weeks (b/w *Last Christmas*)

France
13.04.85: 29-26-31-29-28-29-**21**-35-38-33-26-33-41-45-37-46-42-48-38-37-50-x-48

Germany
4.02.85: 22-**8-8**-14-18-28-43-52-67

Ireland
12.01.85: **2-2**-3-22 (b/w *Last Christmas*)

Japan
21.03.85: peaked at no.**25**, charted for 4 weeks

Netherlands
15.12.84: 24-**2-2-2-2**-6-6-9-16-22-39-48 (b/w *Last Christmas*)

New Zealand
17.02.85: 16-**6**-12-13-13-24-31-41

Norway
26.01.85: 5-5-**4**-8-9

South Africa
13.04.85: peaked at no.**5**, charted for 14 weeks

Sweden
25.01.85: 7-5-3-**2**-5-18 (bi-weekly) (b/w *Last Christmas*)

USA
23.03.85: 60-46-38-30-19-16-11-8-4-**1-1**-2-8-13-21-39-48-67-75-94

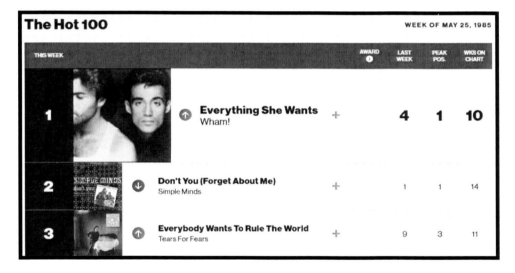

George wrote *Everything She Wants* and, as he had done with *Last Christmas*, he played all the instruments and produced the recording himself, although the song featured on Wham!'s *MAKE IT BIG* album.

'It's the only song I've written that successfully came from a backing track first,' he said. 'I wrote the Linn drum pattern and found a synthesizer program I liked, and wrote the backing track in one evening, took it back to the hotel, and wrote the vocal in the hotel room the next morning.'

The song's lyrics were about a man who is six or eight months into a marriage that isn't going well.

'He's faced with the happy news of an arriving baby,' George explained in an interview with Dick Clark, 'so he's in that situation where he can't back out … It's not the kind of thing I usually write about. Our lyrics are usually a lot closer to the kind of pop lightweight lyric we enjoy, but it's a departure, and I think it worked.'

George recorded *Everything She Wants* at Marcadet Studios in Paris, France, before completing the song at London's Sarm West Studio 2.

'Because it was thrown together that way,' said George, 'I never looked at it as a single 'til everybody started saying it's great!'

In the UK and a few other countries, *Everything She Wants* was issued as a double A-side with *Last Christmas*, in an attempt to lengthen the chart life of the single beyond the festive season. As a double A-side, largely due to the popularity of *Last Christmas*, the single achieved no.2 in Ireland, the Netherlands, Sweden and the UK, and no.5 in Finland.

Elsewhere, *Everything She Wants* was issued as a single in its own right, as the follow-up to either *Freedom* or *Last Christmas*. The single was especially popular in North America, where it went to no.1 in both Canada and the United States. The single also charted at no.4 in Norway, no.5 in Austria and South Africa, no.6 in New Zealand, no.7 in Australia, no.8 in Germany, no.9 in Belgium, no.21 in France and no.25 in Japan.

When he was interviewed during his 25 Live Tour, which took place between 2006 and 2008, George stated that *Everything She Wants* was his favourite Wham! song.

The Last Kiss

UK: Arista ARIST 589 (1985).
  B-side: *The Letter* (David Cassidy).

23.02.85: 67-34-11-**6**-8-11-19-33-49

Germany
22.04.85: 32-23-13-**10**-12-11-14-22-21-32-31-45-54-66-67

The Last Kiss started life as a song titled *Young Love*, which was composed by Alan Tarney and was recorded by Cliff Richard, for his 1981 album, *WIRED FOR SOUND*.

David Cassidy re-wrote the song's lyrics with Alan Tarney, and re-titled it *The Last Kiss*. With George contributing backing vocals, David Cassidy recorded *The Last Kiss* for his 1985 album, *ROMANCE*.

The Last Kiss was issued as the album's lead single, and achieved no.6 in the UK and no.10 in Germany.

Nikita

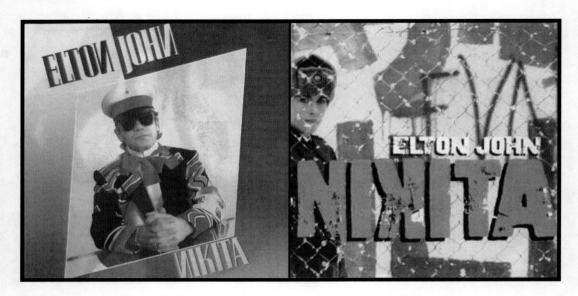

UK: Rocket Record Company EJS 9 (1985).
  B-side: *The Man Who Never Died* (Elton John).

12.10.85: 41-19-9-4-**3**-4-6-15-11-18-33-45-57

Australia
11.11.85: peaked at no.**3**, charted for 18 weeks

Belgium
9.11.85: 34-21-9-5-3-2-**1-1-1-1-1-1-1-1**-2-6-9-13-15-30-36

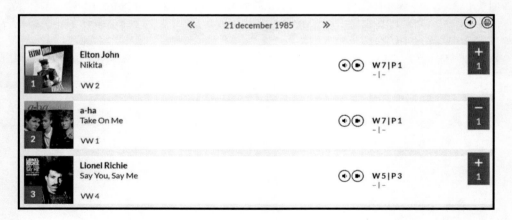

Austria
1.12.85: **3**-4-4-4-**3-3**-5-13-21 (bi-weekly)

France
4.01.86: 44-44-41-25-17-20-16-15-17-10-10-10-7-**6**-12-12-17-22-28-30-36-x-43

Germany
11.11.95: 37-18-5-2-2-**1-1-1**-2-2-5-12-12-19-26-27-42-45-58-65

Italy
14.12.85: peaked at no.**20**, charted for 6 weeks

Netherlands
2.11.85: 47-9-8-3-2-**1-1-1-1-1-1-1-1-1-1**-6-7-11-12-18-31-36-43

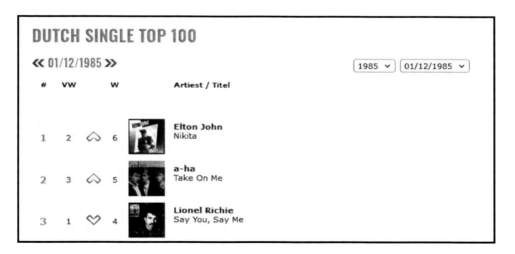

Norway
16.11.85: 6-6-3-3-3-3-3-3-3-3-**2-2-2**-4-5-8-9

South Africa
21.12.85: peaked at no.**1** (4), charted for 20 weeks

New Zealand
8.12.85: 17-7-2-**1-1-1-1-1-1-1**-2-5-6-11-16-24-36-39

Sweden
13.12.85: 15-12-10-**7**-15-x-17 (bi-weekly)

Switzerland
17.11.85: 7-3-2-**1-1-1-1-1**-2-4-4-6-6-10-9-14-20-21-24-x-23

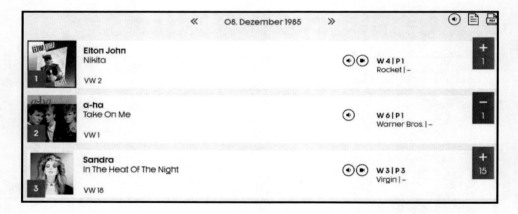

USA
18.01.86: 71-54-44-35-30-22-19-13-10-**7-7**-10-17-32-41-56-67-99

Zimbabwe
11.01.86: peaked at no.**1** (3), charted for 15 weeks

Nikita was written by Elton John and Bernie Taupin, and was recorded by Elton John ~ with George on backing vocals ~ for his 1985 album, *ICE ON FIRE*.

Nikita was released as the lead single from the album. In the song, Nikita is an East German border guard, who was played by Anya Major in the accompanying music video.

Nikita hit no.1 in Belgium, Germany, the Netherlands, New Zealand, South Africa, Switzerland and Zimbabwe, and charted at no.2 in Norway, no.3 in Australia, Austria and the UK, no.6 in France, no.7 in Sweden and the United States, and no.20 in Italy.

Wrap Her Up

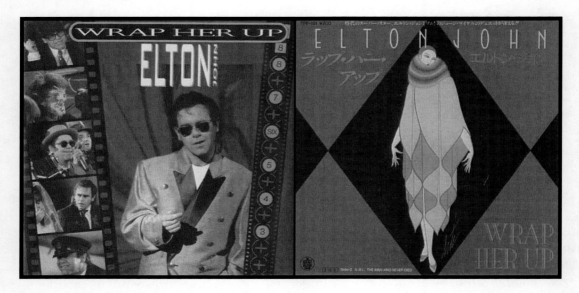

UK: Rocket Record Company EJS 10 (1985).
  B-side: *Restless (Live)* (Elton John).

7.12.85: 43-34-23-20-19-**12**-16-25-50-70-x-94

Australia
3.02.86: peaked at no.**22**, charted for 13 weeks

Germany
24.02.86: 58-59-**54**-60-69

New Zealand
9.03.86: **33**-37-46

USA
26.10.85: 53-40-38-33-28-26-**20-20**-21-35-38-43-65-75

Wrap Her Up was written by Elton John and Bernie Taupin with Charlie Morgan, Davey Johnstone, Fred Mandel and Paul Westwood. Elton recorded the song, with George singing prominent falsetto backing vocals throughout most of the song and duetting with Elton towards the end of the song, for his *ICE ON FIRE* album.

George's involvement with the song began when Elton John sang it to him over a backing track.

'I thought, "Christ, that sounds like a massive hit",' he said, 'so I asked if I was going to do any more singing on his album could I do it on that track.'

When he was in the studio, listening to Elton John sing *Wrap Her Up*, George kept hearing an answer line in his head but, being falsetto, he thought Elton might not like it as it changed the whole character of the song. As it happened, Elton did like it, and it worked out just fine. However, George was adamant he didn't want the song to be a duet, for two reasons.

'One, because it's Elton's song and I didn't want to feel I'd imposed on him,' he explained. 'Two, I didn't know how I'd mime in the video to this falsetto vocal without looking a total ponce ... Up till the end of the song it doesn't sound like me. Well, it sounds like me ~ but with a garrotte on my willy!'

George did feature in the music video, but only towards the end, when he dropped the falsetto voice and was duetting with Elton John.

Wrap Her Up was released as the follow-up to *Nikita*, but it wasn't the massive hit George thought it deserved to be. Nevertheless, it did achieve no.12 in the UK, no.20 in the United States, no.22 in Australia, no.33 in New Zealand and no.54 in Germany.

11 ~ I'm Your Man

UK: Epic A 6716 (1985).
  B-side: *Do It Right (Instrumental)*.

23.11.85: 2-**1**-**1**-2-4-8-8-9-27-33-49-73-x-85

Pos	LW	Title, Artist			Peak Pos	WoC
1	2 ↑	**I'M YOUR MAN** WHAM!		EPIC	1	2
2	1 ↓	**A GOOD HEART** FEARGAL SHARKEY		VIRGIN	1	8
3	3	**DON'T BREAK MY HEART** UB40		DEP INTERNATIONAL	3	6

Australia
23.12.85: peaked at no.**3**, charted for 17 weeks

Austria
1.01.86: 23-18-**14**-19-23 (bi-weekly)

Belgium
23.11.85: 31-9-7-5-5-5-**3**-**3**-4-6-9-25-36

Canada
30.85: 82-50-31-17-15-15-15-12-9-**7**-**7**-8-16-29-41-49-72-98

Finland
11.85: peaked at no.**2**, charted for 8 weeks

France
4.01.86: 49-x-x-39-**34**-41-42-35-34-41-x-45

Germany
9.12.85: 60-11-**7**-10-12-20-25-27-35-43-65-72

Ireland
24.11.85: 7-2-**1**-4-8-14-14

Italy
23.11.85: peaked at no.**1** (1), charted for 15 weeks

Japan
5.12.85: peaked at no.**50**, charted for 9 weeks

Netherlands
30.11.85: 5-4-**3**-5-5-5-6-11-21-36-42

New Zealand
26.01.86: 12-5-**1**-2-3-4-8-10-17-25-44

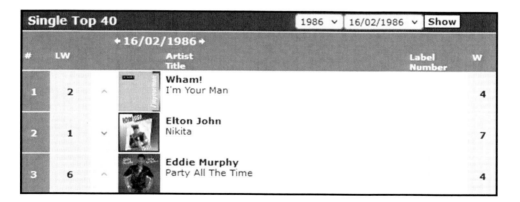

Norway
30.11.85: 8-6-**4**-5-6-6-8

South Africa
16.02.86: peaked at no.**13**, charted for 9 weeks

Spain
12.01.87: **33**

Sweden
13.12.85: 16-**15** (bi-weekly)

Switzerland
8.12.85: 14-10-**7**-10-10-10-10-10-18-23

USA
30.11.85: 55-45-37-25-20-15-14-12-5-**3-3**-6-13-24-41-58-69-97

Zimbabwe
18.01.86: peaked at no.**3**, charted for 15 weeks

George wrote *I'm Your Man* while Wham! were in the United States on their Whamamerica! tour.

'*I'm Your Man* was written very quickly,' he said. 'The whole of the first verse and chorus came to me in five minutes on an internal flight in America.'

I'm Your Man was one of two options for the next Wham! single, the other being *The Edge Of Heaven*, but George favoured *I'm Your Man*.

'*The Edge Of Heaven* you can tie fairly strongly to the last album,' he said. 'It's like a more raunchy *Wake Me Up*, while *I'm Your Man* is pretty different to anything we've ever done. Also, I got pretty sick of *Edge* because we played it all summer in America.'

Wham! promoted *I'm Your Man* with a black and white music video directed by Andy Morahan, which was filmed at London's Marquee nightclub, with George and Andrew Ridgeley performing the song on stage.

I'm Your Man gave Wham! their third no.1 single in the UK, and it topped the chart in Ireland, Italy and New Zealand as well. In other countries, the single charted at no.2 in Finland, no.3 in Australia, Belgium, the Netherlands, the United States and Zimbabwe, no.4 in Norway, no.7 in Canada, Germany and Switzerland, no.13 in South Africa, no.14 in Austria, no.15 in Sweden, no.33 in Spain, no.34 in France and no.50 in Japan.

At the time of its release, *I'm Your Man* was a non-album single, but it subsequently featured on Wham!'s *THE FINAL* album internationally, and on *MUSIC FROM THE EDGE OF HEAVEN* in North America.

George recorded a funkier, solo version of *I'm Your Man*, which featured as one of the tracks on his 1996 hit, *Fastlove*. This same version was also released on the 1997 compilation, *THE BEST OF WHAM!*

12 ~ A Different Corner

UK: Epic A 7033 (1986).
  B-side: *A Different Corner (Instrumental)*.

5.04.86: 4-2-**1**-**1**-**1**-6-12-21-36-48

Pos	LW	Title, Artist		Peak Pos	WoC
1	2 ↑	**A DIFFERENT CORNER** GEORGE MICHAEL	EPIC	1	3
2	1 ↓	**LIVING DOLL** CLIFF RICHARD AND THE YOUNG ONES	WEA	1	5
3	5 ↑	**ROCK ME AMADEUS** FALCO	A&M	3	5

Australia
28.04.86: peaked at no.**4**, charted for 15 weeks

Austria
1.06.86: **6**-8-**6**-13-25 (bi-weekly)

Belgium
12.04.86: 26-15-7-3-**2**-**2**-3-5-5-4-7-14-23

Canada
3.05.86: 76-54-34-20-11-3-**1**-3-4-6-8-12-17-18-27-41-50-57-61-76

Finland
04.86: peaked at no.**8**, charted for 4 weeks

France
17.05.86: 45-37-29-24-18-18-**16**-19-**16**-21-25-31-32-34-34-50-x-x-45

Germany
21.04.86: 32-18-11-10-10-**7**-15-19-27-37-49-48-52-67

Ireland
6.04.86: 15-**2-2**-3-5-6-14-25

Italy
29.03.86: peaked at no.**2**, charted for 20 weeks

Japan
21.05.86: peaked at no.**78**, charted for 4 weeks

Netherlands
5.04.86: 10-3-**2-2-2**-3-3-**2**-5-9-11-26-40-37

New Zealand
25.05.86: 12-4-4-**3**-5-9-17-21-33-42-35-43-x-50

South Africa
15.06.86: peaked at no.**1** (4), charted for 18 weeks

Norway
12.04.86: 3-3-3-**1-1-1**-6-5-8

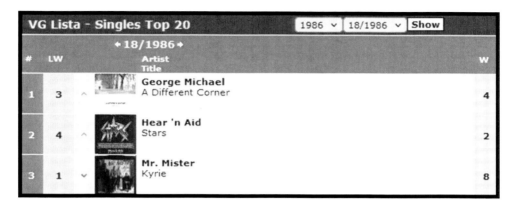

Sweden
28.05.86: **18** (bi-weekly)

Switzerland
27.04.86: 17-10-5-**3-3-3**-5-9-10-14-19-21-28

USA
26.04.86: 57-44-37-26-21-15-10-**7-7-7**-16-28-44-60-80-94

Zimbabwe
28.06.86: peaked at no.1 (2), charted for 23 weeks

Wham! were still at their peak when *A Different Corner* was released ~ however, George and Andrew Ridgeley had already announced they were to split in the summer, going out with a farewell Wham! concert, single and album.

George took just 14 or so hours to write and record *A Different Corner*, and he described it as the most honest and personal song he had ever done.

'That was about a quick relationship,' he said, 'a here today, gone tomorrow one. It's amazing how emotional you can get in a short period of time and how long it can last. Someone can really shake you up, and it takes a long time to get yourself back on your feet ~ that was what it was all about.

'I went in and recorded it exactly the way I felt, and that's the way it sounds. It was partly Wham! and partly the end of a relationship. It was the furthest I'd ever fallen, and in a very short period of time. I had to get rid of it somehow, I had to write about it. That's a really perverse side that I'm sure a lot of writers have ~ I feel like shit, but maybe I'll get a good song out of it.'

The music video George filmed to promote *A Different Corner* was equally sparse, and was set in an anonymous white room with a window. George, also dressed in white, is seen sitting and pacing the room as he sings the song.

A Different Corner gave George his second solo no.1 from two releases in the UK, and the single also topped the chart in Canada, Norway, South Africa and Zimbabwe. Elsewhere, the single achieved no.2 in Belgium, Ireland, Italy and the Netherlands, no.3 in New Zealand and Switzerland, no.4 in Australia, no.6 in Austria, no.7 in Germany and the United States, no.8 in Finland, no.16 in France and no.18 in Sweden.

Like *I'm Your Man* before it, *A Different Corner* was included on the Wham! farewell compilation albums, *THE FINAL* and *MUSIC FROM THE EDGE OF HEAVEN*.

13 ~ The Edge Of Heaven

UK: Epic A FIN 1 (1986).
  B-side: *Wham! Rap '86*

21.06.86: 2-**1**-**1**-2-5-12-28-33-46-66-x-78-95

Pos	LW	Title, Artist		Peak Pos	WoC
1	2 ↑	**THE EDGE OF HEAVEN** WHAM!	EPIC	1	2
2	3 ↑	**I CAN'T WAIT** NU SHOOZ	ATLANTIC	2	6
3	12 ↑	**HAPPY HOUR** THE HOUSEMARTINS	GO! DISCS	3	4

Australia
21.07.86: peaked at no.**2**, charted for 12 weeks

Austria
15.07.86: 17-16-**11**-**11**-16-28 (bi-weekly)

Canada
12.07.86: 79-51-37-26-18-12-**10**-**10**-13-16-18-27-32-38-47-61-72

Belgium
28.06.86: 17-6-6-2-**1-1**-2-2-3-7-13-29-35

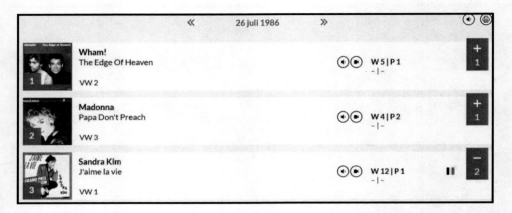

France
19.07.86: 34-38-33-26-23-23-**22**-25-27-30-44-36-x-x-x-46

Germany
30.06.86: 68-13-6-**4-4**-5-6-6-9-10-20-25-42-51-75

Ireland
22.06.86: 6-**1**-2-5-7-19

Italy
14.06.86: peaked at no.**2**, charted for 18 weeks

Netherlands
21.06.86: **1-1-1**-3-2-2-4-7-14-20-30-48

Japan
21.07.86: peaked at no.**66**, charted for 5 weeks

New Zealand
3.08.86: 7-5-7-**3**-4-4-8-24-23-37-39-48

Norway
5.07.86: 4-4-**2**-4-3-4-5-5-4-9

South Africa
3.08.86: peaked at no.**7**, charted for 12 weeks

Spain
20.10.86: peaked at no.**17**, charted for 6 weeks

Sweden
9.07.86: **10**-11-18 (bi-weekly)

Switzerland
13.07.86: 6-6-**4-4**-5-7-9-9-12-21

USA
5.07.86: 47-41-31-22-16-12-**10-10**-17-38-43-70-98

Zimbabwe
30.08.86: peaked at no.**2**, charted for 18 weeks

George wrote *The Edge Of Heaven*, and he said the song's lyrics were 'deliberately and overtly sexual, especially the first verse' ~ he thought he would get away with it because he didn't think anyone listened to Wham! lyrics anymore. The recording featured an uncredited guest appearance by Elton John on piano.

The Edge Of Heaven was released as a single ahead of Wham!'s farewell concert, which was staged at London's Wembley Arena on 28th June 1986. The music video, once again, was directed by Andy Morahan, and was filmed in black and white at Twickenham Film Studios in June 1986.

In the UK, *The Edge Of Heaven* was issued as standard 7" single, with an updated version of *Wham Rap!* on the B-side, and as a limited edition 2 x 7" single pack. The second 7" single featured two new songs, *Battlestations* and *Where Did Your Heart Go?*

The Edge Of Heaven continued George and Wham!'s run of chart topping singles in the UK, deposing *Spirit In The Sky* by Doctor & The Medics in its second week on the chart. The single also hit no.1 in Belgium, Ireland and the Netherlands, no.2 in Australia, Italy, Norway and Zimbabwe, no.3 in New Zealand, no.4 in Germany and Switzerland, no.7 in South Africa, no.10 in Canada, Sweden and the United States, no.11 in Austria, no.17 in Spain and no.22 in France.

14 ~ Where Did Your Heart Go?

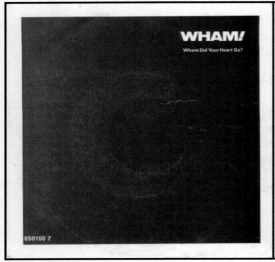 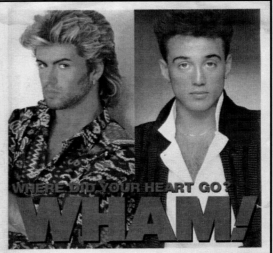

Europe: Epic 650239 7 (1986).
 B-side: *Wham! Rap '86.*

UK: Released as part of *The Edge Of Heaven* 2 x 7" singles pack.

Australia
10.11.86: peaked at no.**54**, charted for 10 weeks

Austria
15.02.87: **23**-30 (bi-weekly)

Canada
25.10.87: 94-86-**81-81**-100

France
29.11.86: 44-45-49-**42**-48-46-46

Japan
25.10.86: peaked at no.**88**, charted for 2 weeks

Netherlands
25.10.86: 42-45-38-**37**

USA
11.10.86: 75-67-59-**50-50**-57-67-85

Where Did Our Heart Go? was written by two American musicians, David & Don Was (*aka* David Weiss and Don Fagenson), and as Was (Not Was) they recorded the song in 1981. In the UK, *Where Did Our Heart Go?* was issued as a double A-sided single with *Wheel Me Out*, but it wasn't a hit.

Wham! recorded a cover of *Where Did Our Heart Go?*, which was issued as part of *The Edge Of Heaven* limited edition 2 x 7" single pack in the UK.

    Where Did Our Heart Go? was promoted as a single in its own right outside the UK and, although it wasn't a big hit, it did chart at no.23 in Austria, no.37 in the Netherlands, no.42 in France, no.50 in the United States and no.54 in Australia. The single was also a minor hit in Canada and Japan, where it peaked at no.81 and no.88, respectively.

15 ~ Battlestations

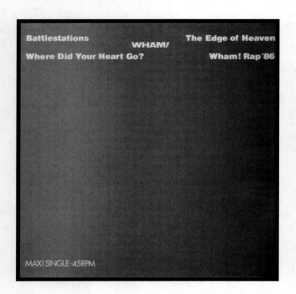

UK: Released as part of *The Edge Of Heaven* 2 x 7" singles pack.

Spain: Epic EPC A 12.7183 (1986).
  Tracks: *Where Did Your Heart Go?/The Edge Of Heaven/Wham! Rap '86.*

12.01.87: **28**

Battlestations was written by George, and was recorded by Wham! for their 1986 farewell albums, *THE FINAL* and *MUSIC FROM THE EDGE OF HEAVEN.*
  Battlestations owes its Top 40 status to its performance in Spain, where it was the lead song on a 4-track maxi-single, which spent a solitary week at no.28.

16 ~ I Knew You Were Waiting (For Me)

UK: Epic DUET 2 (1987).
  B-side: *I Knew You Were Waiting (For Me) (Instrumental)*.

31.01.87: 2-**1**-**1**-2-5-17-28-35-58

Pos	LW	Title, Artist		Peak Pos	WoC
1	2 ↑	**I KNEW YOU WERE WAITING (FOR ME)** GEORGE MICHAEL AND ARETHA FRANKLIN	EPIC	1	2
2	7 ↑	**HEARTACHE** PEPSI AND SHIRLIE	POLYDOR	2	4
3	1 ↓	**JACK YOUR BODY** STEVE 'SILK' HURLEY	DJ INTERNATIONAL	1	5

Australia
9.02.87: peaked at no.**1** (4), charted for 21 weeks

Austria
15.03.87: 12-**9**-10-21-25-28 (bi-weekly)

Canada
28.02.87: 89-77-55-38-27-15-6-6-**4**-**4**-6-6-9-12-24-28-33-53-65-78

Belgium
7.02.87: 34-10-4-2-2-**1**-**1**-2-2-7-11-22-35

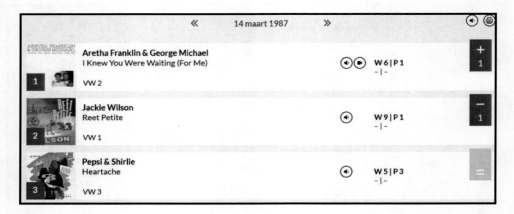

Finland
02.87: peaked at no.**5**, charted for 4 weeks

Germany
16.02.87: 17-10-7-**5**-7-7-11-14-20-29-35-53-63

Ireland
25.01.87: 18-**1**-**1**-**1**-3-15

Netherlands
31.01.87: 36-6-2-2-**1**-**1**-2-2-5-7-16-26-35-57-84

New Zealand
8.03.87: 8-5-5-**3**-5-7-9-11-15-24-39-44-30

Norway
7.02.87: 10-x-10-9-7-**4**-7

South Africa
8.03.87: peaked at no.**10**, charted for 16 weeks

Spain
9.03.87: peaked at no.**14**, charted for 4 weeks

Sweden
11.02.87: 19-9-**4**-6-17-19 (bi-weekly)

Switzerland
15.02.87: 11-6-**5**-**5**-6-7-7-11-13-20-30

USA
21.02.87: 59-44-31-23-17-10-6-3-**1**-**1**-7-10-22-34-46-69-81

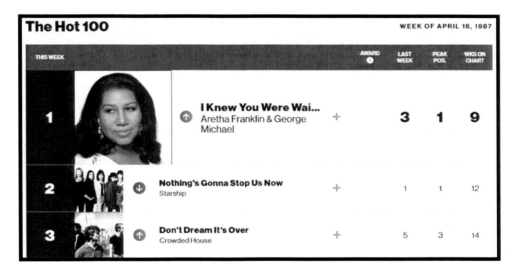

Zimbabwe
4.04.87: peaked at no.**1** (3), charted for 30 weeks

George was far too busy with Wham! when he was approached, and asked to write and produce a song for Aretha Franklin, for a 1984 soundtrack album. Aretha also happened to be one of George's favourite artists, so just the thought of writing a song for her made him feel anxious, and he thought the very idea she might sing a song he had written was 'ludicrous'.

I Knew You Were Waiting (For Me) was composed not by George, but by Dennis Morgan and Simon Climie, and George recorded the song as a duet with Aretha Franklin for her 1986 album, *ARETHA*.

'The first time I heard George was with Wham! and I liked it then,' said Aretha. 'He had a very unique sound, very different from anything that was out there. When Clive (Davis) suggested we get together for *I Knew You Were Waiting*, I was all ready.'

'Standing in the studio looking across at Aretha trading lines,' said George, 'was something that I would never, ever, even a couple of years ago, have dreamed of.'

The accompanying music video, which Andy Morahan directed, saw George and Aretha on stage together as the second chorus ended, while footage on other famous duet partners including Ike & Tina Turner, Marvin Gaye & Tammi Terrell and Sonny & Cher, was shown on a viewing screen.

'We spent eight or ten hours making the video and he (George) was great,' said Aretha. 'He is an absolute pro. I'm very happy with the look and quality of the video. It was nice that we performed together.'

I Knew You Were Waiting (For Me) completed a hat-trick of solo no.1 singles for George in the UK. The single also topped the charts in Australia, Belgium, Ireland, the Netherlands, the United States and Zimbabwe. In the United States, the single was Aretha's first no.1 on the Hot 100 since *Respect* way back in 1967 ~ it was also her first and only chart topping single in the UK.

Around the world, *I Knew You Were Waiting (For Me)* also achieved no.3 in New Zealand, no.4 in Canada, Norway and Sweden, no.5 in Finland, Germany and Switzerland, no.9 in Austria, no.10 in South Africa and no.14 in Spain.

George and Aretha won a Grammy for *I Knew You Were Waiting (For Me)*, for Best R&B Vocal Performance by a Duo or Group.

I Knew You Were Waiting (For Me) featured on one of George's albums for the first time in 1988, when it was included on the compilation, *LADIES & GENTLEMEN – THE BEST OF GEORGE MICHAEL*.

17 ~ I Want Your Sex

UK: Epic LUST 1 (1987).
  B-side: *I Want Your Sex (Rhythm 2 Brass In Love).*

13.06.87: 4-**3**-4-8-19-29-40-56-66-68-x-84-99

Pos	LW	Title, Artist		Peak Pos	WoC
1	13 ↑	**STAR TREKKIN'** THE FIRM	BARK	1	3
2	1 ↓	**I WANNA DANCE WITH SOMEBODY (WHO LOVES ME)** WHITNEY HOUSTON	ARISTA	1	5
3	4 ↑	**I WANT YOUR SEX** GEORGE MICHAEL	EPIC	3	2

Australia
6.07.87: peaked at no.**2**, charted for 19 weeks

Austria
15.07.87: 13-7-**2**-3-8-14 (bi-weekly)

Finland
06.87: peaked at no.**3**, charted for 12 weeks

Belgium
27.06.87: 13-7-3-2-**1-1**-2-4-5-10-22

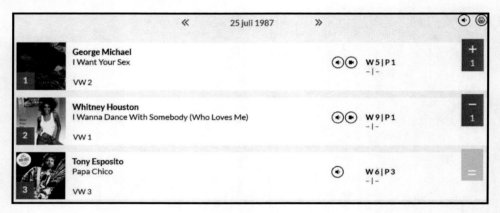

Canada
20.08.87: 83-62-39-22-15-12-12-12-9-7-3-3-3-**2-2**-5-9-20-31-40-48-53-68-68-71-81-91-91-91

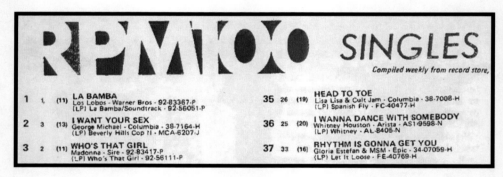

France
25.07.87: 44-45-36-30-30-16-13-18-12-**11**-17-21-22-33-41-45-43
31.12.16: 86

Germany
22.06.87: 56-9-5-4-**3-3-3**-4-6-7-7-9-12-24-33-43-59-75-74

Ireland
7.06.87: 14-2-**1**-6-24

Italy
20.06.87: peaked at no.**2**, charted for 21 weeks

New Zealand
12.07.87: 27-6-3-3-3-**2**-3-4-11-13-21-41-34

Netherlands
13.06.87: 20-14-2-2-2-**1**-3-4-4-6-19-27-36-56-81

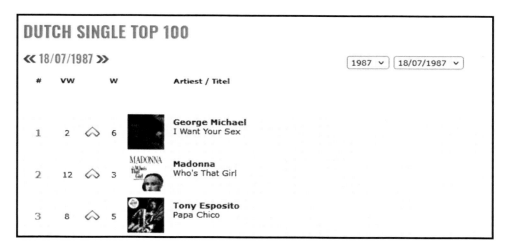

Norway
13.06.87: 6-**3**-5-4-5-7-7

Spain
5.10.87: peaked at no.**4**, charted for 33 weeks

Sweden
17.06.87: 14-9-**8**-11 (bi-weekly)

USA
6.06.87: 51-47-36-28-21-11-9-5-4-**2**-3-5-13-19-29-32-48-61-82-99

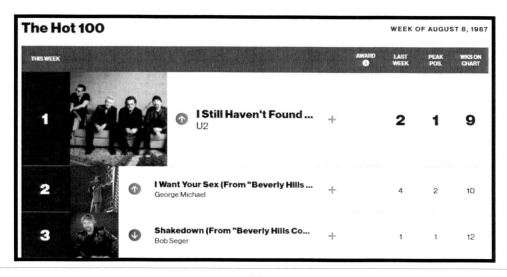

Switzerland
28.06.87: 6-**4-4-4**-5-5-9-12-13-16-19-21-28-27

George wrote and recorded *I Want Your Sex* in three parts, or 'rhythms'.

The first part ~ Rhythm 1: Lust ~ was recorded at London's Sarm West Studios in August 1986, and was first released on the soundtrack to the 1987 action comedy, *Beverly Hills Cop II*, which starred Eddie Murphy.

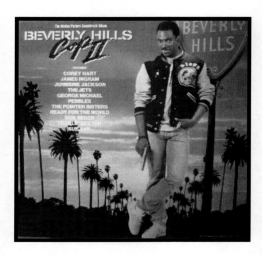

George wrote the song in the studio, and he played all the instruments on the recording himself, that is, a LinnDrum, a Roland Juno-106 and a Yahaha DX7.

'I didn't want to write a song as such,' he said, 'I wanted to make a record. When it comes to making dance records, I'm much more able to do them as I go along in the studio, because it's much more about sound and rhythm. I deliberately wanted to make a record where if you stripped it down to what was left of the song, there wasn't much of a song there.'

Originally, George had a much faster paced pop song titled 'Johnny Sex' in his head, but that didn't quite work. Instead, he accidentally found a rhythm he thought sounded really good, really tribal, which gave him a totally different idea which he worked around, and turned into *I Want You Sex*.

The popularity of *I Want Your Sex*, following the release of *BEVERLY HILLS COP II* in the United States, led to the scheduled release of the track as a single to be brought forward. However, the song's title and lyrics led to the song being banned in some countries. In the UK, the BBC banned day-time radio airplay, stating it was feared the song may promote casual sex and undermine AIDS awareness campaigns. The single was also banned from daytime radio play be independent radio stations across the UK.

'I wasn't expecting the blanket ban.' George admitted. 'I think it's unfair because it's the first ban of its kind in a long time, and I think that if it were not George Michael then I would have no problem being played on those stations, and it's incredibly irritating, having a record out for a couple of weeks and knowing that people haven't heard it.'

George promoted *I Want Your Sex* with another music video directed by Andy Morahan, which featured George's girlfriend at the time, Kathy Jeung.

'It was totally real,' said George. 'Kathy was in love with me but she knew that I was in love with a guy at that point in time. I was still saying I was bisexual … She was the only female that I ever brought into my professional life. I put her in a video. Of course she looked like a beard. It was all such a mess, really. My own confusion, and then on top of that what I was prepared to let the public think.'

Despite all the controversy, *I Want Your Sex* gave George another big hit, and it topped the chart in Belgium, Ireland and the Netherlands. The single achieved no.2 in Australia, Austria, Canada, Italy, New Zealand and the United States, no.3 in Finland, Germany, Norway and the UK, no.4 in Spain and Switzerland, no.8 in Sweden and no.11 in France.

'When I released *I Want Your Sex* and the music video,' said George, 'I didn't think the image would have such a lasting effect. The image still seems to overshadow the music.'

George recorded the second two parts of *I Want Your Sex* at PUK Studios in Denmark in February 1987:

- *Rhythm 2: Brass In Love.*
- *Rhythm 3: A Last Request.*

The second part was issued as the B-side of the *I Want Your Sex* single, and the first two parts featured on George's debut solo album, *FAITH*, which was released in October 1987. The third part was added to the CD edition of *FAITH* as a bonus track.

Jive Talkin'

UK: Hardback 7 BOSS 4 (1987).
  B-side: *Rhythm Talkin' (Part 1)* (Boogie Box High).

4.07.87: 75-31-14-10-**7**-9-17-26-36-55-75

Australia
2.11.87: peaked at no.**82**, charted for 5 weeks

Belgium
29.08.87: 33-13-8-8-**7**-12-13-18-38

Netherlands
22.08.87: 27-11-5-**4**-10-15-20-35-48-76

New Zealand
15.11.87: 50-40-x-**38**-49-46

Originally titled 'Drive Talking', *Jive Talkin'* was composed by Barry, Maurice and Robin Gibb, and was recorded by the Bee Gees for their 1975 album, *MAIN COURSE*. A couple of years later, the Bee Gees recording also featured on the *SATURDAY NIGHT FEVER* soundtrack album.

   As the lead single from *MAIN COURSE*, the Bee Gees took *Jive Talkin'* to no.1 in Canada and the United States, no.4 in New Zealand, no.5 in Ireland and the UK, no.14 in Australia, no.23 in Germany and the Netherlands, and no.24 in Belgium.

Boogie Box High recorded a cover of *Jive Talkin'* in 1987.

Boogie Box High was a musical project put together by George's cousin, Andros Georgiou, and George sang uncredited lead vocals on the project's cover of *Jive Talkin'*, with Haircut One Hundred's Nick Heyward on backing vocals. As a single, *Jive Talkin'* charted at no.4 in the Netherlands, no.7 in Belgium and the UK, and no.38 in New Zealand.

Jive Talkin' subsequently featured on Boogie Box High's 1989 album, *OUTRAGEOUS*, which was released exclusively in Japan and the United States. The album included four additional tracks featuring a vocal contribution by George, namely *Nervous*, *Soul Boy*, *Gave It All Away* and *Lover*.

Nervous and *Gave It All Away* were also issued as singles, but neither was a hit anywhere.

18 ~ Faith

UK: Epic EMU 3 (1987).
  B-side: *Hand To Mouth*.

24.10.87: 10-**2-2**-5-12-21-31-42-63-54-50-67

Pos	LW	Title, Artist		Peak Pos	WoC
1	1	**YOU WIN AGAIN** THE BEE GEES	WARNER BROTHERS	1	7
2	10 ↑	**FAITH** GEORGE MICHAEL	EPIC	2	2
3	5 ↑	**LOVE IN THE FIRST DEGREE** BANANARAMA	LONDON	3	4

5.01.17: 64-65

Australia
16.11.87: peaked at no.**1** (1), charted for 27 weeks
8.01.17: 50

Austria
15.12.87: 10-**4**-5-11-13-17-30 (bi-weekly)

Belgium
30.10.87: 9-5-5-**1-1-1-1-1-1-1**-8-8-11-28

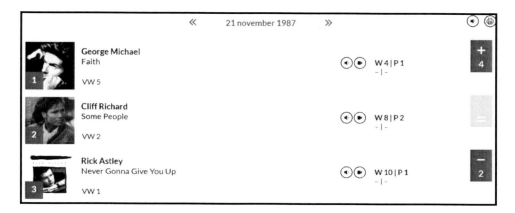

Canada
24.10.87: 92-70-49-31-14-5-5-3-**1-1-1-1**-2-2-4-4-6-11-23-28-37-45-57-65-72-78-86

14.01.17: 47

Finland
11.87: peaked at no.**7**, charted for 4 weeks

France
21.11.87: 44-23-29-**22-22**-25-28-26-31-37-33-43-47-47
31.12.16: 34-60

Germany
2.11.87: 55-15-9-9-**5**-6-10-13-17-21-27-40-48-x-72

Ireland
18.10.87: 11-**2-2-2**-6-19
29.12.16: 86

Italy
24.10.87: peaked at no.**1** (3), charted for 17 weeks

Japan
21.11.87: peaked at no.**86**, charted for 4 weeks

Netherlands
24.10.87: 29-4-3-**1-1-1-1-1**-3-3-7-17-23-28-56-91

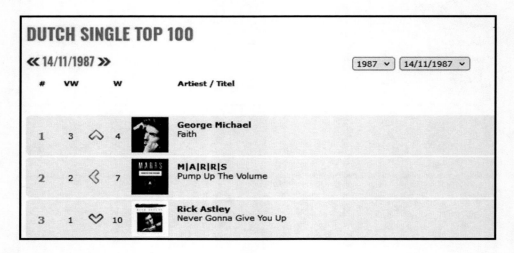

New Zealand
29.11.87: 5-**1-1-1-1-1-1-1-1**-2-3-6-8-9-15-22-25-45-41

Norway
31.10.87: 4-4-4-**3**-5-6-7-9-10-10-10

South Africa
10.12.87: peaked at no.**3**, charted for 18 weeks

Spain
7.12.87: peaked at no.**4**, charted for 33 weeks

Sweden
28.10.87: 15-**9**-11-17-x-18 (bi-weekly)

Switzerland
8.11.87: 11-5-5-**4-4**-8-10-10-18-17-26-16-x-20
1.01.17: 81

USA
24.10.87: 54-37-27-19-10-5-3-**1-1-1-1**-3-9-16-28-37-47-61-78-95

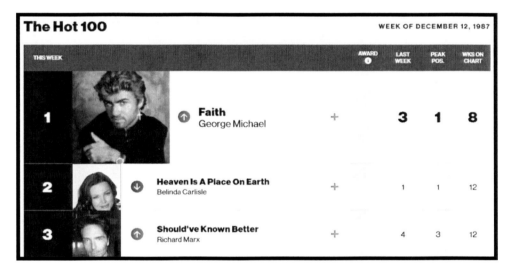

Zimbabwe
16.01.88: peaked at no.**8**, charted for 8 weeks

George wrote and recorded *Faith* for his debut solo album, which he gave the same title. His inspiration for the song came courtesy of a suggestion by publisher Dick Leahy that he write a rock 'n' roll pastiche.

Originally, George wrote and recorded a short, two minute song that he saw as 'a small track on the album, a really short track', which he never planned to release as a single.

'And then I listened to it more and more,' he said. 'Originally there was no guitar solo. There was no real guitar sound on it or anything. And everyone said it's great, it's great but it's too short … So I thought, well, maybe I should put it out as a single …'

But, thinking two minutes was too short for a single, George went into London's Sarm West Studio 2 on the first two days of September 1987, to extend the track by adding a guitar solo and middle section, before mixing the recording.

Faith was released as the follow-up to *I Want Your Sex*, and George promoted it with a music video directed by Andy Morahan. In it, George was seen with a new image: designer stubble, wearing a black 'Rocker's Revenge' leather jacket, old Levi jeans, cowboy boots and Ray-Ban Aviator shades.

'They were my own jeans,' George revealed. 'The rips were genuine, because I wore them so much. I used to ask my mum to sew up new rips. In the end, they were so worn out, she refused. The whole *Faith* image was all me. I came up with the leather jacket and everything else. I didn't use a stylist ~ I don't think I could have afforded one!'

The promo opened with *I Want You Sex* playing, and a Wurlitzer jukebox. Then, a brief snippet of Wham!'s *Freedom* was played on a church organ by Chris Cameron, before George finally appeared, dancing and playing a guitar as he sang *Faith*.

Faith was issued as a 12" picture disc single in the UK, where George had to settle for two weeks at no.2, behind the Bee Gees and *So You Win Again*.

Faith did hit no.1 in Australia, Belgium, Canada, Italy, the Netherlands, New Zealand and the United States, and the single charted at no.2 in Ireland, no.3 in Norway and South Africa, no.4 in Austria, Spain and Switzerland, no.5 in Germany, no.7 in Finland, no.8 in Zimbabwe, no.9 in Sweden and no.22 in France.

19 ~ Father Figure

UK: Epic EMU 4 (1987).
 B-side: *Love's In Need Of Love Today*.

9.01.88: 35-**11**-13-23-41-67

Australia
8.02.88: peaked at no.**5**, charted for 16 weeks

Austria
15.03.88: 26-**17**-25-23-23 (bi-weekly)

Canada
23.01.88: 91-70-53-37-32-22-8-4-**2-2-2**-5-9-14-25-31-41-49-58-75-83-86

Belgium
16.01.88: 26-16-7-6-3-**2**-5-6-14-26

France
5.03.88: 49-50-47-45-45-49-48-**37**-39-45-47

Germany
1.02.88: 60-**18**-23-20-**18**-23-25-31-38-40-44-60-66-63

Ireland
10.01.88: 20-**2**-6

Italy
6.02.88: peaked at no.**14**, charted for 4 weeks

Netherlands
9.01.88: 73-24-7-3-**2**-4-6-14-25-37-46-61-95

New Zealand
6.03.88: 11-**7**-13-11-18-16-31-37-28-43

Norway
30.01.88: **10**

Spain
7.03.88: peaked at no.**4**, charted for 15 weeks

Switzerland
31.01.88: 17-15-**13**-19-21-28-30

USA
16.01.88: 49-37-30-19-12-4-**1**-**1**-2-3-8-19-26-34-43-74-88

George wrote and recorded *Father Figure* for his *FAITH* album ~ however, the song didn't turn out as he'd originally intended.

'The initial concept for *Father Figure* was to make a kind of mid-temp dance track,' he said, 'and what happened was I wanted to hear something in my mix, so I happened to cut out the snare on the board, and suddenly it changed the whole entire mood of the track. Suddenly, it seemed really dreamy … and I just thought, hey, this is actually much better! So I worked the rest of the feel of the track around this spacey type sound, and it ended up, in my mind, being the most original sounding thing on the album.'

Father Figure was issued as the follow-up to *Faith* in most countries, and as the follow-up to *Hard Day* in Australasia and North America, which had been issued as a 12" single only and wasn't a hit. Surprisingly, *Father Figure* became only George's second single ~ solo and with Wham! ~ to miss the Top 10 in the UK (the first was *Club Fantastic Megamix*), where it peaked at no.11.

The single did much better in the United States, where it gave George another no.1 single. *Father Figure* also achieved no.2 in Belgium, Canada, Ireland and the Netherlands, no.4 in Spain, no.5 in Australia, no.7 in New Zealand, no.10 in Norway, no.13 in Switzerland, no.14 in Italy, no.17 in Austria, no.18 in Germany and no.37 in France.

Andy Morahan, once again, was responsible for directing the accompanying music video, which explored the relationship between George, as a cab driver, and a fashion model played by Tania Coleridge. At the 1988 MTV Video Music Awards, Andy Morahan picked up an award for the promo, for Best Direction of a Music Video.

20 ~ One More Try

One More Try.

UK: Epic EMU 5 (1988).
  B-side: *Look At Your Hands*.

23.04.88: 14-**8**-9-19-26-43-67

Australia
26.06.88: **49**

Austria
15.06.88: **19**-29-26-29 (bi-weekly)

Canada
23.04.88: 79-49-40-30-15-6-3-**1-1**-3-3-4-7-8-10-19-31-46-70

Belgium
30.04.88: 23-12-9-4-4-**3-3**-4-6-11-24

Finland
04.88: peaked at no.**12**, charted for 4 weeks

France
4.06.88: 30-24-19-7-**5**-7-**5-5**-6-**5**-6-7-8-8-12-17-22-31-35
31.12.16: 40-91

Germany
9.05.88: 32-31-**22**-24-31-31-34-40-46-47-61-68

Ireland
24.04.88: 5-**1**-9-27

Italy
30.04.88: peaked at no.**11**, charted for 8 weeks

Netherlands
23.04.88: 43-11-6-5-**4-4-4**-8-12-24-29-33-55-98

New Zealand
26.06.88: 21-**8**-12-12-15-25-42

USA
16.04.88: 40-31-22-14-4-2-**1-1-1**-2-7-16-32-38-48-61-73-95

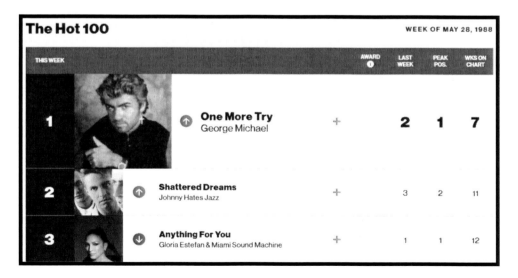

Norway
30.04.88: 9-**7**-**7**-**7**

Spain
20.06.88: peaked at no.**20**, charted for 6 weeks

Sweden
25.05.88: 11-5-**4**-6-20 (bi-weekly)

Switzerland
15.05.88: 12-11-16-**4**-7-7-12-10-11-15-15-25

George wrote and recorded *One More Try* for his *FAITH* album and, at the time, he thought it was the best thing he had ever done.

'It's certainly my best vocal,' he said. 'I actually wrote the whole thing, from start to finish, in eight hours. We recorded it the same day.'

George was actually working on another song, which wasn't going well, and then *One More Try* 'just came out'.

'I don't find *One More Try* hard to listen to,' he said, 'the way I did *A Different Corner*. It's more engaging. When I wrote *A Different Corner* I was still in the middle of feeling that way about the relationship, while *One More Try* is after I'd decided.'

George promoted *One More Try* with a simple music video filmed at The Carrington Hotel, an empty and derelict establishment in New South Wales, Australia. The promo was directed by Tony Scott, who was best known as the director of the popular 1986 film, *Top Gun*.

As the follow-up to *Father Figure*, *One More Try* continued George's run of success in North America, topping the chart in both Canada and the United States. In the latter, the single also went to no.1 on Billboard's Adult Contemporary and Hot R&B/Hip-Hop Songs charts.

Father Figure also achieved no.1 in Ireland, and charted at no.3 in Belgium, no.4 in the Netherlands, Sweden and Switzerland, no.5 in France, no.7 in Norway, no.8 in New Zealand and the UK, no.11 in Italy, no.12 in Finland, no.19 in Austria, no.20 in Spain, no.22 in Germany and no.49 in Australia.

Divine, an American trio of teenage girls, recorded a cover of *One More Try* for their debut album, *FAIRY TALES*, released in 1999. As a single, their version of *One More Try* rose to no.29 on the Hot 100 in the United States.

Other artists to have recorded covers of *One More Try* include Beverley Knight, Hazel O'Connor, Joan Baez and Mariah Carey.

21 ~ Monkey

 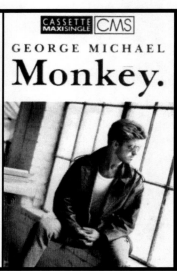

UK: Epic EMU 6 (1988).
   B-side: *Monkey (A 'Cappella)*.

16.07.88: 19-**13**-14-20-32-54

Australia
28.08.88: 33-13-**12**-17-14-23-30-40

Austria
15.09.88: **22**-29-25 (bi-weekly)

Canada
23.07.88: 72-56-40-29-12-7-6-4-**1-1**-2-10-14-22-72

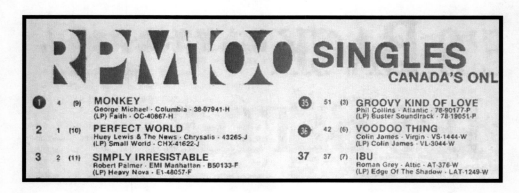

Belgium
23.07.88: 30-19-9-7-**5-5**-8-14

Finland
07.88: peaked at no.**5**, charted for 4 weeks

France
15.10.88: 46-43-43-x-35-39-**34**-44

Germany
1.08.88: 41-30-30-**24**-25-25-38-42-61-64

Ireland
17.07.88: 9-**8**-15

Italy
10.09.88: **25**

Japan
26.08.88: peaked at no.**90**, charted for 3 weeks

Netherlands
16.07.88: 59-19-8-8-**7**-12-19-32-38-52-81

USA
9.07.88: 42-36-21-16-10-8-2-**1-1**-4-13-25-36-49-71-86

New Zealand
11.09.88: 24-10-**9**-12-15-36-42-50

Spain
15.08.88: peaked at no.**23**, charted for 8 weeks

Switzerland
31.07.88: 12-11-**5**-8-7-13-14-20-19

George wrote and recorded *Monkey* for his *FAITH* album.

George promoted the release of *Monkey* as a single with a music video directed by Andy Morahan, which was choreographed by Paula Abdul. The promo featured footage from George's 1988 concert tour.

Like *One More Try* before it, *Monkey* proved most successful in North America, where it topped the charts in both Canada and the United States. George became only the third artist, after Michael Jackson and Whitney Houston, to achieved four consecutive no.1 singles from one album in the United States (Michael Jackson went one better, with five chart toppers from his *BAD* album). Courtesy of a remix by Jimmy Jam & Terry Lewis, *Monkey* also gave George his first no.1 single on Billboard's Hot Dance Club Play chart.

Outside North America, *Monkey* charted at no.5 in Belgium, Finland and Switzerland, no.7 in the Netherlands, no.8 in Ireland, no.9 in New Zealand, no.12 in Australia, no.13 in the UK, no.22 in Austria, no.23 in Spain, no.24 in Germany, no.25 in Italy and no.34 in France.

22 ~ Kissing A Fool

UK: Epic EMU 7 (1988).
  B-side: *Kissing A Fool (Instrumental)*.

3.12.88: 24-**18**-26-37-42-59-x-87

Belgium
3.12.88: 23-15-12-11-**10-10**-16-28

Canada
22.10.88: 70-53-43-22-15-9-4-2-**1**-5-5-5-12-17-27-34-68

France
4.02.89: 46-48-46-**45**

Germany
19.12.88: **44**-47-47-47-65-75

Ireland
27.11.88: 25-**9**-12

Netherlands
26.11.88: 53-21-14-**13-13**-14-26-36-52-64

USA
8.10.88: 47-34-28-22-15-9-7-**5**-9-16-37-58-58-65-82

George wrote *Kissing A Fool* en-route to Japan as part of Wham!'s The Big Tour in early 1985, however, as the song didn't fit with the duo's image he didn't record it at the time. Two years on, George did record *Kissing A Fool* for his debut solo album, *FAITH*, and he later confirmed he had recorded his vocals *a cappella* in one take.

'I don't think I've ever really been influenced by other friends as to who I should or shouldn't go out with,' he stated. '*Kissing A Fool* isn't really about that. It's about a relationship I had with someone who couldn't handle the situation because of who I was, George Michael. At the time it did surprise me. First, I hadn't realised how much I'd achieved, and secondly, I hadn't realised it could have its limitations. I wrote it in that swing style because I think that period of music had that feeling of resignation ~ it's very much a late night giving up feeling.'

Kissing A Fool was the final single lifted from George's *FAITH* album. It broke his run of chart topping singles in the United States, where it peaked at no.5, but it did go all the way to no.1 in Canada. Success elsewhere was harder to find, but *Kissing A Fool* did achieve no.9 in Ireland, no.10 in Belgium, no.13 in the Netherlands, no.18 in the UK, no.44 in Germany and no.45 in France.

23 ~ Heaven Help Me

UK: Mika Records MIKAZ 2 (1989).
  B-side: *It's A Party* (Deon Estus).

29.04.89: 49-**41**-42-62

Canada
25.03.89: 89-82-73-47-28-19-12-6-**4**-5-9-26-32-39-82

Netherlands
13.05.89: 69-39-**27**-**27**-31-43-78-94

USA
25.02.89: 67-50-37-29-24-19-15-12-7-**5**-11-22-36-57-73-90

Heaven Help Me was written by George and Deon Estus, and was recorded by Deon Estus ~ with George on backing vocals ~ for his one and only solo album, *SPELL*, which was released in 1989. Deon Estus was no stranger to George, having formerly worked as a bassist with both Wham! and George solo.

When it was issued as a single, the record sleeve for *Heaven Help Me* credited either Deon Estus alone, or 'Deon Estus with additional vocals by George Michael'. However, even where George was credited on the record sleeve, only Deon Estus was named on the record itself, and only Deon Estus was listed wherever the single charted.

Heaven Help Me achieved no.4 in Canada, no.5 in the United States, no.27 in the Netherlands and no.41 in the UK.

24 ~ Praying For Time

UK: Epic GEO 1 (1990).
  B-side: *If You Were My Woman*.

25.08.90: 8-**6**-10-12-29-47-66
2.11.17: 93

Australia
2.09.90: 34-24-19-**16**-20-19-19-22-29-24-31-45

Canada
1.09.90: 100-41-29-20-11-7-5-2-**1-1**-2-6-23-64-79

Austria
23.09.90: 24-21-21-**20**-24-27

Belgium
1.09.90: 37-24-13-10-6-**4**-5-11-11-21-29-38-42

Finland
09.90: peaked at no.**20**, charted for 4 weeks

France
15.09.90: 40-45-36-36-27-27-**19**-26-25-25-31-37-50

Germany
10.09.90: 47-43-**19**-24-25-30-30-35-44-48-53-58-71-83-95

Ireland
19.08.90: 22-**3**-4-11-15

Italy
15.09.90: peaked at no.**5**, charted for 20 weeks

Japan
30.08.90: peaked at no.**89**, charted for 3 weeks

USA
1.09.90: 41-23-18-8-5-2-**1**-3-8-20-36-51-70-90

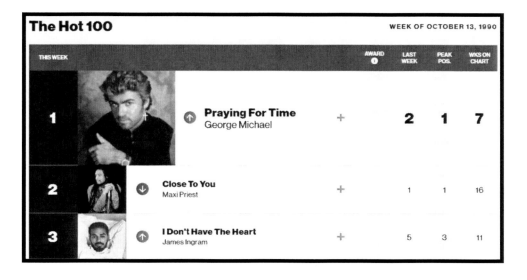

Netherlands
25.08.90: 65-26-14-**11**-14-19-29-39-60-89

New Zealand
9.09.90: 42-28-21-13-14-12-9-**8**-27-17-29-33-33-29-47-44-44-44-44-44-42

Norway
18.08.90: 9-6-**2**-**2**-5-4-7-7-5

Sweden
26.09.90: 14-**9**-17 (bi-weekly)

Switzerland
9.09.90: 13-9-9-**6**-7-10-18-28-29

Zimbabwe
20.10.90: peaked at no.**3**, charted for 5 weeks

George wrote and recorded *Praying For Time* for his second solo album, *LISTEN WITHOUT PREJUDICE VOL.1*, which was released in September 1990.

'It's very difficult to really express what I was trying to say with *Praying For Time*,' said George. 'When there is any subject which you feel really strongly about, especially if its complex, it's very difficult to actually be eloquent about it and really get your point across. I think the actual lyric has much more power than me trying to explain it. I think it's the type of song that so many people will have different interpretations. I wrote it, really, thinking just in terms of the way people act.'

George wrote *Praying For Time* in just two or three days, but he claimed he had no idea why he wrote it.

'The first two lines of the chorus, the lines "It's so hard to love, there's so much hate", came into my head,' he said, 'and very often that's the way a song will start with me, just a lyric will come into my head … Then you have to work around that, think of a melody for those words, and once you've got that nucleus then you're inspired to write the rest of the song.'

The music video used to promote *Praying For Time* was directed by Michael Borofsky, and was essentially an animated lyric video, as George declined to appear in the promo himself. An alternate music video, which did feature George recording and performing the song, was released at a later date.

Praying For Time was issued as the lead single from *LISTEN WITHOUT PREJUDICE VOL.1*, and it gave George his seventh ~ and what proved to be his last ~ solo no.1 single in the United States. The single also topped the chart in Canada, and achieved no.2 in Norway, no.3 in Ireland and Zimbabwe, no.4 in Belgium, no.5 in Italy, no.6 in Switzerland and the UK, no.8 in New Zealand, no.9 in Sweden, no.11 in the Netherlands, no.16 in Australia, no.19 in France and Germany, and no.20 in Austria and Finland.

The B-side of *Praying For Time* was a live version of a 1970-71 hit by Gladys Knight & The Pips, *If I Were Your Woman*, re-titled *If You Were My Woman*, which was recorded at George's Wembley Stadium concert on 11th June 1988.

25 ~ Waiting For That Day

UK: Epic GEO 2 (1990).
  B-side: *Fantasy*.

27.10.90: 32-26-**23**-34-60

Australia
2.06.91: **50**

Canada
26.01.91: 89-80-72-65-38-26-11-**9-9-9**-18-23-28-40-64-91

Ireland
28.10.90: **11**-15

Netherlands
22.06.91: 93-81-**79**-84

USA
19.01.91: 68-53-43-40-35-31-**27**-31-60-94

George wrote and recorded *Waiting For That Day* for his *LISTEN WITHOUT PREJUDICE VOL.1* album. Keith Richard and Mick Jagger were also given a songwriting credit, as the song's rhythm was very similar to the Rolling Stones' 1973 hit, *You Can't Always Get What You Want* ~ this title can also be heard towards the end of *Waiting For That Day*, which also sampled James Brown's 1970 hit, *Funky Drummer*.

Waiting For That Day was released as the follow-up to *Praying For Time* in most countries, however, *Freedom! '90* preceded it in Australasia and North America. It proved to be George's least successful single to date, and only achieved no.9 in Canada, no.11 in Ireland, no.23 in the UK, no.27 in the United States and no.50 in Australia. *Waiting For That Day* was also a minor no.79 hit in the Netherlands, but it failed to chart in many countries.

26 ~ Freedom! '90

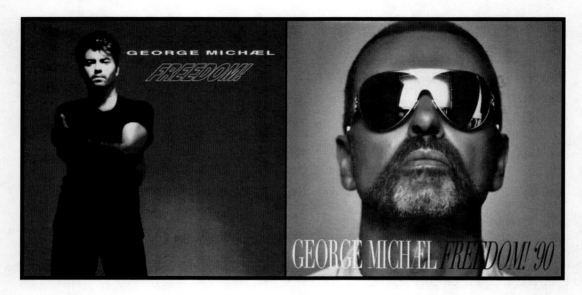

UK: Epic GEO 3 (1990).
  B-side: *Freedom! (Back To Reality Mix).*

15.12.90: 30-**28**-32-32-44-54
2.11.17: 49

Australia
13.01.91: 38-34-22-23-21-19-**18**-26-19-**18-18**-24-25-30-35-38-45

Austria
23.12.90: 27-29-26-29-30-**25**

Canada
17.11.90: 83-47-23-17-12-7-7-7-4-**1**-4-6-17-28-49-88

Belgium
17.11.90: 27-**26-26**-34-41-50

France
2.02.91: 41-**23**-26-25-29-34-31-33-38-35-45
31.12.16: 58-84

Germany
3.12.90: 62-64-43-56-53-**41**-49-47-58-60-66-65-71-84-96

Ireland
16.12.90: **17**-21-21-28-30

Italy
9.02.91: peaked at no.**21**, charted for 3 weeks

Netherlands
27.10.90: 62-37-20-16-**15**-30-45-65-90

New Zealand
2.12.90: 31-30-20-**13-13-13-13-13**-23-36-45-38

Sweden
16.01.91: **20** (bi-weekly)

USA
27.10.90: 53-39-33-26-20-15-12-9-**8-8**-12-16-30-42-67-96

Zimbabwe
9.02.91: peaked at no.**1** (1), charted for 4 weeks

George wrote and recorded *Freedom! '90* for his *LISTEN WITHOUT PREJUDICE VOL.1* album ~ the '90 was added to the song's title, to avoid any confusion with Wham!'s 1984 hit, *Freedom*. The recording, like *Waiting For That Day*, sampled James Brown's *Funky Drummer*.

Once again, George refused to appear in the accompanying music video himself.

'At some point in your career,' he said, by way of explanation, 'the situation between yourself and the camera reverses. For a certain number of years, you court it and you need it, but ultimately, it needs you more and it's a bit like a relationship. The minute that happens, it turns you off, and it does feel like it is taking something from you.'

Instead, George recruited five supermodels, including Cindy Crawford and Naomi Campbell, to appear in the promo and lip-synch *Freedom! '90*, along with four male models and the fashion photographer, Mario Sorrenti. The music video was directed by David Fincher.

Freedom! '90 was issued as a limited edition 12" picture disc single in Europe, including the UK, and North America, and the single fared better that *Waiting For That Day* in most countries.

Freedom! '90 hit no.1 in Canada and Zimbabwe, and peaked at no.8 in the United States, no.13 in New Zealand, no.15 in the Netherlands, no.17 in Ireland, no.18 in Australia, no.20 in Sweden, no.21 in Italy, no.23 in France, no.25 in Austria, no.26 in Belgium, no.28 in the UK and no.41 in Germany.

George performed *Freedom! '90*, along with a new song *White Light*, when he appeared during the closing ceremony of the 2012 Summer Olympics, which were staged in London.

27 ~ Heal The Pain

UK: Epic 656647 7 (1991).
  B-side: *Soul Free*.

16.02.91: 40-**31**-37-63

Belgium
23.02.91: 39-38-**36**-46

Ireland
17.02.91: **16**-18

Netherlands
16.02.91: 89-61-36-**25**-32-42-58-82

George wrote and recorded *Heal The Pain* for his *LISTEN WITHOUT PREJUDICE VOL.1* album.

   Outside North America, *Heal The Pain* was issued as the fourth single from the album, but it was only a modest hit, charting at no.16 in Ireland, no.25 in the Netherlands, no.31 in the UK and no.36 in Belgium.

   In North America, *Soul Free* b/w *Cowboys And Angels* was preferred, but it failed to chart in either Canada or the United States. *Soul Free* was also issued as a single in Australasia and Japan, but it wasn't a hit anywhere.

Towards the end of 2005, George recorded a duet version of *Heal The Pain* with Paul McCartney ~ this version was released a year later, when it featured on George's greatest hits compilation, *TWENTY FIVE*. In 2008, a promo CD single of the duet version was released as a single in the United States, but it wasn't a hit.

28 ~ Cowboys And Angels

UK: Epic 656774 7 (1991).

30.03.91: 59-**45**-61

Belgium
4.05.91: 38-**26**-35-35-40-41-45

France
1.06.91: 49-47-48-x-x-x-**36**-49

Ireland
31.03.91: **15**

Netherlands
6.04.91: 81-59-40-32-24-**20-20**-27-38-56-73

George wrote and recorded *Cowboys And Angels* for his *LISTEN WITHOUT PREJUDICE VOL.1* album ~ at 7:14 minutes, it was the longest song he had released, and featured a saxophone solo by Andy Hamilton.

In a 2004 interview, George revealed *Cowboys And Angels* was inspired by a short-lived love triangle.

'She was in love with me because she couldn't get me,' he said, 'and I was in love with him because I couldn't get him … It's a very personal lyric, but it's about the ridiculousness of wanting what you can't have.'

Cowboys And Angels was released as the fifth and final single from *LISTEN WITHOUT PREJUDICE VOL.1* in Europe, including the UK, where it became the first single by George to miss the Top 40 ~ it peaked at no.45.

The single did achieve Top 40 status in four countries, charting at no.15 in Ireland, no.20 in the Netherlands, no.26 in Belgium and no.36 in France, but it failed to chart in most European countries where it was released.

Cowboys And Angels was also released as a single in Australasia, but it failed to chart in Australia or New Zealand. In North America, *Cowboys And Angels* was released as the B-side of another flop single, *Soul Free*.

29 ~ Don't Let The Sun Go Down On Me

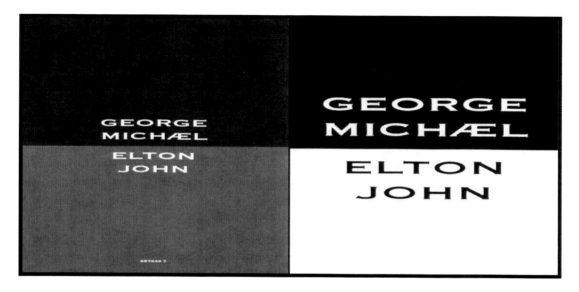

UK: Epic 657646 7 (1991).
  B-side: *I Believe (When I Fall In Love It Will Be Forever)*.

7.12.91: **1-1**-2-3-4-8-24-42-56-70

Pos	LW	Title, Artist		Peak Pos	WoC
1	New	**DON'T LET THE SUN GO DOWN ON ME** GEORGE MICHAEL AND ELTON JOHN	EPIC	1	1
2	1 ↓	**BLACK OR WHITE** MICHAEL JACKSON	EPIC	1	3
3	6 ↑	**RIDE LIKE THE WIND** EAST SIDE BEAT	FFRR	3	2

5.01.17: 91

Australia
12.01.92: 6-4-4-**3-3**-5-5-10-12-14-27-35-50

Austria
26.01.92: 16-13-12-10-7-3-**2**-3-8-3-6-6-6-7-5-7-8-8-11-15-10-11-11-15-24

Finland
01.92: peaked at no.**12**, charted for 4 weeks

Belgium
28.12.91: 37-9-6-3-**1-1-1-1-1-1**-2-2-5-8-11-24-28

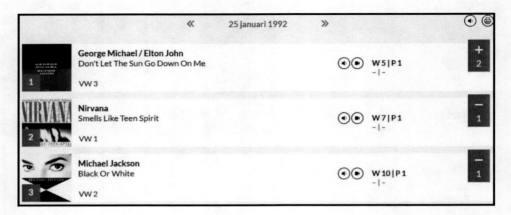

Canada
21.12.91: 49-49-49-49-35-10-4-2-**1-1-1**-2-8-12-28-52-57-100

France
4.01.92: 37-32-18-7-5-3-2-**1-1-1-1-1-1-1-1**-2-5-3-5-5-6-6-6-15-15-31

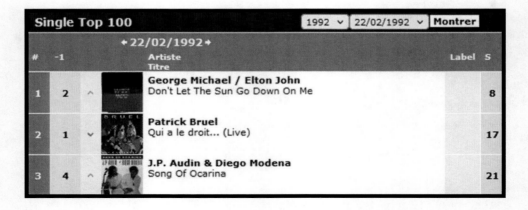

31.12.16: 52-95

Germany
23.12.91: 84-28-10-10-6-**4-4**-5-8-9-10-11-11-15-21-29-32-34-33-39-82-95-87

Ireland
8.12.91: **2**-3-**2-2-2-2**-7-23-23-29

Italy
7.12.91: peaked at no.**1** (7), charted for 26 weeks

Netherlands
30.11.91: 92-70-41-15-4-2-**1-1-1-1-1**-2-2-3-5-11-18-30-37-65-94

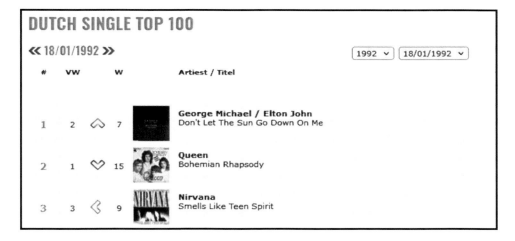

Norway
7.12.91: 7-2-2-**1-1-1-1-1-1-1**-2-5-6-8

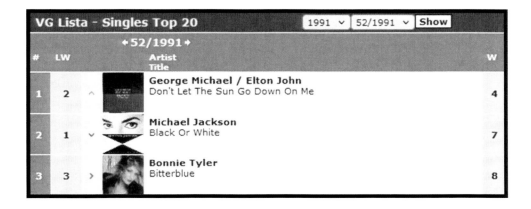

New Zealand
2.02.92: 7-**4-4**-7-6-5-9-13-19-23-29-35-39

Spain
3.02.92: peaked at no.**8**, charted for 8 weeks

Sweden
18.12.91: 17-6-**2**-3-4-7-14-34 (bi-weekly)

Switzerland
22.12.91: 9-4-4-3-**1-1-1-1-1-1**-2-2-2-2-2-6-8-3-5-6-17-9-33-31-24-x-35

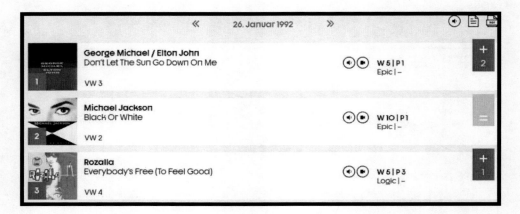

1.01.17: 51

USA
7.12.91: 72-34-19-19-12-8-4-3-**1**-3-4-6-7-11-18-24-32-43-51-57

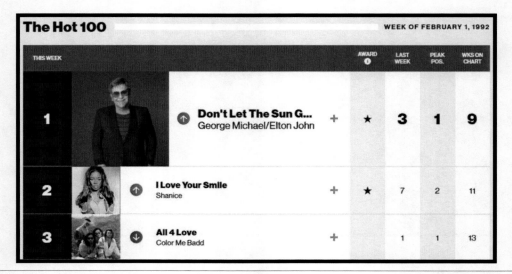

Zimbabwe
29.02.92: peaked at no.**5**, charted for 4 weeks

Don't Let The Sun Go Down On Me was written by Elton John and Bernie Taupin, and was originally recorded by Elton John for his 1974 album, *CARIBOU*. As a single, Elton took the song to no.1 in Canada, no.2 in the United States, no.13 in Australia, no.16 in the UK, no.17 in Ireland and no.30 in the Netherlands.

George first performed *Don't Let The Sun Go Down On Me* with Elton John at the Live Aid concert, staged at London's Wembley Stadium on 13th July 1985. George and Elton were joined on stage by Andrew Ridgeley and Kiki Dee, as backing singers.

Six years on, George regularly performed *Don't Let The Sun Go Down On Me* during his Cover To Cover Tour, and at the final concert at London's Wembley Arena on 23rd March 1991, George took everyone by surprise by having Elton John join him on stage to sing the song. Later the same year, this live recording was released as a single.

George and Elton promoted their duet version of *Don't Let The Sun Go Down On Me* with a music video that featured footage from a 'live' concert filmed in front of 70,000 fans, which was directed by Andy Morahan.

'The video was actually shot over several days,' said George's publicist, Michael Pagnotta. 'It was shot in an airline hanger in Burbank, California, where George had been rehearsing. Elton came in for a night and they ran through the song a couple of times. Then the song was filmed in its entirety live in Chicago in the middle of October, as part of that Cover To Cover Tour, and when Elton came out from the wings that place went crazy.'

Don't Let The Sun Go Down On Me was a huge success, and topped the charts in Belgium, Canada, France, Italy, the Netherlands, Norway, Switzerland, the UK and the United States. The single also achieved no.2 in Austria, Ireland and Sweden, no.3 in Australia, no.4 in Germany and New Zealand, no.5 in Zimbabwe and no.8 in Spain.

George and Elton picked up a Grammy nomination for *Don't Let The Sun Go Down On Me*, but the award went to Celine Dion & Peabo Bryson, for *Beauty And The Beast*.

George performed *Don't Let The Sun Go Down On Me* with Joe McElderry, when he appeared as a celebrity guest during the final of the sixth series of the UK's *The X-Factor*, which was aired on 12th December 2009 ~ the following evening, Joe McElderry was declared the winner.

Oleta Adams recorded a cover of *Don't Let The Sun Go Down On Me* for the 1991 tribute album, *TWO ROOMS – CELEBRATING THE SONGS OF ELTON JOHN & BERNIE TAUPIN*. Her version was issued as a single, and was a no.33 hit in the UK.

George's contribution to the *TWO ROOMS* tribute album was a cover of *Tonight*, a song Elton had recorded for his 1976 album, *BLUE MOVES*.

30 ~ Too Funky

UK: Epic 658058 7 (1992).
  B-side: *Crazyman Dance*.

13.06.92: **4**-5-6-8-14-27-38-52-75

Australia
21.06.92: 8-5-4-4-6-4-**3**-5-6-11-11-15-21-24-37-41-43

Austria
5.07.92: 28-15-16-14-15-**9**-14-10-10-19-**9**-20-17

Belgium
20.06.92: 29-19-9-6-4-3-**2-2**-5-8-14-15-29-35

Canada
27.06.92: 65-39-31-26-7-**6-6**-8-9-10-18-33-42-81-99

France
27.06.92: 33-20-17-10-7-**5**-6-6-12-11-13-11-19-18-22-32-38

Germany
6.07.92: 59-56-16-14-**12**-13-14-15-20-23-27-34-41-42-73-79-96

Italy
6.06.92: peaked at no.**2**, charted for 26 weeks

Japan
16.07.92: **95**

Netherlands
6.06.92: 98-47-23-8-7-**3**-6-10-12-17-36-58-92

New Zealand
12.07.92: 9-**5-5**-10-11-6-14-11-19-31-46

Norway
13.06.92: 7-4-**2-2-2**-5-3-x-9

Sweden
10.06.92: 19-13-10-**7-7**-9-13-29 (bi-weekly)

Switzerland
21.06.92: 36-29-9-9-8-7-**6**-9-9-13-12-17-15-20-25-24-38-30

USA
13.06.92: 41-30-17-12-13-13-12-12-**10**-16-17-25-34-46-55-65-71-75-85-93

George wrote and recorded *Too Funky* with the intention of including the track on the follow-up to his *LISTEN WITHOUT PREJUDICE VOL.1* album ~ the song's hook sampled Jocelyn Brown's 1984 hit, *Somebody Else's Guy*. Instead, George decided to donate it, along with another two songs ~ *Do You Really Want To Know* and *Happy* ~ to the *RED HOT + DANCE* album, which was released to raise funds for AIDS research and relief.

Of the three new songs George donated to *RED HOT + DANCE*, only *Too Funky* was issued as a single, and George promoted it with a music video in which he made several brief appearances, playing a fashion designer directing supermodels on a fictitious catwalk. Originally, the plan was to ask the same supermodels who had featured in the *Freedom! '90* music video back again, but only one ~ Linda Evangelista ~ actually appeared in both videos. A 'making of' video was also filmed, as was a rarely seen alternate edit which also featured several male models.

Too Funky was a sizeable hit, and achieved no.2 in Belgium, Italy and Norway, no.3 in Australia and the Netherlands, no.4 in the UK, no.5 in France and New Zealand, no.6 in Canada and Switzerland, no.7 in Sweden, no.9 in Austria, no.10 in the United States, no.12 in Germany and no.16 in Zimbabwe.

Too Funky was the last single George released, before he took legal action against Sony Music (Columbia Records in North America, Epic Record internationally), to break free of his recording contract with the company. George filed his lawsuit against Sony on 30th October 1992.

'My reason for wanting to part with Sony,' he stated, 'is because I don't believe that one particular area of the world which is very important to me has any belief in me or any motivation to exploit my work. If there's a relationship between artist and record company it should be a mutual thing.'

George had to wait until 1st June 1994, before Justice Jonathan Parker delivered his judgement ~ and wholly rejected George's claims.

'I am shocked and extremely disappointed,' said George, following the verdict. 'It means that even though I both created and paid for my work, I will never own it or have any rights over it. In fact, there is no such thing as resignation of an artist in the music industry.'

Following the court battle, George re-negotiated his contract with Sony Music, which was then sold to DreamWorks Records in North America, and to Virgin Records internationally, in July 1995 for around $40 million.

31 ~ Somebody To Love

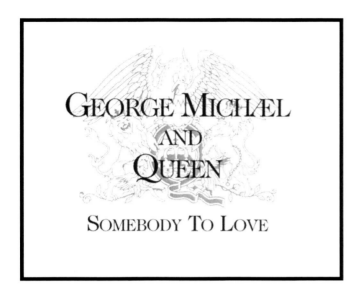

UK: Parlophone G&Q1 (1-track promo CD, 1993).

Somebody To Love (Live) charted as part of the *Five Live* EP in the UK ~ see albums.

Australia
2.05.93: 37-27-**19**-20-20-20-21-28-28-35-41

Austria
30.05.93: 17-17-**15**-21-21-21-23-25-27

Belgium
8.05.93: 34-29-14-**8-8**-9-9-11-12-16-35-40-47

Canada
24.04.93: 91-67-48-36-24-24-20-15-**13-13**-37-55-78-90

France
19.06.93: 36-20-28-19-**16**-23-22-36-21-32-24-37

Germany
24.05.93: 59-51-24-26-**21**-23-26-30-39-44-48-49-83-88-85

Italy
1.05.93: peaked at no.**9**, charted for 10 weeks

Netherlands
8.05.93: 20-9-**6**-7-11-12-20-24-27-33-46

New Zealand
16.05.93: 23-13-**8-8**-10-13-20-21-21

Spain
14.06.93: peaked at no.**1** (4), charted for 20 weeks

USA
15.05.93: 49-37-**30**-34-38-46-59-67-98

Freddie Mercury wrote *Somebody To Love*, and the song was originally recorded by Queen for their 1976 album, *A DAY AT THE RACES*. As a single, Queen took *Somebody to Love* to no.1 in the Netherlands, no.2 in Belgium and the UK, no.5 in Canada, no.6 in Ireland, no.7 in South Africa, no.13 in the United States, no.15 in Australia, no.19 in Denmark and no.21 in Germany.

Freddie Mercury died of AIDS on 24th November 1991.

George performed *Somebody To Love* with the three remaining members of Queen at The Freddie Mercury Tribute Concert for AIDS Awareness, which was staged at London's Wembley Stadium on 20th April 1992.

'George Michael was the best,' said Queen's Brian May. 'There's a certain note in his voice when he did *Somebody To Love* that was pure Freddie.'

George's live performance of *Somebody To Love* with Queen was released on *FIVE LIVE*, a 5-6 track EP, and as a single in its own right in many countries. The EP charted as an album in most countries, and the single achieved at no.1 in Spain, no.6 in the Netherlands, no.8 in Belgium and New Zealand, no.9 in Italy, no.13 in Canada, no.15 in Austria, no.16 in France, no.19 in Australia, no.21 in Germany and no.21 in the United States.

32 ~ Killer/Papa Was A Rollin' Stone

UK: Parlophone 12R 6340 (1993).
  B-side: *Killer/Papa Was A Rollin' Stone (PM Dawn Remix – Instrumental)*.

5.06.93: **89**

Canada
3.07.93: 95-76-44-39-33-22-**19-19**-33-49-60-60-95

USA
3.07.93: 95-99-91-**69-69**-79-91

Killer/Papa Was A Rollin' Stone was a medley of two performances by George.

  Killer was written by Adamski and Seal, and was originally recorded by Adamski ~ with uncredited lead vocals by Seal ~ for his 1990 album, *DOCTOR ADAMSKI'S MUSICAL PHARMACY*. As a single, Adamski took *Killer* to no.1 in Belgium, the UK and Zimbabwe, no.2 in Germany and the Netherlands, no.5 in Ireland and Sweden, no.11 in Austria, no.14 in Finland, and no.15 in Spain and Switzerland.

  Seal re-recorded *Killer* for his self-titled debut album, which was released in 1991. Once again, *Killer* was issued as a single, and second time around it achieved no.6 in Ireland and no.8 in the UK.

Papa Was A Rollin' Stone was written by Barrett Strong and Norman Whitfield, and was originally recorded by The Undisputed Truth. Their version was issued as a single in North America in May 1972, and was a minor no.63 hit on the Hot 100 in the United States.

The song is much better known for the Grammy winning 12 minute version recorded by The Temptations for their 1972 album, *ALL DIRECTIONS*. An edited version was issued as a single, and went all the way to no.1 in the United States. Elsewhere, The Temptations took *Papa Was A Rollin' Stone* to no.3 in the Netherlands, no.6 in New Zealand and South Africa, no.11 in Germany, no.12 in Canada, no.14 in the UK, no.16 in Belgium and no.42 in France.

George's performance of *Killer* at London's Wembley Stadium on 22nd March 1991 was mixed with his recording of *Papa Was A Rollin' Stone*, and the resultant medley was released on his *Five Live* EP. The medley fared best in Canada, where it rose to no.19.

The medley was a minor no.69 hit in the United States, and in the UK, where a 12" single of *Killer/Papa Was A Rollin' Stone* was issued, the medley spent a solitary week at no.89.

The German DJ/musician ATB (*aka* André Tanneberger) recorded a cover of *Killer* in 1999, with lead vocals by Drue Williams. His version of the song charted at no.4 in the UK, no.16 in Finland, no.24 in Sweden, no.25 in the Netherlands, no.31 in Germany and no.41 in Belgium.

Bill 'Wolf' Wolfer recorded a cover of *Papa Was A Rollin' Stone*, with Michael Jackson on backing vocals, for his 1983 album, *WOLF*. As a single, his version was a minor no.55 hit in the United States.

More successful, Was (Not Was) recorded *Papa Was A Rollin' Stone* for their 1990 album, *ARE YOU OKAY?* Released as a single, they took the song to no.6 in Switzerland, no.11 in Ireland, no.12 in the UK, no.14 in the Netherlands, no.15 in Austria, no.22 in New Zealand, no.40 in Belgium and no.57 in Canada.

33 ~ Jesus To A Child

UK: Virgin VSCDX 1571 (1996).
 Tracks: *Freedom '94 (Live Version)/One More Try (Live Gospel Version)/Older (Instrumental Version).*

20.01.96: **1**-2-4-10-22-39-50-61-71-66-82-100-x-68-87-65-75

Pos	LW	Title, Artist		Peak Pos	WoC
1	New	**JESUS TO A CHILD** GEORGE MICHAEL	VIRGIN	1	1
2	1 ↓	**EARTH SONG** MICHAEL JACKSON	EPIC	1	7
3	2 ↓	**FATHER AND SON** BOYZONE	POLYDOR	2	9

Austria
21.01.96: **11-11**-13-15-20-21-19-24-23-31-37

Belgium
20.01.96: 29-**3**-4-5-6-16-16-18-25-41-49-35-44-48

Canada
15.01.96: 89-66-52-51-42-34-24-16-12-12-12-**10**-14-17-22-23-28-42-73-91

Australia
21.01.96: **1-1**-6-7-14-17-34-48

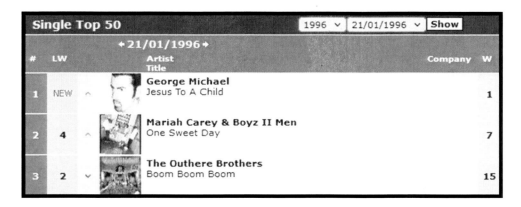

Finland
13.01.96: **1-1-1**-2-2-3-7-x-x-14

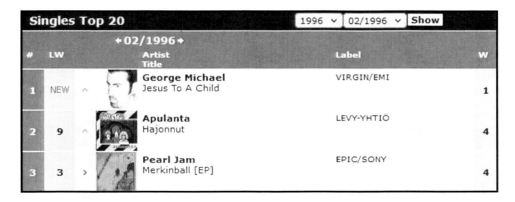

France
6.01.96: 31-9-10-8-**7**-9-11-11-9-11-14-17-15-19-21-29-31-40-48
31.12.16: 61

Germany
15.01.96: 86-20-16-14-**12**-14-15-22-26-32-41-40-55-59-68-80

Ireland
11.01.96: **1**-2-2-2-3-4-14-20-28-x-28

Italy
13.01.96: peaked at no.**2**, charted for 18 weeks

Japan
17.01.96: peaked at no.**62**, charted for 2 weeks

Netherlands
20.01.96: 12-**2**-4-6-11-15-23-48

New Zealand
21.01.96: 9-**5-5**-7-15-11-21-24-19-45

Norway
20.01.96: **1**-2-4-2-4-7-9-12-12-16-20

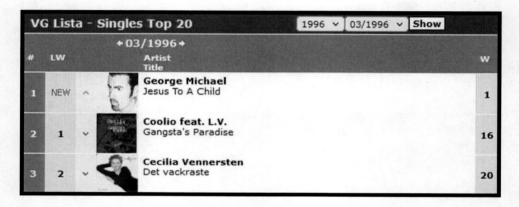

Spain
15.01.96: peaked at no.**1** (7), charted for 16 weeks

Sweden
19.01.96: **2**-4-6-4-4-7-11-14-22-25-25-38-52

Switzerland
21.01.96: 7-7-**4**-8-8-9-11-11-13-13-16-17-22-26-31-40

USA
24.02.96: **7-7**-12-20-39-45-53-62-68-72-80-86-93-97

When his Brazilian lover Anselmo Feleppa, who has been described as his first and biggest love, died suddenly in March 1993 of an AIDS-related brain haemorrhage, George was understandably devastated ~ so much so, he couldn't motivate himself to write any new music for nearly two years.

George had first met Anselmo Feleppa, a dress designer, in the lobby of a hotel in Rio de Janeiro in 1991, when he was on tour in Brazil.

'It was a very strange first love,' he said. 'It was a very distorted situation. This was the first love of my entire life. It was tragic that I lost him, but it was a wonderful experience meeting him.'

Two years after Anselmo Feleppa's passing, George was sat at a keyboard at the same Notting Hill studio where he'd recorded much of his *FAITH* album. Here, tinkering away, he played a very simple string part, and added a very gentle guitar part.

'My way of making music is very strange,' he said. 'Generally, I put my backing tracks together very simply on keyboards. In this case, I think I'd added a little guitar. But the moment I think there's something coming, there's something important coming, I shove everybody out of the room. I go in. I know how to work the vocal recorder that we use, and then I just sing on repeat, repeat, repeat, repeat … and then I sang "Like Jesus to a child" ~ simple as that.'

George immediately knew he had hit upon something special.

'And I thought, "Oh my God, that's him! That's him and me, like Jesus to a child." And within probably a day, the track was almost finished, which is really unusual for me. And within a week, I was singing it in front of the Brandenburg Gate because I was so excited I was writing again. I could write again and not only that but I'd written probably the most personal song I'd ever written in the space of a day, day and a half, and it was all systems go.'

George later described *Jesus To A Child* as the best thing he'd ever done.

'It's a special song,' he said. 'It was one of those songs that just felt like it was handed to me. I didn't have to try very hard. It came naturally. It was recorded over five days but written in just a couple of hours. Yes, it's a sad song, but I hope it has a positive message too ~ I didn't want it to be all "woe is me, woe is me". It is a song about bereavement, but also about hope.'

Writing *Jesus To A Child* inspired George to start work on what would be his first new album for more than five years ~ titled *OLDER*, it was released in May 1996. *Jesus To A Child* was issued as the album's lead single, and George promoted the song with a simple music video directed by Howard Greenhalgh, which featured George standing in a darkened room, with a light shining on his face, as he sang the song.

Jesus To A Child was George's first single to make its chart debut in the UK at no.1, deposing Michael Jackson's *Earth Song*. The single also topped the charts in Australia, Finland, Ireland, Norway and Spain, and achieved no.2 in Italy, the Netherlands and Sweden, no.3 in Belgium, no.4 in Switzerland, no.5 in New Zealand, no.7 in France and the United States, no.10 in Canada, no.11 in Austria and no.12 in Germany.

Following his passing on 25th December 2016, Dame Esther Rantzen revealed that George had secretly donated all his royalties from *Jesus To A Child* to the childrens charity she had founded, ChildLine.

'George helped us to reach out to hundreds of thousands of children through his generosity,' she said. 'I met him a couple of times. He approached us, rather than us going cap in hand to him, but it was an intensely personal gift. He didn't want it to be known or part of his image.'

34 ~ Fastlove

UK: Virgin VSCDT 1579 (1996).
  Tracks: *I'm Your Man/Fastlove (Part II – Fully Extended Mix)*.

4.05.96: **1-1-1**-2-8-10-15-24-34-34-44-63-59-70-85-95-91

Pos	LW	Title, Artist		Peak Pos	WoC
1	New	**FASTLOVE** GEORGE MICHAEL	VIRGIN	1	1
2	1 ↓	**RETURN OF THE MACK** MARK MORRISON	WEA	1	8
3	3	**OOH AAH...JUST A LITTLE BIT** GINA G	ETERNAL	2	5

Austria
5.05.96: 22-x-25-**13**-30-20-24-20-26-28-35-35-35

Belgium
11.05.96: 37-28-28-35-32-**25**-30-41-33-34-35-40-50

Canada
29.04.96: 94-87-71-53-33-24-10-7-5-5-**4**-9-13-18-22-26-36-48-54-80

Australia
5.05.96: 2-2-**1**-**1**-2-**1**-**1**-5-8-9-10-12-13-13-27-27-35-38

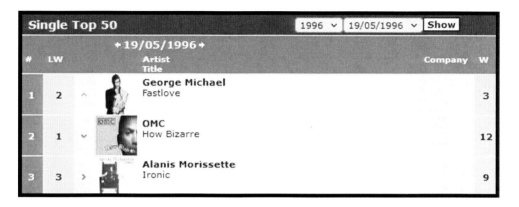

Finland
27.04.96: 8-**5**-9-10-12-18-19

France
27.04.96: 22-20-17-14-13-**10**-14-14-13-15-15-12-13-**10**-**10**-14-13-19-20-20-35-29-47
31.12.16: 88

Germany
6.05.96: 49-74-34-36-30-30-**25**-30-30-28-36-39-50-52-57-59-61-64-75-75-77-86-85

Ireland
25.04.96: **5**-**5**-6-9-8-11-17-17-20-28-29

Italy
27.04.96: peaked at no.**1** (2), charted for 13 weeks

Netherlands
4.05.96: 35-22-13-**12**-21-30-31-34-45

New Zealand
5.05.96: 11-10-**5**-**5**-14-32-22-24-x-39-39

Norway
4.05.96: **11**-**11**-15-12-x-19

Spain
22.04.96: peaked at no.**1** (4), charted for 10 weeks

Sweden
3.05.96: 8-8-**7**-12-16-15-21-23-29-28-28-39-43-45-53-x-x-60

Switzerland
5.05.96: **13**-24-17-22-25-19-23-26-27-21-27-26-21-28-38-36-37-45-x-36

USA
11.05.96: 34-23-15-**8-8**-9-11-13-12-19-24-35-42-55-65-74-78-87-100

Zimbabwe
12.08.96: peaked at no.**6**, charted for 4 weeks

George wrote and recorded *Fastlove* for his *OLDER* album ~ the track sampled Patrice Rushen's 1982 hit, *Forget Me Nots*, so she, Freddie Washington and Terri McFaddin also received a songwriting credit.

Fastlove was issued as the follow-up to *Jesus To A Child*, and George promoted its release with a music video directed by Anthea Benton and Vaughan Arnell. In it, one of the dancers was seen wearing headphones with 'FONY' in the style of Sony's logo ~ a none too subtle reference to George's legal battle with Sony Music.

Fastlove, like *Jesus To A Child*, made its chart debut in the UK at no.1, taking over the top spot from Mark Morrison's *Return Of The Mack*. The single also went to no.1 in Australia, Italy and Spain, and charted at no.4 in Canada, no.5 in Finland, Ireland and New Zealand, no.6 in Zimbabwe, no.7 in Sweden, no.8 in the United States (where it was George's last solo Hot 100 hit), no.10 in France, no.11 in Norway, no.12 in the Netherlands, no.13 in Austria and Switzerland, and no.25 in Belgium and Germany.

George picked up three BRIT Award nominations, including two for *Fastlove*. He won British Male Solo Artist, but lost out to the Spice Girls and *Wannabe* in the British Single of the Year and British Video of the Year categories.

35 ~ Spinning The Wheel

UK: Virgin VSCDG 1595 (1996).
  Tracks: *You Know That I Want To/Safe/Spinning The Wheel (Forthright Mix)*.

31.08.96: **2**-6-11-17-22-27-29-35-39-47-62-75-81-97-x-96-x-90-96

Pos	LW		Title, Artist		Peak Pos	WoC
1	1		**WANNABE** SPICE GIRLS	VIRGIN	1	7
2	New		**SPINNING THE WHEEL** GEORGE MICHAEL	VIRGIN	2	1
3	New		**VIRTUAL INSANITY** JAMIROQUAI	SONY S2	3	1

Australia
1.09.96: 19-**14**-20-15-19-17-24-22-32-33-39-46

Austria
8.09.96: 38-**29**-32-34

Belgium
14.09.96: **36**-44

Finland
24.08.96: **13**-16

Germany
2.09.96: 97-x-**67-67**-68-74-69-72-86-96

Ireland
22.08.96: **14**-19-16-24-29

Italy
7.09.96: peaked at no.**10**, charted for 7 weeks

Netherlands
7.09.96: 46-31-25-**24**-42

New Zealand
15.09.96: 29-31-26-**17**-x-47-47

Sweden
30.08.96: **18**-23-57-38

Switzerland
1.09.96: **24**-50-45-48-x-42-x-48

George co-wrote *Spinning The Wheel* with Jon Douglas, and he recorded the song for his *OLDER* album. The song's title alludes to the risks a lover knows he is taking, when he is aware his partner is sexually promiscuous in an age when AIDS was still relatively new, and was increasingly prevalent within the gay community.

George promoted the release of *Spinning The Wheel* as a single with a black and white music video directed by Anthea Benton and Vaughan Arnell, in which he fronts a band in a nightclub setting.

Spinning The Wheel entered the UK chart at no.2, behind the debut hit by the Spice Girls, *Wannabe*, and rose no higher. The single was less successful in other countries, but it did chart at no.10 in Italy, no.13 in Finland, no.14 in Australia and Ireland, no.17 in New Zealand, no.18 in Sweden, no.24 in the Netherlands and Switzerland, no.29 in Austria, no.36 in Belgium and no.67 in Germany.

Spinning The Wheel broke George's run of success in North America ~ it wasn't a hit in Canada or the United States, and neither were any of George's future singles. George himself blamed his lack of success on Sony Music.

'People talk about me losing my career in America because I cruised,' he said. 'No. I lost my career in America 'cos I took on Sony. Simple. It was already kamikazed there, so it didn't really make much difference. If I'd been successful in America, then I probably wouldn't have cruised there.'

36 ~ Older

UK: Virgin VSCDG 1626 (1997).
　Tracks: *I Can't Make You Love Me/Desafinado/The Strangest Thing (Live)*.

1.02.97: **3**-11-27-30-50-49-57-63-80-82-70-92-80

Pos	LW		Title, Artist		Peak Pos	WoC
1	New		**BEETLEBUM** BLUR	FOOD	1	1
2	1 ↓		**YOUR WOMAN** WHITE TOWN	CHRYSALIS	1	2
3	New		**OLDER/I CAN'T MAKE YOU LOVE ME** GEORGE MICHAEL	VIRGIN	3	1

Ireland
23.01.97: 12-16-9-7-**6-6**-9-10-11-16-22-30-x-x-25

Netherlands
25.01.97: 76-**46**-47-57-59-66-75-86-93-98

Spain
20.01.97: peaked at no.**3**, charted for 6 weeks

Sweden
31.01.97: **60**

George wrote and recorded *Older* for his album with the same title.

   Older was released as the fourth single from the album, with a cover of Bonnie Raitt's 1991 hit *I Can't Make You Love Me* as the B-side, or as one of the tracks on a 4-track CD single/EP. *I Can't Make You Love Me* was written by Allen Shamblin and Mike Reid, and Bonnie Raitt recorded the song for her 1991 album, *LUCK OF THE DRAW*. As a single, Bonnie Raitt took *I Can't Make You Love Me* to no.18 in the United States, no.22 in New Zealand, no.40 in Canada, no.43 in the Netherlands and no.50 in the UK.

In the UK, both *Older* and *I Can't Make You Love Me* were listed, when the single/EP made its chart debut at no.3, kept off the top spot by Blur's *Beetlebum* and White Town's *Your Woman*.

   Older, listed on its own, peaked at no.3 in Spain as well, and achieved no.6 in Ireland. However, the single was only a modest no.46 and no.60 hit in the Netherlands and Sweden, respectively, and it failed to chart in most countries.

37 ~ Star People '97

UK: Virgin VSCDG1641 (1997).
  Tracks: *Everything She Wants (Unplugged)/Star People (Unplugged)*.

10.05.97: **2**-14-32-37-43-59-58-62-74-86-59-63-59-75

Pos	LW	Title, Artist			Peak Pos	WoC
1	New		**LOVE WONT WAIT** GARY BARLOW	RCA	1	1
2	New		**STAR PEOPLE '97** GEORGE MICHAEL	VIRGIN	2	1
3	New		**LOVE IS THE LAW** SEAHORSES	GEFFEN	3	1

Austria
25.05.97: 39-**37**

Finland
17.05.97: **15**

Germany
26.05.97: **64**-72-71-75-72-78-77-81-93

Ireland
1.05.97: **7-7**-8-14-20-28-24

Netherlands
10.05.97: 47-41-**40**-44-56-68-82

Spain
5.05.97: peaked at no.**4**, charted for 2 weeks

Sweden
9.05.97: 60-59-x-x-**37**-55-50-57-x-57

Switzerland
25.05.97: **28**-30-31-35-43-44-46

George wrote and recorded *Star People* for his *OLDER* album ~ the lyrics alluded to the frivolity and materialism of certain, unnamed people in show business.

George re-recorded, remixed and re-titled the track as *Star People '97*, prior to its release as the fifth single from the album. *Star People '97*, unlike the album version of the song, sampled The Gap Band's *Burn Rubber On Me (Why You Wanna Hurt Me)*, which they recorded for their 1980 album, *THE GAP BAND III. Burn Rubber On Me (Why You Wanna Hurt Me)* was written by Charlie Wilson, Lonnie Simmons and Rudy Taylor, and it was a minor no.84 hit on the Hot 100 in the United States for The Gap Band.

Star People '97 debuted at no.2 in the UK, beaten to the top spot by another new entry, Gary Barlow's *Love Won't Wait*. The single also achieved no.4 in Spain, no.7 in Ireland, no.15 in Finland, no.28 in Switzerland, no.37 in Austria and Sweden, and no.40 in the Netherlands. Although it failed to enter the Hot 100 in the United States, *Star People '97* did give George his second chart topper on Billboard's Hot Dance Club Songs chart.

38 ~ Waltz Away Dreaming

UK: Aegean AECD01 (1997).
  Tracks: *Things I Said Tonight (Live Demo Version)* (Toby Bourke).

7.06.97: **10**-22-33-55-86

George wrote *Waltz Away Dreaming* with a little known Irish singer, Toby Bourke, and the pair recorded the song as a duet at London's Denmark Street Studio.

  Waltz Away Dreaming was issued as a single in the UK only in 1997, and made its chart debut at no.10 ~ it was Toby Bourke's first and only hit single.

  In 1999, Tim Hammill remixed *Waltz Away Dreaming*, and this version ~ titled *Waltz Away Dreaming '99* ~ was issued as a single in continental Europe, but it wasn't a hit anywhere.

Both versions of *Waltz Away Dreaming* featured on Toby Bourke's album, *ROOM 21*.

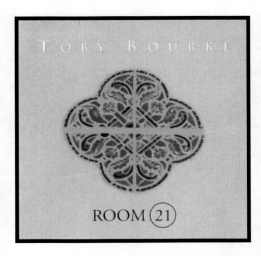

Waltz Away Dreaming was released on one of George's albums for the first time in 1998, when it was included on the cassette edition of the compilation, *LADIES & GENTLEMEN – THE BEST OF GEORGE MICHAEL* ~ however, it was omitted from the CD and vinyl editions of the album.

39 ~ You Have Been Loved

UK: Virgin VSCDG 1663 (1997).
  Tracks: *The Strangest Thing '97 (Radio Mix)/Father Figure (Unplugged)/Praying For Time (Unplugged).*

20.09.97: **2**-6-19-34-51-67-71-71-81-90-84-94-82-99

Pos	LW	Title, Artist		Peak Pos	WoC
1	New	**SOMETHING ABOUT THE WAY YOU LOOK/CANDLE** ELTON JOHN	ROCKET	1	1
2	New	**YOU HAVE BEEN LOVED EP** GEORGE MICHAEL	VIRGIN	2	1
3	1 ↓	**THE DRUGS DON'T WORK** VERVE	HUT	1	2

Ireland
11.09.97: **11**-13-**11**-18-24-30-34

Netherlands
20.09.97: 48-**44**-54-51-58-72

Sweden
12.09.97: **53**-56

George wrote *You Have Been Loved* with David Austin, and he recorded the song for his *OLDER* album ~ like *Jesus To A Child*, the song was inspired by George's late lover, Anselmo Feleppa.

You Have Been Loved was issued as the sixth and final single from *OLDER*, and was released as a double A-side with a remixed version of another track from the album, *The Strangest Thing*. However, only *You Have Been Love* was listed in the few countries where the single charted.

In the UK, *You Have Been Loved* made its chart debut at no.2 behind another new entry, Elton John's tribute the Diana, Princess of Wales, *Candle In The Wind 1997*, which was backed with *Something About The Way You Look*. Diana lost her life on 31st August 1997, when the car she was travelling in crashed in the *Pont de l'Alma* tunnel in Paris, France.

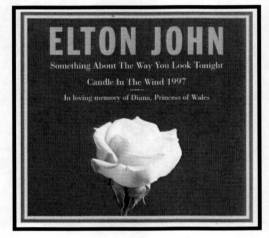

Like Elton's re-working of his 1974 hit, *Candle In The Wind*, the lyrics of *You Have Been Loved* resonated with nation, but it was never going to outsell Elton's tribute.

Outside the UK, *You Have Been Loved* achieved no.11 in Ireland, no.44 in the Netherlands and no.53 in Sweden, but it failed to chart in many countries.

40 ~ Outside

UK: Epic 666249 3 (1998).
  Tracks: *Fantasy 98/Outside (Jon Douglas Remix)*.

31.10.98: **2-2**-7-13-27-35-36-37-43-42-45-48-60-73-82-66-61-87

Pos	LW	Title, Artist		Peak Pos	WoC
1	New	**BELIEVE** CHER	WEA	1	1
2	New	**OUTSIDE** GEORGE MICHAEL	EPIC	2	1
3	New	**SWEETEST THING** U2	ISLAND	3	1

Australia
1.11.98: 19-22-18-**13**-20-26-30-36-42-30-39-38-44

Austria
8.11.98: 28-**17**-21-18-18-19-22-26-28-37-40-40

Belgium
24.10.98: 48-22-21-**20**-25-27-32-34-37-47-47-50-49

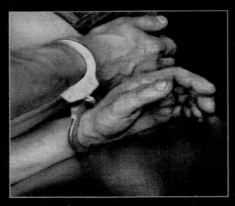

OUTSIDE

GEORGE MICHAEL

CD1 19·10·98 26·10·98 CD2

Finland
31.10.98: 9-**8-8**

France
24.10.98: 32-31-**26**-32-40-40-58-68-59-68-61-67-65-77-74-89-88

Germany
2.11.98: **30**-39-34-34-37-44-55-62-63

Ireland
22.10.98: 9-**7-7**-8-17-26-32-33-39-34-35-35

Italy
24.10.98: peaked at no.**3**, charted for 16 weeks

Netherlands
24.10.98: 44-18-**14**-15-20-20-24-29-39-42-44-55-63-76

New Zealand
15.11.98: 12-12-16-18-17-**11**-18-18-24-47-x-44-48

Norway
31.10.98: 13-12-**10**-13

Sweden
29.10.98: **15**-31-27-22-32-45-58-60-x-x-59-59

Switzerland
1.11.98: 28-24-**19**-22-25-23-27-28-28-28-28-31-32-41-46

George wrote *Outside*, and he recorded the song at London's Sarm West studios, for inclusion on his first solo compilation album, *LADIES & GENTLEMEN – THE BEST OF GEORGE MICHAEL*, which was released in November 1998.

The song was inspired by George's arrest in a public restroom at Will Rogers Memorial Park in Beverly Hills, California, on 7th April 1998. George was arrested 'for engaging in a lewd act' by an undercover police officer, Marcelo Rodriguez.

'I got followed into the restroom,' said George, 'and then this cop ~ I didn't know it was a cop, obviously ~ he started playing this game, which I think is called "I'll show you mine, you show me yours, and then when you show me yours, I'm going to nick you!".'

Following his arrest, George pleaded 'No contest', and was fined $810 and sentenced to 80 hours of community service. The incident also resulted in George coming out publicly as a gay man.

'From the moment I outed myself,' he said, 'when I wrote *Outside*, immediately I thought, "Wouldn't it be great to make a video for all those kids that are now where you where twenty-five years ago, with your only experience being cruising ~ and feeling terrible about it because you're sixteen or whatever?" If someone had made a video like that for my entertainment when I was a young guy, I would have loved it.'

The promo was filmed on 4th July 1998, and was directed by Vaughan 'Von' Arnell, with whom George had previously worked on his *Fastlove* and *Spinning The Wheel* videos.

'Von came to L.A. because he wanted to make something for *Outside*,' said George, 'and he sat with me looking very nervous, and I couldn't work out why, and after about half an hour he said, "Can I be really honest with you?" And I said, "Yeah, of course you can", and he said, "Can we do it in a toilet?"'

'So I sat and looked at him and it took me about ten seconds to say, "Yes, but it's got to be a disco toilet" … and then I immediately had the idea of the revolving urinals and everything, which is probably my favourite three seconds of any video I've ever made.'

In the music video, George dressed as a LAPD police officer ~ the police officer who had arrested him, Marcelo Rodriguez, took offence, and claimed the promo mocked him ~ he took out a $10 million lawsuit against George, which was subsequently dismissed, with the judge ruling that Rodriquez, as a public officer, could not legally recover any damages for emotional distress.

George was well aware the music video would be controversial, but he had no regrets about filming it.

'I thought if it's funny enough,' he said, 'and if the record is good enough, then you can get away with murder!'

Like most of the singles from his *OLDER* album, *Outside* fared best in the UK, where it made its chart debut at no.2, a position it held for two weeks, kept off the top spot by Cher's *Believe*. The single also achieved no.3 in Italy, no.7 in Ireland, no.8 in Finland, no.10 in Norway, no.11 in New Zealand, no.13 in Australia, no.14 in the Netherlands, no.15 in Sweden, no.17 in Austria, no.19 in Switzerland, no.20 in Belgium, no.26 in France and no.30 in Germany.

UK: Epic 667012 2 (1999).
  Tracks: *A Different Corner (Live at Parkinson)*.

13.03.99: **4**-7-13-21-33-38-39-44-47-65-77-82-78-80

Australia
21.03.99: **45**-x-x-49

Belgium
27.03.99: 45-47-**42**-44-46

France
6.03.99: 47-30-**27**-31-31-31-37-38-36-41-48-53-53-78-81-92
31.12.16: 55-93

Germany
15.03.99: 57-44-**38**-43-52-47-49-56-62

Ireland
4.03.99: 15-14-**12**-16-24-32-31

Italy
13.03.99: peaked at no.**8**, charted for 6 weeks

Netherlands
13.03.99: 41-15-12-**9**-11-14-16-18-25-24-31-30-36-45-52-66-73-75

New Zealand
25.04.99: **21**-30-24-35

Spain
13.03.99: 6-8-**5**-6-8-11-12

Sweden
25.03.99: 34-**27**-32-35-37-55-57-59

Switzerland
21.03.99: 28-23-24-23-26-**22**-25-29-41-44-46-42

As was written and originally recorded by Stevie Wonder, for his 1976 album, *SONGS IN THE KEY OF LIFE*. As a single, Stevie Wonder took *As* to no.36 on the Hot 100 in the United States.

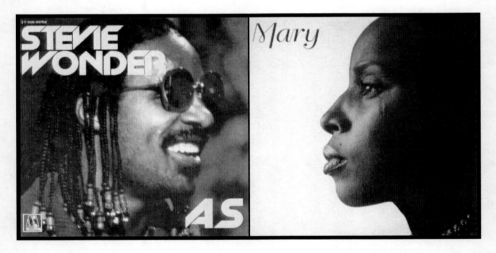

George recorded a cover of *As*, as a duet with Mary J. Blige, for his *LADIES & GENTLEMEN – THE BEST OF GEORGE MICHAEL* album. The recording also featured on Mary J. Blige's 1999 album, *MARY*.

However, *As* was omitted from the American editions of both albums ~ George blamed Jay Boberg, President of Mary J. Blige's record company, who took the decision after George was arrested for engaging in a lewd act in a public restroom. Kirk Burrowes, the Executive Producer of Mary J. Blige's *MARY* album, later confirmed Jay Boberg was indeed the man responsible.

'He (Jay Boberg) did not want to let George Michael, who initiated that original production,' said Kirk Burrowes, 'to use it as a single in the US to launch his greatest hits album. It pissed everyone off at Sony. It pissed George Michael off. It pissed everyone off, but we couldn't make Jay Boberg bend. He should have put it on the *MARY* album, but we couldn't put it on the album in the States because he wouldn't let George Michael put it on *LADIES & GENTLEMEN* in the States.'

Outside the United States, *As* was released as the follow-up to *Outside*, and was promoted with a music video directed by Big TV! Although not as successful as *Outside*, *As* charted at no.4 in the UK, no.5 in Spain, no.8 in Italy, no.9 in the Netherlands, no.12 in Ireland, no.21 in New Zealand, no.22 in Switzerland, no.27 in France and Sweden, no.38 in Germany, no.42 in Belgium and no.45 in Australia.

Two dance covers of *As*, both re-titled *As Always*, have charted in the UK. Farley Jackmaster Funk Presents Ricky Dillard took the song to no.49 in 1989, and Secret Life scored a no.45 hit with their version three years later.

42 ~ If I Told You That

UK: Arista 74321 76628 2 (2000).
   Tracks: *If I Told You That (Johnny Douglas Mix)/Fine (Album Version)* (Whitney Houston).

17.06.00: **9**-19-25-34-48-47-49-54-63-93-62-51

Australia
24.09.00: **37-37**-41-44

Belgium
17.06.00: **41**

Germany
19.06.00: 60-66-**58**-60-62-62-69-77-87

Ireland
8.06.00: **25**

Italy
15.06.00: peaked at no.**9**, charted for 6 weeks

Netherlands
3.06.00: 62-**31**-35-51-61-61-52-53-68-82

Spain
17.06.00: **18**

Sweden
22.06.00: 46-x-**44**-56

Switzerland
11.06.00: 44-36-38-35-**33**-41-43-47-49-58-60-77-84-90-88

If I Told You That was written by Rodney Jerkins, Fred Jerkins III, LaShawn Daniels and Toni Estes, and was originally recorded by Whitney Houston for her 1998 album, *MY LOVE IS YOUR LOVE*.

A duet version of the song, with George, featured on Whitney's compilation, *THE GREATEST HITS*, released in 2000. This version was co-produced by George, whose vocals were added to Whitney's after she had recorded it for her *MY LOVE IS YOUR LOVE* album.

If I Told You That was originally written as a duet for Whitney Houston and Michael Jackson. 'That song was meant for Whitney and Michael,' Rodney Jerkins confirmed in 1998. 'We didn't make it happen, and the next person was George Michael.'

The duet with George was only released as a promotional single in the United States, so it wasn't eligible to chart on the Hot 100. Elsewhere, the single was issued commercially, and apart from the no.9 it achieved in Italy and the UK, sales were generally disappointing, with *If I Told You That* peaking at no.16 in Denmark, no.18 in Spain, no.25 in Ireland, no.31 in Australia and the Netherlands, no.33 in Switzerland, no.41 in Belgium, no.44 in Sweden and no.58 in Germany.

The music video for *If I Told You That*, directed by Kevin Bray, was shot in a nightclub setting. Both George and Whitney appeared in the promo, and during filming George joked, 'She's gonna un-gay me in a minute!', with Whitney responding, 'Boy, please, I un-gayed you the moment you laid eyes on me!'

The promo was included on Whitney Houston's *Fine* DVD single, which was only released in the United States, and later on George's *Twenty Five* video compilation.

43 ~ Freeek!

UK: Polydor 570 681-2 (2002).
  Tracks: *Freeek! (The Scumfrogs Mix)/(The Moogymen Mix)*.

30.03.02: **7**-17-28-42-47-57-65-54-61-74

Australia
31.03.02: **5**-12-27-33-42-48

Austria
31.03.02: **7**-16-10-21-20-28-27-42-39-60-57-57

Belgium
30.03.02: 30-**21**-35-47

Finland
23.03.02: 10-**6**

France
23.03.02: **7**-19-25-34-45-53-64-69-77-97

Germany
1.04.02: **7**-23-28-34-46-61-68-80-88

Ireland
21.03.02: peaked at no.**14**, charted for 3 weeks

Italy
21.03.02: peaked at no.1 (1), charted for 15 weeks

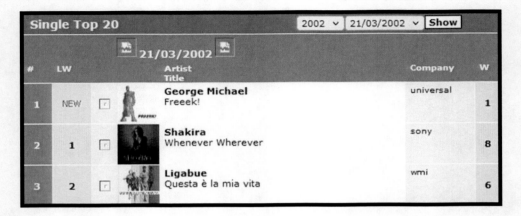

Japan
20.03.02: **93**

Netherlands
30.03.02: **12-12**-17-29-39-61

New Zealand
7.04.02: **15-15**-22-35-47

Norway
30.03.02: **7**-12-9-12-19

Spain
24.03.02: **1-1-1**-2-3-3-6-13-15-17

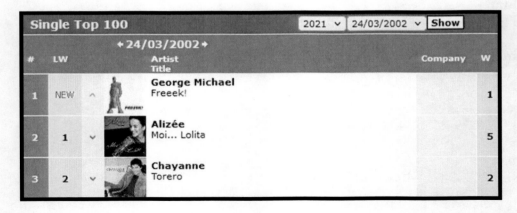

Sweden
29.03.02: **26**-35-42-45-55-55-60-60-53
26.09.02: 59

Switzerland
31.03.02: 5-3-**2**-3-6-14-17-21-39-44-60-74-81-96

George wrote *Freeek!* with Moogymen (*aka* James Jackman, Niall Flynn and Ruadhri Cushnan) ~ a remastered version of the song was later included on George's *PATIENCE* album, which was released in March 2004.

Freeek! sampled three other songs: Aaliyah's *Try Again*, Kool & The Gang's *N.T.*, and Q-Tip's *Breathe And Stop*.

George promoted *Freeek!* with an expensive futuristic music video, featuring cyborgs and innovative technology, which was directed by Joseph Kahn. The promo had a $2 million budget, and included similar effects Joseph Kahn had first used in Janet Jackson's *Doesn't Really Matter* video.

Freeek! hit no.1 in Italy and Spain, and charted at no.2 in Switzerland, no.5 in Australia, no.6 in Finland, no.7 in Austria, France, Germany, Norway and the UK, no.12 in the Netherlands, no.14 in Ireland, no.15 in New Zealand, no.21 in Belgium and no.26 in Sweden.

The B-side of *Freek!* was a live version of John Lennon & Paul McCartney's *The Long And Winding Road*, which George performed at Concert For Linda, a memorial concert staged at the Royal Albert Hall in April 1999 for Linda McCartney, who succumbed to breast cancer on 17th April 1998.

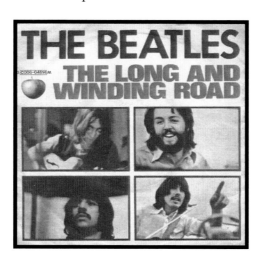

The Beatles recorded *The Long And Winding Road* for their 1970 album, *LET IT BE*. The track was issued as a single in North America, and topped the charts in both Canada and the United States.

44 ~ Shoot The Dog

UK: Polydor 570 924-2 (2002).
 Tracks: *Shoot The Dog (Moogymen Mix)/(Alexkid Shoot The Radio Remix)/(Video).*

10.08.02: **12**-35-54-69-x-73-78

Australia
18.08.02: **36**

Austria
11.08.02: **41**-43-51-60-65

Belgium
17.08.02: **46**

France
3.08.02: 96-**59**-65-78-87-86

Germany
26.08.02: **44**-69-78-96

Ireland
1.08.02: peaked at no.**23**, charted for 2 weeks

Italy
1.08.02: peaked at no.**5**, charted for 10 weeks

Netherlands
10.08.02: 34-**26**-39-54-85

Spain
11.08.02: **4-4**-5-7-13-20-20

Sweden
22.08.02: **39**-48-x-56

Switzerland
18.08.02: **14**-15-17-25-32-42-69-91-94-91

Shoot The Dog is a song George started working on several months before the 9/11 terrorist attack in the United States in 2001 and, as well as the 'Gotta Get up' vocals from George's own *Fastlove*, the recording sampled the Human League's 1981 hit, *Love Action (I Believe In Love)* and Silver Convention's 1976 hit, *Get Up And Boogie*. Consequently, Philip Oakley and Ian Burden were credited alongside George as songwriters.

'I know this is dangerous territory,' said George. 'I've never done anything so political before. I've spent years shouting my mouth off about serious issues over dinner tables, but never really had the confidence to express my views in a song … The truth of the matter is the government didn't want to start talking about Iraq until September because they thought, just like (President George W.) Bush, that if they tied September the 11th into the equation, that they could persuade people … The reason I talk about the Jubilee and the World Cup at the end of *Shoot The Dog* is because I'm talking about things that the government at that time was obviously really thankful for, because they knew it would keep everybody busy.'

Shoot The Dog proved to be hugely controversial, as was the animated music video George used to promote the song. The promo, as well as George in various guises, featured President George W. Bush, the British Prime Minister Tony Blair and his wife Cherie, Iraq's leader Saddam Hussein, HM Queen Elizabeth II, HRH Prince Charles, footballers David Beckham, Paul Scholes and David Seaman, and referee Pierluigi Collina. The music video was directed by 2DTV.

Despite the controversy, *Shoot The Dog* achieved no.4 in Spain, no.5 in Italy, no.12 in the UK, no.14 in Switzerland, no.23 in Ireland, no.26 in the Netherlands, no.36 in Australia, no.39 in Sweden, no.41 in Austria, no.44 in Germany, no.46 in Belgium and no.59 in France.

'I don't regret it for a second,' George stated. 'It was worth the kicking I got because I genuinely believed that I was one of many people that were screaming at the public that they needed to look and be sceptical.'

Like *Freeek!*, *Shoot The Dog* was subsequently included on George's 2004 album, *PATIENCE*.

45 ~ Amazing

UK: Sony Music 674726 2 (2004).
  Tracks: *Freeek! '04.*

13.03.04: **4**-9-11-20-26-37-48-47-47-48-62
10.07.04: 98
9.10.04: 99

Australia
14.03.04: 8-**6**-14-23-25-25-24-27-32-26-33-37-44

Austria
14.03.04: **23**-26-34-37-29-31-38-34-46-50-71

Belgium
13.03.04: 33-**23**-30-34-29-33-45-x-50

Finland
6.03.04: **13**

France
11.04.04: **37**-41-38-45-56-68-77-87-95

Germany
15.03.04: **19**-36-42-44-33-39-44-49-56-64

Ireland
4.03.04: peaked at no.**4**, charted for 6 weeks

Italy
4.03.04: peaked at no.**1** (1), charted for 14 weeks

Netherlands
13.03.04: 15-**9**-18-22-28-42-51-48-69-77

New Zealand
21.03.04: 46-32-33-**30**-37-36-x-x-38-39-39

Norway
13.03.04: **11**-19

Spain
7.03.04: 2-**1**-3-3-6-8-9-9-11-8-13-9-10-12-18-20-9-20

20.02.05: 20

Sweden
12.03.04: **16**-19-32-44-40-42-50

Switzerland
14.03.03: **10-10**-14-22-22-25-27-36-31-41-48-71-80-86-x-88

Amazing was written by George and Johnny Douglas, and George recorded the song for his *PATIENCE* album ~ the song was about, and was dedicated to, George's boyfriend at the time, Kenny Goss.

With *Freeek!* and *Shoot The Dog* having been released in 2002, *Amazing* effectively served as the lead single from *PATIENCE*. George promoted its release with a music video directed by Matthew Rolston, which featured a holographic performance of the song by George in a nightclub setting.

Amazing hit no.1 in Italy and Spain, and charted at no.4 in Ireland and the UK, no.6 in Australia, no.9 in the Netherlands, no.10 in Switzerland, no.11 in Norway, no.13 in Finland, no.16 in Sweden, no.19 in Germany, no.23 in Austria and Belgium, no.30 in New Zealand and no.37 in France.

The single failed to enter the Hot 100 in the United States, but it did give George his third chart topping single ~ after *Monkey* and *Star People '97* ~ on Billboard's Hot Dance Club Songs chart.

46 ~ Flawless (Go To The City)

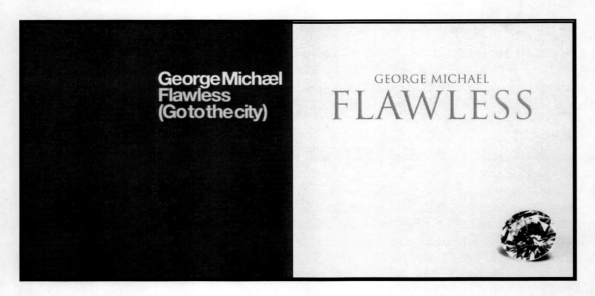

UK: Sony Music 750034 1 (2004).
  Tracks: *Please Send Me Someone (Anselmo's Song) (Alternative Version Edit).*

10.07.04: **8**-14-22-30-34-33-43-50-53-65

Australia
18.07.04: **26**-33-38-39-43

Austria
25.07.04: **72**-73

Belgium
10.07.04: **35**-36-44

Germany
19.07.04: **54**-78-79-84-96-96

Ireland
1.07.04: peaked at no.**23**, charted for 2 weeks

Italy
1.07.04: peaked at no.**7**, charted for 15 weeks

Netherlands
3.07.04: **30**-36-51-63-69-69-68-84

Spain
4.07.04: **2**-5-13-13

Switzerland
11.07.04: 40-**36**-44-38-46-47-70-62-96-97-97

George wrote and recorded *Flawless (Go To The City)* for his *PATEINCE* album. The tracks sampled *Romeo And Juliet* by Alec R. Costandinos and *Flawless* by The Ones ~ the latter, in turn, sampled Gary's Gang's *Keep On Dancin'*. As well as George, Eric Matthew, Gary Turnier, Nashom Wooden, Olivier Stumm and Paul Alexander all received a songwriting credit.

Flawless (Go To The City) was released as the follow-up to *Amazing*, and George promoted its release with a music video directed by Jake Scott, which was set in a hotel room with George seated on the bed while he sings the song, surrounded by dancers who undress and dress themselves. As the songs ends, everyone leaves the hotel room, with George turning out the lights and closing the door as he is the last out.

Although it wasn't as successful as *Amazing*, *Flawless (Go To The City)* was a Top 10 hit in Spain, Italy and the UK, where it peaked at no.2, no.7 and no.8, respectively. Elsewhere, the single charted at no.23 in Ireland, no.26 in Australia, no.30 in the Netherlands, no.35 in Belgium, no.36 in Switzerland, no.54 in Germany and no.72 in Austria.

In common with all George's post-*Fastlove* singles, *Flawless (Go To The City)* missed the Hot 100 in the United States, but it did give him his fourth no.1 on Billboard's Hot Dance Club Songs chart.

47 ~ Round Here

UK: Sony Music 675470 2 (2004).
  Tracks: *Patience/Round Here (Video)*.

13.11.04: **32**-62-x-x-x-97

Italy
4.11.04: peaked at no.**30**, charted for 2 weeks

Switzerland
21.11.04: **55**-94-65-90

George wrote and recorded *Round Here* for his *PATEINCE* album ~ the song was inspired by George's childhood, and in particular his first day at school.

Round Here was the fifth track from *PATIENCE* to be released as a single, and the accompanying music video ~ directed by Andy Morahan ~ featured George in the studio, recording the song, plus footage of Kingsbury, London, which is where George spent most of his childhood years.

Round Here only achieved Top 40 status in two counties, Italy and the UK, where it achieved no.30 and no.32, respectively. The single was also a minor no.55 hit in Switzerland, but it failed to chart in most countries, and was passed over for release in North America.

48 ~ An Easier Affair

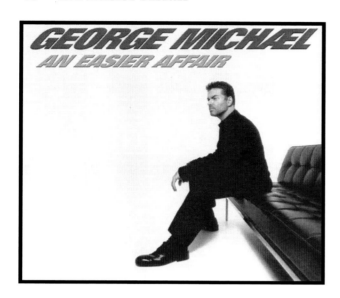

UK: Sony BMG Music Entertainment 82876869462 (2006).
  Tracks: *Brother, Can You Spare A Dime*.

8.07.06: 74-**13**-26-39-51-64-87

Australia
13.08.06: **36**-49

Austria
14.07.06: **58**

France
8.07.06: **87**

Germany
14.07.06: **44**-61-62-67-84-88-94-100

Ireland
6.07.06: **20**

Netherlands
8.07.06: **37**-42-44-55-57-66-79

Sweden
10.08.06: **23**-50-46-44-44-59-46

Italy
6.07.06: peaked at no.**1** (1), charted for 22 weeks

Switzerland
16.07.06: **28**-36-41-68-77-77-61-85-82-79-95-x-x-x-x-98-98-68-98

An Easier Affair was written by George with Kevin Ambrose, Niall Flynn and Ruadhri Cushnan, and he recorded the song for his second greatest hits compilation, *TWENTY FIVE*, which was released in November 2006.

An Easier Affair was released as the lead single from the album ~ it was most successful in Italy, where it made its chart debut at no.1. Elsewhere, the single was less well received, but it did achieve no.13 in the UK, no.20 in Ireland, no.23 in Sweden, no.28 in Switzerland, no.36 in Australia, no.37 in the Netherlands, no.44 in Germany and no.58 in Austria.

The B-side of *An Easier Affair* was a live recording of *Brother, Can You Spare A Dime?*, which George sang when he was a guest at Luciano Pavarotti's 'Pavarotti & Friends' charity concert, staged in the tenor's home town of Modena, Italy, on 6th June 2006. The song was originally composed by Jay Gorney, with lyrics by Yip Harburg, way back in 1932, and is best known for Bing Crosby's recording. At the Pavarotti & Friends concert, as well as performing *Brother, Can You Spare A Dime?*, George also sang *Don't Let The Sun Go Down On Me* as a duet with Luciano Pavarotti.

49 ~ This Is Not Real Love

UK: Sony BMG Music Entertainment 88697019792 (2006).
  Tracks: *Edith & The Kingpin (Recorded Abbey Road Dec. '04).*

11.11.06: 79-**15**-21-36-53-87

Austria
17.11.06: **62**-67

Belgium
25.11.06: 46-**41**

Italy
9.11.06: peaked at no.**4**, charted for 16 weeks

Netherlands
11.11.06: 34-**32**-46-67-91-97

Switzerland
19.11.06: **36**-48-58-82-80

George wrote *This Is Not Real Love* with James Jackman and Ruadhri Cushnan, and he recorded the song with Mutya Buena ~ formerly a member of Sugababes ~ for his *TWENTY FIVE* compilation.

This Is Not Real Love was released as the follow-up to *An Easier Affair*, and was promoted with a music video that featured brief clips of George in the studio and Mutya Buena singing the song, but mostly focussed on actors playing out various love scenes.

Like *An Easier Affair*, *This Is Not Real Love* was most successful in Italy, where it was a no.4 hit. The single also charted at no.15 in the UK, no.32 in the Netherlands, no.36 in Switzerland, no.41 in Belgium and no.62 in Austria.

This Is Not Real Love wasn't issued as a single in the United States until 2008, when it rose to no.8 on Billboard's Hot Dance Club Songs chart, but failed to enter the Hot 100.

Mutya Buena included a remixed version of *This Is Not Real Love* on her debut solo album, *REAL GIRL*, which was released in 2007.

50 ~ December Song (I Dreamed Of Christmas)

UK: Aegean 2729330 (2009).
   Tracks: *Jingle (A Musical Interlude)/Edith & The Kingpin (Live at Abbey Road)/*
      Praying For Time (Live at Abbey Road).

26.12.09: **14**-32

Austria
25.12.09: **63**

Germany
25.12.09: **37**-55

Ireland
17.12.09: **40**

Netherlands
19.12.09: 38-**18**-50-100

Sweden
25.12.09: **43**

George co-wrote *December Song (I Dreamed Of Christmas)* with David Austin, whom he had known since childhood ~ the song sampled Frank Sinatra's *The Christmas Waltz*, which Julie Styne and Sammy Cahn wrote in 1954, and Frank Sinatra recorded for the B-side of his cover of *White Christmas*.

Originally, George and David Austin wrote *December Song (I Dreamed Of Christmas)* with the Spice Girls in mind, and considered offering the song to Michael Bublé, before George decided to record it himself.

December Song (I Dreamed Of Christmas) was only the second festive song George had recorded, after the perennially popular *Last Christmas*. He first made the song available, for free, on his official website on the 25th and 26th December 2008.

George performed *December Song (I Dreamed Of Christmas)* song live, when he appeared as a celebrity guest on the final of sixth series of the UK's *The X-Factor*, which was aired on 13th December 2009. This coincided with the song being released physically for the first time. Within twenty-four hours of George's appearance, all physical copies of the single sold out, forcing the record company to hastily press more copies.

As well as his *The X-Factor* appearance, George promoted *December Song (I Dreamed Of Christmas)* with only his second animated music video, after *Shoot The Dog*, which was directed by MIE. The promo revolved around George's view of Christmas as a young boy.

December Song (I Dreamed Of Christmas) made its chart debut in the UK at no.14, but the following week it dropped to no.32, before falling off the chart a week later. Elsewhere, the single achieved no.18 in the Netherlands, no.37 in Germany, no.40 in Ireland, no.43 in Sweden and no.63 in Austria.

51 ~ True Faith

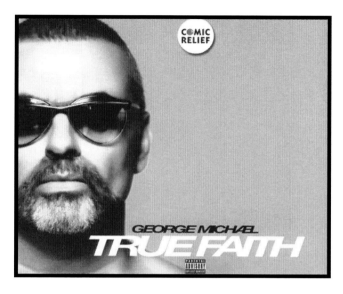

UK: Aegean CDAEG 1 (2011).
  Tracks: *True Faith (Instrumental)*.

26.03.11: **27**-70

Netherlands
19.03.11: **38**-66

True Faith was written by Bernard Sumner, Gillian Gilbert, Peter Hook, Stephen Hague and Stephen Morris, and was originally recorded by New Order for their 1987 album, *SUBSTANCE 1987*.

New Order took *True Faith* to no.4 in New Zealand and the UK, no.5 in Ireland, no.8 in Australia and Germany, no.13 in Switzerland, no.32 in the United States and no.33 in Belgium.

George recorded a cover of *True Faith* in 2001, in support of the Comic Relief charity ~ his vocals were electronically disguised using a vocoder, which pleased some of his fans but alienated others. The music video, directed by MIE, premiered on the BBC's Red Nose Day TV show on 18th March 2011.

True Faith entered the UK chart at no.27, which proved to be its peak position. The single also achieved no.38 in the Netherlands, but it was largely ignored and failed to chart in most countries where it was released.

52 ~ White Light

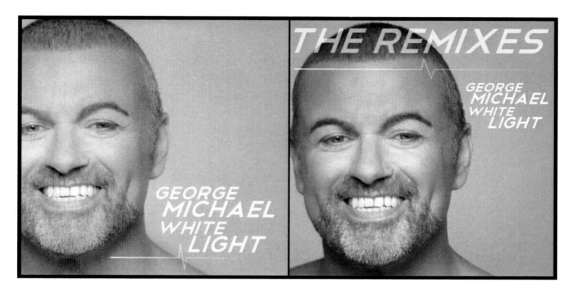

UK: Aegean 3710020 (2012).
Tracks: *Song Of The Siren/White Light (Voodoo Sonics Remix)/(Kinky Roland Remix)*.

25.08.12: **15**-66

Austria
31.08.12: **53**

Belgium
25.08.12: **50**

France
18.08.12: 75 (*White Light* EP) (LP chart)
1.09.12: **73**

Germany
24.08.12: **21**-63-87

Netherlands
21.07.12: 98-x-x-x-**6**-79

Spain
19.08.12: **35**

Switzerland
26.08.12: **34**-74

George wrote and recorded *White Light* in 2012, and the song was released to radio on 2nd July 2012, a date chosen to mark the 30th anniversary of when George first single *Wham Rap!* entered the UK chart.

'When I first wrote it,' said George, 'I thought "Can I be this corny?" To go, "I'm alive, I'm alive, I'm alive" … When I thought about it, there was nothing wrong with that. It was absolutely what I felt, you know, it was an absolute joy.'

George promoted the release of *White Light*, when he performed the song live ~ along with *Freedom! '90* ~ at the closing ceremony of the Summer Olympics, staged in London, on 12th August 2012. The accompanying music video was directed by Ryan Hope.

White Light, which proved to be George's final chart success during his lifetime with a new song, achieved no.6 in the Netherlands, no.15 in the UK, no.21 in Germany, no.34 in Switzerland, no.35 in Spain, no.50 in Belgium, no.53 in Austria and no.73 in France.

THE ALMOST TOP 40 SINGLES

Only one of George's singles has made the Top 50 in one or more countries, but failed to enter the Top 40 in any.

Mothers Pride

George wrote and recorded *Mothers Pride* for his 1990 album, *LISTEN WITHOUT PREJUDICE VOL.1*. In North America, it was issued as the B-side of *Waiting For That Day*, and it picked up enough airplay in the United States to chart in its own right. *Mothers Pride* rose to no.46 on the Hot 100, and spent nine weeks on the chart.

Note: none of George's albums, solo or with Wham!, have been a Top 50 hit, without achieving Top 40 status in at least one country.

GEORGE'S TOP 40 SINGLES

In this Top 40, each of George's singles has been scored according to the following points system.

Points are given according to the peak position reached on the singles chart in each of the countries featured in this book:

No.1:   100 points for the first week at no.1, plus 10 points for each additional week at no.1.

No.2:   90 points for the first week at no.2, plus 5 points for each additional week at no.2.

No.3:   85 points.

No.4-6:   80 points.
No.7-10:   75 points.
No.11-15:   70 points.
No.16-20:   65 points.

No.21-30:   60 points.
No.31-40:   50 points.
No.41-50:   40 points.

No.51-60:   30 points.
No.61-70:   20 points.
No.71-80:   10 points.
No.81-100:   5 points.

Total weeks charted in each country are added, to give the final points score.

Reissues, re-entries and re-recordings of a single are counted together.

1   *Last Christmas* ~ 2842 points

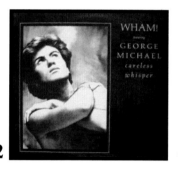

2   *Careless Whisper* ~ 2622 points

3   *Don't Let The Sun Go Down On Me* ~ 2312 points

4   *Wake Me Up Before You Go-Go* ~ 2249 points

5 *Faith* ~ 2234 points

6. *A Different Corner* ~ 1903 points
7. *I Knew You Were Waiting (For Me)* ~ 1823 points
8. *Jesus To A Child* ~ 1821 points
9. *Freedom* ~ 1803 points
10. *I'm Your Man* ~ 1797 points

11. *The Edge Of Heaven* ~ 1782 points
12. *I Want Your Sex* ~ 1773 points
13. *Fastlove* ~ 1765 points
14. *Everything She Wants* ~ 1564 points
15. *Praying For Time* ~ 1533 points

16. *One More Try* ~ 1496 points
17. *Too Funky* ~ 1436 points
18. *Father Figure* ~ 1339 points
19. *Freeek!* ~ 1302 points
20. *Monkey* ~ 1243 points

21. *Amazing* ~ 1237 points
22. *Outside* ~ 1168 points
23. *Freedom! '90* ~ 1081 points
24. *Bad Boys* ~ 1020 points
25. *Young Guns (Go For It!)* ~ 997 points
26. *Somebody To Love* ~ 958 points
27. *As* ~ 860 points
28. *Spinning The Wheel* ~ 834 points
29. *Shoot The Dog* ~ 730 points
30. *Club Tropicana* ~ 707 points

31. *Flawless (Go To The City)* ~ 626 points
32. *Kissing A Fool* ~ 615 points

33. *Star People '97* ~ 601 points
33. *An Easier Affair* ~ 601 points
35. *If I Told You That* ~ 597 points
36. *Wham Rap!* ~ 564 points
37. *White Light* ~ 405 points
38. *Older* ~ 363 points
39. *Waiting For That Day* ~ 353 points
40. *This Is Not Real Love* ~ 347 points

No surprise, given its popularity every festive season, *Last Christmas* is George's most successful chart single, with his most successful solo single *Careless Whisper* not too far behind. George's live duet with Elton John, *Don't Let The Sun Go Down On Me*, is in third place, with Wham!'s *Wake Me Up Before You Go-Go* and George's solo hit *Faith* rounding off the Top 5.

    White Light, George's last Top 40 success while he was still alive, is ranked at no.37.

SINGLES TRIVIA

To date, George has achieved 52 Top 40 singles in one or more of the countries featured in this book, including 13 with Wham! (14 if *Careless Whisper* is included).

There follows a country-by-country look at the most successful hits by George, starting with his homeland.

Note: The *Five Live* EP was classed as an album in most countries, and is only included here where it was listed on the singles chart.

GEORGE IN THE UK

George has achieved 50 hit singles in the UK, which spent 580 weeks on the Top 100.

No.1 Singles

1984	*Wake Me Up Before You Go-Go*
1984	*Careless Whisper*
1984	*Freedom*
1985	*I'm Your Man*
1986	*A Different Corner*
1986	*The Edge Of Heaven*
1987	*I Knew You Were Waiting (For Me)*
1991	*Don't Let The Sun Go Down On Me*
1993	*Five Live* EP
1996	*Jesus To A Child*
1996	*Fastlove*
2021	*Last Christmas*

Most weeks at No.1

3 weeks	*Careless Whisper*
3 weeks	*Freedom*
3 weeks	*A Different Corner*
3 weeks	*Fastlove*
2 weeks	*Wake Me Up Before You Go-Go*
2 weeks	*I'm Your Man*
2 weeks	*The Edge Of Heaven*
2 weeks	*I Knew You Were Waiting (For Me)*
2 weeks	*Don't Let The Sun Go Down On Me*

Singles with the most weeks

105 weeks	*Last Christmas*
25 weeks	*Everything She Wants*
23 weeks	*Careless Whisper*
18 weeks	*Outside*
17 weeks	*Young Guns (Go For It)*
17 weeks	*Fastlove*
16 weeks	*Wake Me Up Before You Go-Go*
16 weeks	*Jesus To A Child*
16 weeks	*Spinning The Wheel*
15 weeks	*Bad Boys*

The Brit Certified/BPI (British Phonographic Industry) Awards

The BPI began certifying Silver, Gold & Platinum singles in 1973. From 1973 to 1988: Silver = 250,000, Gold = 500,000 & Platinum = 1 million. From 1989 onwards: Silver = 200,000, Gold = 400,000 & Platinum = 600,000. Awards are based on shipments, not sales; however, in July 2013 the BPI automated awards, based on actual sales (including streaming 'sales') since February 1994.

4 x Platinum	*Last Christmas* (December 2021) = 2.4 million
Platinum	*Careless Whisper* (September 1984) = 1 million
Platinum	*Fastlove* (April 2019) = 600,000
Platinum	*Wake Me Up Before You Go-Go* (May 2019) = 600,000
Platinum	*Faith* (October 2020) = 600,000
Gold	*Freedom* (November 1984) = 500,000
Gold	*A Different Corner* (May 1986) = 500,000
Gold	*I Knew You Were Waiting (For Me)* (March 1987) = 500,000
Gold	*Five Live* EP (May 1993) = 400,000
Gold	*Jesus To A Child* (October 2019) = 400,000
Gold	*Outside* (January 2020) = 400,000
Gold	*Club Tropicana* (June 2020) = 400,000
Gold	*Don't Let The Sun Go Down On Me* (October 2020) = 400,000
Gold	*As* (April 2021) = 400,000
Gold	*Freedom! '90* (May 2021) = 400,000
Silver	*Young Guns (Go For It)* (November 1982) = 250,000
Silver	*Bad Boys* (June 1983) = 250,000
Silver	*I'm Your Man* (November 1985) = 250,000
Silver	*The Edge Of Heaven* (July 1986) = 250,000
Silver	*Spinning The Wheel* (August 1996) = 200,000
Silver	*You Have Been Loved* (October 1997) = 200,000
Silver	*Star People '97* (January 2019) = 200,000

Silver	*Amazing* (March 2020) = 200,000
Silver	*Father Figure* (July 2020) = 200,000
Silver	*Everything She Wants* (April 2021) = 200,000
Silver	*Somebody To Love* (January 2022) = 200,000

GEORGE IN AUSTRALIA

George has achieved 36 hit singles in Australia, which spent 578 weeks on the chart.

No.1 Singles

1984	*Wake Me Up Before You Go-Go*
1984	*Careless Whisper*
1987	*I Knew You Were Waiting (For Me)*
1987	*Faith*
1996	*Jesus To A Child*
1996	*Fastlove*

Most weeks at No.1

7 weeks	*Wake Me Up Before You Go-Go*
4 weeks	*Careless Whisper*
4 weeks	*I Knew You Were Waiting (For Me)*
4 weeks	*Fastlove*
2 weeks	*Jesus To A Child*

Singles with the most weeks

43 weeks	*Last Christmas*
28 weeks	*Careless Whisper*
28 weeks	*Faith*
24 weeks	*Wake Me Up Before You Go-Go*
21 weeks	*I Knew You Were Waiting (For Me)*
20 weeks	*Freedom*
19 weeks	*I Want Your Sex*
18 weeks	*Young Guns (Go For It!)*
18 weeks	*Wham Rap (Enjoy What You Do)*
18 weeks	*Too Funky*
18 weeks	*Fastlove*

ARIA (Australian Recording Industry Association) Awards

Platinum = 70,000, Gold = 35,000

4 x Platinum	*Last Christmas* = 280,000	
2 x Platinum	*Wake Me Up Before You Go-Go* = 140,000	
2 x Platinum	*Careless Whisper* = 140,000	
2 x Platinum	*Faith* = 140,000	
Platinum	*Freedom! '90* = 70,000	
Platinum	*Too Funky* = 70,000	
Platinum	*Fastlove* = 70,000	
Gold	*I Knew You Were Waiting (For Me)* = 35,000	
Gold	*Father Figure* = 35,000	
Gold	*One More Try* = 35,000	
Gold	*Outside* = 35,000	
Gold	*Freeek!* = 35,000	
Gold	*Amazing* = 35,000	

GEORGE IN AUSTRIA

George has achieved 33 hit singles in Austria, which spent 379 weeks on the chart.

No.1 Singles

2021   *Last Christmas*

Last Christmas topped the chart for one week.

Singles with the most weeks

102 weeks	*Last Christmas*
25 weeks	*Don't Let The Sun Go Down On Me*
14 weeks	*Careless Whisper*
14 weeks	*Faith*
13 weeks	*Too Funky*
12 weeks	*Wake Me Up Before You Go-Go*
12 weeks	*Everything She Wants*
12 weeks	*The Edge Of Heaven*
12 weeks	*I Knew You Were Waiting (For Me)*
12 weeks	*I Want Your Sex*
12 weeks	*Father Figure*
12 weeks	*Fastlove*
12 weeks	*Outside*
12 weeks	*Freeek!*

GEORGE IN BELGIUM (Flanders)

George has achieved 38 hit singles in Belgium (Flanders), which spent 343 weeks on the chart.

No.1 Singles

1984	*Wake Me Up Before You Go-Go*
1986	*The Edge Of Heaven*
1987	*I Knew You Were Waiting (For Me)*
1987	*I Want Your Sex*
1987	*Faith*
1992	*Don't Let The Sun Go Down On Me*

Most weeks at No.1

7 weeks	*Faith*
6 weeks	*Don't Let The Sun Go Down On Me*
4 weeks	*Wake Me Up Before You Go-Go*
2 weeks	*The Edge Of Heaven*
2 weeks	*I Knew You Were Waiting (For Me)*
2 weeks	*I Want Your Sex*

Singles with the most weeks

17 weeks	*Don't Let The Sun Go Down On Me*
16 weeks	*Wake Me Up Before You Go-Go*
14 weeks	*Careless Whisper*
14 weeks	*Faith*
14 weeks	*Too Funky*
14 weeks	*Jesus To A Child*
13 weeks	*I'm Your Man*
13 weeks	*The Edge Of Heaven*
13 weeks	*A Different Corner*
13 weeks	*I Knew You Were Waiting (For Me)*
13 weeks	*Praying For Time*
13 weeks	*Somebody To Love*
13 weeks	*Fastlove*
13 weeks	*Outside*

GEORGE IN CANADA

George has achieved 25 hit singles in Canada, which spent 488 weeks on the chart.

No.1 Singles

1984	*Wake Me Up Before You Go-Go*
1985	*Careless Whisper*
1985	*Everything She Wants*
1986	*A Different Corner*
1987	*Faith*
1988	*One More Try*
1988	*Monkey*
1988	*Kissing A Fool*
1990	*Praying For Time*
1991	*Freedom! '90*
1992	*Don't Let The Sun Go Down On Me*

Most weeks at No.1

4 weeks	*Wake Me Up Before You Go-Go*
4 weeks	*Faith*
2 weeks	*Careless Whisper*
2 weeks	*Everything She Wants*
2 weeks	*One More Try*
2 weeks	*Monkey*
2 weeks	*Praying For Time*

Singles with the most weeks

32 weeks	*Wake Me Up Before You Go-Go*
30 weeks	*Careless Whisper*
29 weeks	*I Want Your Sex*
28 weeks	*Faith*
28 weeks	*Last Christmas*
22 weeks	*Everything She Wants*
22 weeks	*Father Figure*
20 weeks	*A Different Corner*
20 weeks	*I Knew You Were Waiting (For Me)*
20 weeks	*Jesus To A Child*
20 weeks	*Fastlove*

GEORGE IN FINLAND

George has achieved 23 hit singles in Finland, which spent 161 weeks on the chart.

No.1 Singles

1996   *Jesus To A Child*

Jesus To A Child topped the chart for three weeks.

Singles with the most weeks

33 weeks	*Last Christmas*
16 weeks	*Wake Me Up Before You Go-Go*
16 weeks	*Careless Whisper*
12 weeks	*I Want Your Sex*
8 weeks	*Bad Boys*
8 weeks	*Freedom*
8 weeks	*I'm Your Man*
8 weeks	*Jesus To A Child*
7 weeks	*Fastlove*

GEORGE IN FRANCE

George has achieved 31 hit singles in France, which spent 421 weeks on the chart.

No.1 Singles

1992   *Don't Let The Sun Go Down On Me*

Don't Let The Sun Go Down On Me topped the chart for seven weeks.

Singles with the most weeks

29 weeks	*Careless Whisper*
27 weeks	*Don't Let The Sun Go Down On Me*
24 weeks	*Fastlove*
22 weeks	*Everything She Wants*
21 weeks	*One More Try*
20 weeks	*Wake Me Up Before You Go-Go*
20 weeks	*Jesus To A Child*
18 weeks	*I Want Your Sex*
18 weeks	*As*
18 weeks	*Last Christmas*

GEORGE IN GERMANY

George has achieved 39 hit singles in Germany, which spent 616 weeks on the chart.

No.1 Singles

2021   *Last Christmas*

Last Christmas topped the chart for three weeks.

Singles with the most weeks

155 weeks	*Last Christmas*
23 weeks	*Don't Let The Sun Go Down On Me*
23 weeks	*Fastlove*
20 weeks	*Careless Whisper*
19 weeks	*I Want Your Sex*
17 weeks	*Bad Boys*
17 weeks	*Wake Me Up Before You Go-Go*
17 weeks	*Too Funky*
16 weeks	*Young Guns (Go For It!)*
16 weeks	*Jesus To A Child*

GEORGE IN IRELAND

George has achieved 41 hit singles in Ireland, which spent 287 weeks on the chart.

No.1 Singles

1984	*Wake Me Up Before You Go-Go*
1984	*Freedom*
1984	*Careless Whisper*
1985	*I'm Your Man*
1986	*The Edge Of Heaven*
1987	*I Knew You Were Waiting (For Me)*
1987	*I Want Your Sex*
1988	*One More Try*
1993	*Five Live* EP
1996	*Jesus To A Child*

Most weeks at No.1

3 weeks   *Freedom*

3 weeks	*Careless Whisper*
3 weeks	*I Knew You Were Waiting (For Me)*
3 weeks	*Five Live* EP
2 weeks	*Wake Me Up Before You Go-Go*

Singles with the most weeks

53 weeks	*Last Christmas*
14 weeks	*Five Live* EP
13 weeks	*Older*
12 weeks	*Careless Whisper*
12 weeks	*Outside*
11 weeks	*Fastlove*
10 weeks	*Don't Let The Sun Go Down On Me*
10 weeks	*Jesus To A Child*

GEORGE IN ITALY

George has achieved 30 hit singles in Italy, which spent 440 weeks on the chart.

No.1 Singles

1984	*Careless Whisper*
1985	*Last Christmas*
1985	*I'm Your Man*
1987	*Faith*
1991	*Don't Let The Sun Go Down On Me*
1996	*Fastlove*
2002	*Freeek!*
2004	*Amazing*
2006	*An Easier Affair*

Most weeks at No.1

9 weeks	*Careless Whisper*
7 weeks	*Don't Let The Sun Go Down On Me*
3 weeks	*Last Christmas*
3 weeks	*Faith*
2 weeks	*Fastlove*

Most weeks on the chart

| 48 weeks | *Last Christmas* |

27 weeks	*Careless Whisper*
26 weeks	*Too Funky*
26 weeks	*Don't Let The Sun Go Down On Me*
22 weeks	*An Easier Affair*
21 weeks	*I Want Your Sex*
20 weeks	*A Different Corner*
20 weeks	*Praying For Time*
18 weeks	*The Edge Of Heaven*
18 weeks	*Jesus To A Child*

GEORGE IN JAPAN

George has achieved 16 hit singles in Japan, which spent 151 weeks on the chart.

His highest charting singles are *Careless Whisper* and *Last Christmas*, which both peaked at no.12.

Singles with the most weeks

49 weeks	*Last Christmas*
26 weeks	*Careless Whisper*
17 weeks	*Bad Boys*
13 weeks	*Freedom*
9 weeks	*I'm Your Man*
8 weeks	*Club Tropicana*

GEORGE IN THE NETHERLANDS

George has achieved 47 hit singles in the Netherlands, which spent 557 weeks on the chart.

No.1 Singles

1984	*Wake Me Up Before You Go-Go*
1984	*Careless Whisper*
1986	*The Edge Of Heaven*
1987	*I Knew You Were Waiting (For Me)*
1987	*I Want Your Sex*
1987	*Faith*
1991	*Don't Let The Sun Go Down On Me*

Most weeks at No.1

7 weeks	*Careless Whisper*
5 weeks	*Faith*
5 weeks	*Don't Let The Sun Go Down On Me*
3 weeks	*The Edge Of Heaven*
2 weeks	*I Knew You Were Waiting (For Me)*

Singles with the most weeks

113 weeks	*Last Christmas*
21 weeks	*Don't Let The Sun Go Down On Me*
18 weeks	*As*
17 weeks	*Careless Whisper*
16 weeks	*Wake Me Up Before You Go-Go*
16 weeks	*Faith*
15 weeks	*Freedom*
15 weeks	*I Knew You Were Waiting (For Me)*
15 weeks	*I Want Your Sex*
14 weeks	*A Different Corner*
14 weeks	*One More Try*
14 weeks	*Outside*

GEORGE IN NEW ZEALAND

George has achieved 30 hit singles in New Zealand, which spent 361 weeks on the chart.

No.1 Singles

1986	*I'm Your Man*
1987	*Faith*

Faith topped the chart for eight weeks, and *I'm Your Man* for one week.

Singles with the most weeks

24 weeks	*Careless Whisper*
24 weeks	*Last Christmas*
21 weeks	*Praying For Time*
19 weeks	*Faith*
16 weeks	*Freedom*
14 weeks	*Club Tropicana*
14 weeks	*Wake Me Up Before You Go-Go*

13 weeks	*Bad Boys*
13 weeks	*A Different Corner*
13 weeks	*I Knew You Were Waiting (For Me)*
13 weeks	*I Want Your Sex*
13 weeks	*Don't Let The Sun Go Down On Me*

GEORGE IN NORWAY

George has achieved 24 hit singles in Norway, which spent 233 weeks on the chart.

No.1 Singles

1984	*Wake Me Up Before You Go-Go*
1984	*Freedom*
1986	*A Different Corner*
1991	*Don't Let The Sun Go Down On Me*
1996	*Jesus To A Child*

Most weeks at No.1

9 weeks	*Wake Me Up Before You Go-Go*
7 weeks	*Don't Let The Sun Go Down On Me*
3 weeks	*A Different Corner*

Singles with the most weeks

66 weeks	*Last Christmas*
16 weeks	*Wake Me Up Before You Go-Go*
16 weeks	*Careless Whisper*
14 weeks	*Don't Let The Sun Go Down On Me*
11 weeks	*Faith*
11 weeks	*Jesus To A Child*
10 weeks	*Freedom*
10 weeks	*I'm Your Man*
10 weeks	*The Edge Of Heaven*

GEORGE IN SOUTH AFRICA

George has achieved 10 hit singles in South Africa, which spent 147 weeks on the chart.

No.1 Singles

| 1984 | *Careless Whisper* |
| 1986 | *A Different Corner* |

Most weeks at No.1

| 4 weeks | *A Different Corner* |
| 3 weeks | *Careless Whisper* |

Singles with the most weeks

21 weeks	*Careless Whisper*
18 weeks	*A Different Corner*
18 weeks	*Faith*
17 weeks	*Wake Me Up Before You Go-Go*
16 weeks	*I Knew You Were Waiting (For Me)*
14 weeks	*Everything She Wants*
12 weeks	*Freedom*
12 weeks	*The Edge Of Heaven*
10 weeks	*Club Tropicana*

GEORGE IN SPAIN

George has achieved 25 hit singles in Spain, which spent 290 weeks on the chart.

No.1 Singles

1993	*Somebody To Love (Live)*
1996	*Jesus To A Child*
1996	*Fastlove*
2002	*Freeek!*
2004	*Amazing*

Most weeks at No.1

7 weeks	*Jesus To A Child*
4 weeks	*Somebody To Love (Live)*
4 weeks	*Fastlove*
3 weeks	*Freeek!*

Singles with the most weeks

42 weeks	*Last Christmas*
33 weeks	*Faith*
33 weeks	*I Want Your Sex*
20 weeks	*Somebody To Love (Live)*
20 weeks	*Amazing*
16 weeks	*Wake Me Up Before You Go-Go*
16 weeks	*Jesus To A Child*
15 weeks	*Father Figure*
11 weeks	*Careless Whisper*
10 weeks	*Fastlove*
10 weeks	*Freeek!*

GEORGE IN SWEDEN

George has achieved 32 hit singles in Sweden, which spent 371 weeks on the chart.

No.1 Singles

1983	*Young Guns (Go For It!)*
1984	*Wake Me Up Before You Go-Go*
2017	*Last Christmas*

Last Christmas returned to no.1 in 2018, 2019 and 2021.

Most weeks at No.1

6 weeks	*Last Christmas*
2 weeks	*Young Guns (Go For It!)*
2 weeks	*Wake Me Up Before You Go-Go*

Singles with the most weeks

101 weeks	*Last Christmas*
20 weeks	*Careless Whisper*
16 weeks	*Wake Me Up Before You Go-Go*
16 weeks	*Don't Let The Sun Go Down On Me*
16 weeks	*Too Funky*
16 weeks	*Fastlove*
14 weeks	*Young Guns (Go For It!)*
13 weeks	*Jesus To A Child*

| 12 weeks | *Everything She Wants* |
| 12 weeks | *I Knew You Were Waiting (For Me)* |

GEORGE IN SWITZERLAND

George has achieved 32 hit singles in Switzerland, which spent 476 weeks on the chart.

No.1 Singles

| 1984 | *Careless Whisper* |
| 1992 | *Don't Let The Sun Go Down On Me* |

Most weeks at No.1

| 6 weeks | *Don't Let The Sun Go Down On Me* |
| 4 weeks | *Careless Whisper* |

Singles with the most weeks

103 weeks	*Last Christmas*
28 weeks	*Don't Let The Sun Go Down On Me*
19 weeks	*Fastlove*
18 weeks	*Careless Whisper*
18 weeks	*Too Funky*
16 weeks	*Jesus To A Child*
15 weeks	*Wake Me Up Before You Go-Go*
15 weeks	*Outside*
15 weeks	*If I Told You That*
15 weeks	*Amazing*
15 weeks	*An Easier Affair*

GEORGE IN THE USA

George has achieved 27 hits in the United States, which spent 433 weeks on the Hot 100.

No.1 Singles

1984	*Wake Me Up Before You Go-Go*
1985	*Careless Whisper*
1985	*Everything She Wants*
1987	*I Knew You Were Waiting (For Me)*
1987	*Faith*

1988	*Father Figure*
1988	*One More Try*
1988	*Monkey*
1990	*Praying For Time*
1991	*Don't Let The Sun Go Down On Me*

Most weeks at No.1

4 weeks	*Faith*
3 weeks	*Wake Me Up Before You Go-Go*
3 weeks	*Careless Whisper*
3 weeks	*One More Try*
2 weeks	*Everything She Wants*
2 weeks	*I Knew You Were Waiting (For Me)*
2 weeks	*Father Figure*
2 weeks	*Monkey*

Singles with the most weeks

25 weeks	*Last Christmas*
24 weeks	*Wake Me Up Before You Go-Go*
21 weeks	*Careless Whisper*
20 weeks	*Everything She Wants*
20 weeks	*I Want Your Sex*
20 weeks	*Faith*
20 weeks	*Don't Let The Sun Go Down On Me*
20 weeks	*Too Funky*
19 weeks	*Fastlove*
18 weeks	*Freedom*
18 weeks	*I'm Your Man*
18 weeks	*One More Try*

RIAA (Recording Industry Association of America) Awards

The RIAA began certifying Gold singles in 1958 and Platinum singles in 1976. From 1958 to 1988: Gold = 1 million, Platinum = 2 million. From 1988 onwards: Gold = 500,000, Platinum = 1 million. Awards are based on shipments, not sales (unless the award is for digital sales).

2 x Platinum	*Last Christmas* (December 2019) = 2 million
Platinum	*I Want Your Sex* (November 1989) = 1 million
Platinum	*Wake Me Up Before You Go-Go* (May 1992) = 1 million
Platinum	*Careless Whisper* (May 1992) = 1 million
Gold	*Faith* (November 1989) = 500,000

Gold   *One More Try* (November 1989) = 500,000
Gold   *Freedom! '90* (April 1991) = 500,000
Gold   *Don't Let The Sun Go Down On Me* (January 1992) = 500,000
Gold   *Everything She Wants* (May 1992) = 500,000
Gold   *Too Funky* (August 1992) = 500,000
Gold   *Jesus To A Child* (April 1996) = 500,000
Gold   *Fastlove* (July 1996) = 500,000

GEORGE IN ZIMBABWE

George has achieved 14 hit singles in Zimbabwe, which spent 160 weeks on the chart.

No.1 Singles

1986   *A Different Corner*
1987   *I Knew You Were Waiting (For Me)*
1991   *Freedom! '90*

Most weeks at No.1

5 weeks   *I Knew You Were Waiting (For Me)*
2 weeks   *A Different Corner*

Singles with the most weeks

30 weeks   *I Knew You Were Waiting (For Me)*
23 weeks   *A Different Corner*
18 weeks   *The Edge Of Heaven*
15 weeks   *Young Guns (Go For It!)*
15 weeks   *I'm Your Man*
15 weeks   *Careless Whisper*
11 weeks   *Freedom*

All The Top 40 Albums

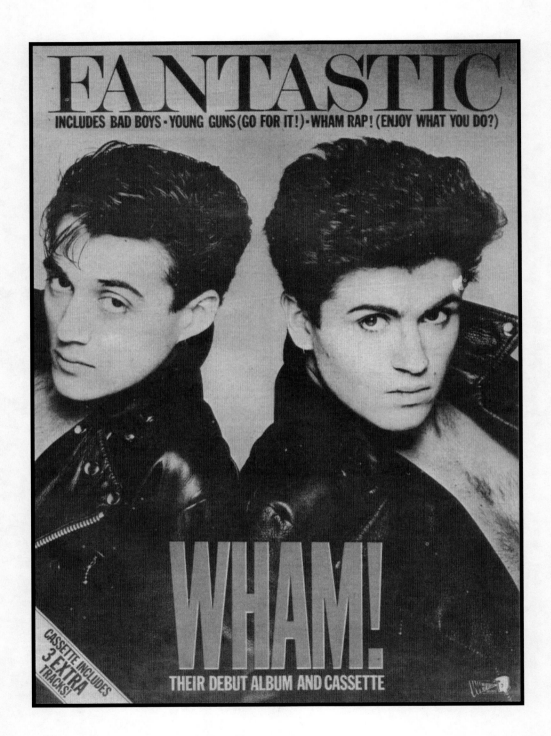

1 ~ FANTASTIC

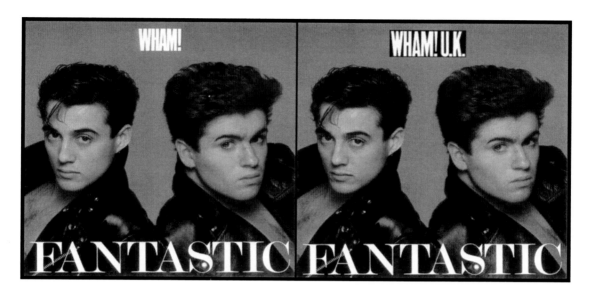

Bad Boys/A Ray Of Sunshine/Love Machine/Wham Rap! (Enjoy What You Do)/Club Tropicana/Nothing Looks The Same In The Light/Come On/Young Guns(Go For It!)

Cassette & CD Bonus Tracks: *A Ray Of Sunshine (Instrumental Remix)/Love Machine (Instrumental Remix)/Nothing Looks The Same In The Light (Instrumental Remix)*

Produced by George Michael, Bob Carter & Steve Brown.

UK: Inner Vision IVL 25328 (1983).

9.07.83: **1-1**-2-4-7-4-3-3-3-3-4-5-7-5-5-7-13-11-14-17-10-10-8-8-11-11-12-11-21-25-19-27-35-40-24-44-48-53-56-82-59-81-77-85-83-x-68-95-54-66-69-80-69-63-58-70-46-48-48-56-37-40-58-51-75-62-76-66-61-57-46-54-60-71-80-79-74-64-54-40-56-40-45-37-49-60-43-48-54-55-54-65-45-33-40-46-62-75-79-69-64-78-86-89-64-73-60-58-77-84-96-86-86-x-91

Pos	LW	Title, Artist		Peak Pos	WoC
1	New	**FANTASTIC** WHAM!	INNER VISION	1	1
2	1 ↓	**SYNCHRONICITY** THE POLICE	A&M	1	3
3	2 ↓	**THRILLER** MICHAEL JACKSON	EPIC	1	31

5.07.86: 58-47-89

Australia
25.07.83: peaked at no.**6**, charted for 28 weeks

Finland
02.83: peaked at no.**8**, charted for 15 weeks

Germany
18.07.83: 61-13-9-**7**-8-**7**-8-**7-7-7**-8-8-12-16-20-27-33-36-34-53-47-64

Japan
21.09.83: peaked at no.**17**, charted for 44 weeks

Netherlands
16.07.83: 26-14-13-9-**8**-13-11-12-16-21-22-24-24-18-23-19-28-39-44
25.08.84: 40-38-42-38-39-39-45-44-x-38-37-38-38-33-50
1.12.84: 28-x-42-41-44-43-39-37-x-x-x-x-38-31-45-37-38-37-49-48

New Zealand
14.08.83: 12-4-2-**1-1-1**-2-3-5-10-13-12-13-14-16-31-35-31-33-33-33-33-33-46-x-44-x-x-
   x-x-41

Norway
16.07.83: 14-9-**8**-12-13-14-18-19-19

South Africa
19.11.83: peaked at no.**3**, charted for 21 weeks

Sweden
8.09.83: **15**-23-22-29 (bi-weekly)

Switzerland
6.11.83: **25**

USA
24.09.83: 96-84-**83**

Zimbabwe
25.09.83: peaked at no.**6**

George and Andrew Ridgeley recorded their debut album, which they cheekily titled *FANTASTIC*, at London's Maison Rouge Studios.

George wrote or co-wrote seven of the eight songs on the album, with Andrew co-writing two songs, *Wham Rap! (Enjoy What You Do)* and *Club Tropicana*. The one exception was a cover of *Love Machine*, which Pete Moore and Billy Griffin wrote, and was originally recorded by The Miracles in 1975. The Miracles took the song to no.1 in the United States and no.3 in the UK.

George and Andrew wrote a further two songs for the album, *Golden Soul* and *Soul Boy*, but they discarded both as they didn't feel either was strong enough. Neither song has ever been officially released, but both have leaked on the internet. Another song the duo decided against recording for the album, feeling it wasn't in keeping with the image they were trying to portray, was *Careless Whisper*.

Andrew acknowledged, musically, George's talent was greater than his own.

'I can sing a bit, but not as well as him,' he said, 'so what's the point? The same with songwriting. It just so happens he's one of the best songwriters in the world today, along with people like Michael Jackson and Stevie Wonder. He's certainly the best in Britain, so it'd just be nonsense for me to force my position, and say on the next LP I have to write four songs to George's five. To do that at this stage would mean compromising our very, very high standards, so I'm satisfied to step back and leave all that to George.'

In the United States, to avoid confusion with a similarly named American group, *FANTASTIC* was originally credited to Wham! U.K., but the 'U.K.' was quickly dropped.

Four singles, one of which was remixed, re-titled and reissued, plus a megamix medley of three songs, were released from the album:

- *Wham Rap!*
- *Young Guns (Go For It!)*
- *Wham Rap! (Enjoy What You Do)*
- *Bad Boys*
- *Club Tropicana*
- *Club Fantastic Megamix*

Wham Rap!, the duo's debut single, was only a minor hit in the UK when it was first issued, but it fared much better when it was remixed and re-titled, and released as the follow-up to *Young Guns (Go For It!)*.

George and Andrew Ridgeley were in a battle with their record company Inner Vision, desperate to escape what they had realised was a very one-sided record contract not in their favour, when against their wishes *Club Fantastic Megamix* was issued as a single. It was it was a medley of three songs on *FANTASTIC*, namely *A Ray Of Sunshine*, *Love Machine* and *Come On*, and since the songs had already been recorded and released, George and Andrew were powerless to prevent the release of *Club Fantastic Megamix*, but they did urge their fans not to purchase it.

FANTASTIC made its chart debut at no.1 in the UK, a position it held for two weeks. The album also topped the chart in New Zealand, and achieved no.3 in South Africa, no.6 in Australia and Zimbabwe, no.7 in Germany, no.8 in Finland, the Netherlands and Norway, no.15 in Sweden, no.17 in Japan and no.25 in Switzerland. The album was also a minor no.85 hit in the United States.

When *FANTASTIC* was reissued on CD in 1998, as with the original cassette and CD versions of the album, the three instrumental remixes were included as bonus tracks.

2 ~ MAKE IT BIG

*Wake Me Up Before You Go-Go/Everything She Wants/Heartbeat/Like A Baby/Freedom/
If You Were There/Credit Card Baby/Careless Whisper*

Produced by George Michael.

UK: Epic EPC 86311 (1984).

17.11.84: **1-1**-2-3-3-3-3-3-4-3-5-9-7-10-10-6-15-17-15-15-18-12-11-16-20-20-22-29-26-
28-32-35-41-32-38-32-36-37-33-35-45-41-47-51-43-66-72-77-85-93-x-99-x-80-90-78-
63-52-51-40-50-41-69-60-x-94-91-96

Pos	LW	Title, Artist		Peak Pos	WoC
1	New	**MAKE IT BIG** WHAM!	EPIC	1	1
2	1↓	**WELCOME TO THE PLEASUREDOME** FRANKIE GOES TO HOLLYWOOD	ZTT	1	2
3	New	**ALF** ALISON MOYET	CDS	3	1

10.05.86: 97
28.06.86: 96-60-38-100-100-95

Australia
19.11.84: peaked at no.**1** (2), charted for 28 weeks

Austria
15.12.84: 6-5-9-**4-4**-7-7-9-11-18 (bi-weekly)

Canada
3.11.84: 77-56-35-24-19-15-10-7-5-4-3-**1-1-1-1**-2-2-**1**-2-4-4-5-6-9-17-18-18-17-16-15-
10-9-9-9-7-7-10-15-15-14-14-14-13-11-9-8-10-11-13-15-16-20-27-34-35-41-38-35-34-
31-31-31-28-27-27-28-34-48-56-58-58-70

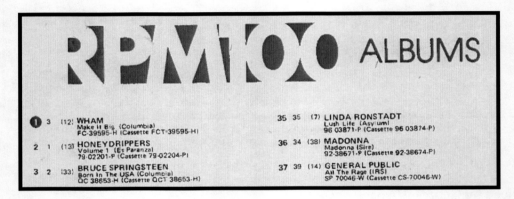

Finland
11.84: peaked at no.**1** (4), charted for 22 weeks

Netherlands
17.11.84: **1-1**-2-3-3-3-2-2-**1-1-1**-4-6-7-11-15-14-15-22-23-22-24-27-23-27-46-36-36-39-
39-40-47-49-44-42-45-42-36-31-23-29-33-50-x-49

Germany
19.11.84: 36-20-7-7-9-7-10-**5-5-5**-8-7-9-11-13-16-17-23-29-37-51-43-51-55-60

Italy
17.11.84: peaked at no.**1** (7), charted for 25 weeks

Japan
21.11.84: peaked at no.**1**, charted for 26 weeks

New Zealand
25.11.84: 6-5-7-11-11-11-11-11-8-2-**1**-2-2-3-3-4-6-7-15-12-18-19-35-33-x-50

Norway
5.11.84: **1-1-1-1-1**-2-2-2-2-2-3-4-8-10-12-16-16-19-18

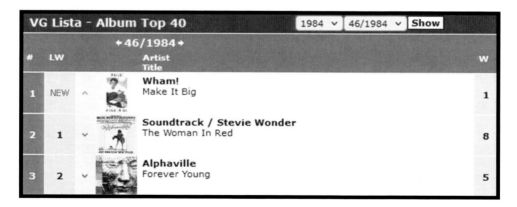

South Africa
24.11.84: peaked at no.**1** (10), charted for 24 weeks

Sweden
23.11.84: 5-**3-3-3**-5-5-4-8-16-28-43 (bi-weekly)

Switzerland
18.11.84: 9-13-3-2-**1**-3-3-4-2-2-3-2-4-8-7-11-15-17-26-28-30-x-28-x-25

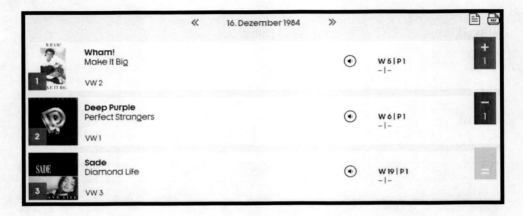

USA
10.11.84: 50-25-24-24-23-23-23-23-19-17-13-10-6-3-3-2-**1-1-1**-4-7-7-7-7-9-10-9-9-8-8-7-6-7-7-7-8-11-15-16-16-17-16-17-15-15-11-11-11-11-14-18-18-18-23-27-31-37-41-56-61-61-55-55-48-48-52-57-66-78-95-95

4.02.17: 93-88

Zimbabwe
20.01.85: peaked at no.**4**

Wham!'s second album *MAKE IT BIG* was mostly written and recorded at Studio Miraval in southern France, primarily for tax reasons.

'We could have gone to Montserrat or Nassau,' said Andrew Ridgeley, 'but it was hot down in France and we fancied a nice summer. Also, it was only one and a half hours from London, and George had to keep going back to do things for *Careless Whisper*.'

'I went over (to France) with five basic ideas,' said George, 'and I thought, Oh, I'll muddle my way through 'cos I felt very good at the time. On the way to the airport in the taxi I got the chorus line for *Freedom*, and when I got there it kept going round in my head, so we worked on it and did *Freedom* on the third day.'

Two tracks ~ *Wake Me Up Before You Go-Go* and *Careless Whisper* ~ were recorded in London, at Sarm West's Studio 2, which is where many of the other songs on the album were mixed and completed. The album itself, incorrectly, credited the album as having been mixed at London's Good Earth Studios and Marcadet Studios in Paris, France. Most of the songs on the album were recorded with a live rhythm section.

George was responsible for writing seven of the eight tracks on *MAKE IT BIG*, with Andrew Ridgeley credited with co-writing *Careless Whisper*. Like FANTASTIC before it, the also featured one cover, *If You Were There*, which Ernie Isley, Marvin Isley and Chris Jasper wrote. The song was originally recorded by the Isley Brothers, for their 1973 album, *3 + 3*, and was issued as the B-side of the single *Need A Little Taste Of Love* in the UK.

Four massive hit singles were released from *MAKE IT BIG*:

- *Wake Me Up Before You Go-Go*
- *Careless Whisper*
- *Freedom*
- *Everything She Wants*

Careless Whisper was issued as a solo single by George in most countries, but was credited to Wham! featuring George Michael in North America. In a few countries, including the UK, *Everything She Wants* was released as a double A-side with *Last Christmas*.

Wham! promoted their second album with The Big Tour, which kicked off at Whitley Bay, England, on 4th December 1984. In total, the duo played 15 dates in the UK, seven in Japan, six in the United States, five in Australia, two in Hong Kong and two in China ~ where Wham! became the first ever Western pop act to play a concert, a momentous event that attracted huge media attention, and resulted in the 1986 documentary film, *Wham! In China: Foreign Skies*. The Big Tour concluded in Canton, China, on 10th April 1985.

MAKE IT BIG mirrored the success of *FANTASTIC* in the UK, where it made its chart debut at no.1, a position it held for two weeks. The album also hit no.1 in Australia, Canada, Finland, Italy, Japan, the Netherlands, New Zealand, Norway, South Africa, Switzerland and the United States, and charted at no.3 in Sweden, no.4 in Austria and Zimbabwe, and no.5 in Germany.

3 ~ THE FINAL

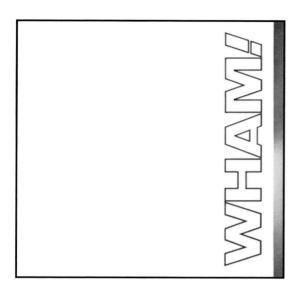

LP1: *Wham Rap! (Enjoy What You Do) (Special US Remix)/Young Guns (Go For It!) (12" Version)/Bad Boys/Club Tropicana/Wake Me Up Before You Go-Go/Careless Whisper (12" Version)/Freedom (7" Version)/Last Christmas (Pudding Mix)*

LP2: *Everything She Wants (Long Remix)/I'm Your Man (Extended Stimulation)/Blue (Armed With Love)/A Different Corner/Battlestations/Where Did Your Heart Go? (David Was, Don Was)/The Edge Of Heaven*

CD: *Wham Rap! (Enjoy What You Do) (Special US Remix)/Young Guns (Go For It!)/Bad Boys/Club Tropicana/Wake Me Up Before You Go-Go/Careless Whisper (7" Version)/ Freedom (7" Version)/Last Christmas (Pudding Mix)/Everything She Wants (Remix)/I'm Your Man/A Different Corner/Battlestations/Where Did Your Heart Go (Dave Was, Don Was)/The Edge Of Heaven*

UK: Epic EPC 88681 (1986).

19.07.86: **2-2-2**-3-4-6-8-11-19-23-26-29-25-21-23-27-32-38-53-45-49-55-23-15-15-18-
   30-33-36-45-47-45-53-51-50-66-63-68-91-96-x-81-88-69-92-x-x-99
10.07.99: 36-40
10.12.11: 50-74-91-97
5.01.17: 40-31-29-21-19-28-29-35-34-30-60-100
26.10.17: 94-80-x-91-86

Pos	LW	Title, Artist			Peak Pos	WoC
1	1	**TRUE BLUE** MADONNA		SIRE	1	2
2	New	**THE FINAL** WHAM!		EPIC	2	1
3	3	REVENGE **REVENGE** EURYTHMICS		RCA	3	2

Australia
28.07.86: peaked at no.**5**, charted for 28 weeks

Austria
1.08.86: 30-**3**-4-**3**-4-9-22 (bi-weekly)

Finland
07.86: peaked at no.**11**, charted for 15 weeks

Germany
14.07.86: 55-19-6-**2-2-2-2**-3-4-4-8-13-18-24-30-32-43-42-58-56-56-64

Italy
12.07.86: peaked at no.**2**, charted for 21 weeks

Japan
6.08.86: peaked at no.**11**, charted for 15 weeks

Norway
19.07.86: 15-11-9-13-8-8-**7**-8-10-14-19

Netherlands

12.07.86: 8-2-2-**1-1-1**-2-2-3-3-7-9-13-14-13-15-15-20-23-32-29-36-37-33-28-19-12-22-31-33-26-30-33-31-46-46-44-35-51-61-72-62-25-24-31-36-40-62-77-82-99

23.11.91: 78-54-44-33-33-x-26-20-19-31-43-47-69-80

New Zealand

10.08.86: 8-**1-1-1-1-1-1-1**-2-2-2-8-10-10-12-13-15-17-19-21-12-18-21-20-23-34-34-47-x-48

7.07.96: 23-13-15-21-29-49

2.01.17: 34

South Africa

17.08.86: peaked at no.**1** (6), charted for 33 weeks

Spain

6.10.86: peaked at no.**3**, charted for 36 weeks

Sweden
9.07.86: 25-**16**-17-31 (bi-weekly)

Switzerland
20.07.86: 26-4-**2-2-2**-3-4-5-6-15-25-16-28
1.01.17: 82

Zimbabwe
28.09.86: peaked at no.**5**

In the spring of 1986, after releasing just two albums together, George and Andrew Ridgeley announced they were breaking up.

'When I decided to split with Andrew I was in the middle of a very, very heavy depression,' said George. 'I had personal problems at the time. I was going through the end of a relationship and I was feeling very negative about the whole Wham! thing. I was feeling trapped by a lot of things.'

The split was amicable, with George keen to start writing and recording new music for an older, more mature audience.

'True, we could have gone on,' he said, 'possibly for many years, but what would the name Wham! stand for in, say, five years' time? Two men approaching their thirties, and singing about ~ what? To us, that name is about being young, optimistic, with everything to gain, and an excitement for the future. Andrew and I have somehow managed to keep hold of these things, and our friendship, for four years, and that's the best reason we can think of for finishing things now, before experience and the music business take their toll.'

George and Andrew did promise a farewell single and concert, plus a greatest hits album, before they went their separate ways. The latter, titled *THE FINAL*, included six Top 40 singles that didn't feature on the first two Wham! albums:

- *Last Christmas*
- *I'm Your Man*
- *A Different Corner*
- *The Edge Of Heaven*
- *Where Did Your Heart Go?*
- *Battlestations*

Battlestations was released exclusively in Spain, while *A Different Corner* ~ like *Careless Whisper* ~ was issued as a solo single by George.

THE FINAL entered the UK chart at no.2, kept off the top spot by Madonna's *TRUE BLUE*. The compilation did hit no.1 in the Netherlands, New Zealand and South Africa, and achieved no.2 in Germany, Italy and Switzerland, no.3 in Austria and Spain, no.5 in Australia and Zimbabwe, no.7 in Norway, no.11 in Finland and Japan, and no.16 in Sweden.

4 ~ MUSIC FROM THE EDGE OF HEAVEN

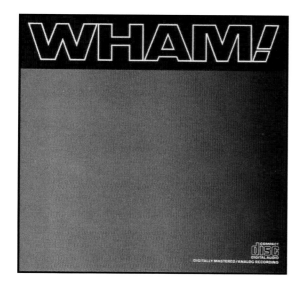

Hot Side: *The Edge Of Heaven/Battlestations/I'm Your Man/Wham! Rap '86*
Cool Side: *A Different Corner/Blue (Live in China)/Where Did Your Heart Go?/Last Christmas*

Produced by George Michael.

UK: Not released.

USA: Columbia OC 40285 (1986).

19.07.86: 41-20-15-13-12-**10-10**-12-12-17-20-28-42-49-56-69-81

Canada
5.07.86: 77-65-41-24-16-**9-9**-10-10-12-12-13-19-19-25-39-49-49-72

MUSIC FROM THE EDGE OF HEAVEN was released exclusively in Japan and North America, instead of *THE FINAL* compilation. The album focussed on the newer songs from *THE FINAL*, leaving off the older hits, and included an exclusive live recording, *Blue (Live in China)*.

There were some differences between the versions of certain songs on *MUSIC FROM THE DGE OF HEAVEN* and *THE FINAL*:

- *THE FINAL* featured 'The Pudding Mix' of *Last Christmas*.

- *A Different Corner* featured the intro from the music video on *MUSIC FROM THE EDGE OF HEAVEN*.

- On *MUSIC FROM THE DGE OF HEAVEN*, an edited version of *I'm Your Man* with a newly recorded spoken bridge featured.

MUSIC FROM THE EDGE OF HEAVEN rose to no.9 in Canada and no.10 in the United States.

In 2015, along with *FANTASTIC* and *MAKE IT BIG*, *MUSIC FROM THE EDGE OF HEAVEN* was released in Europe as part of a three album box-set titled *ORIGINAL ALBUM CLASSICS*.

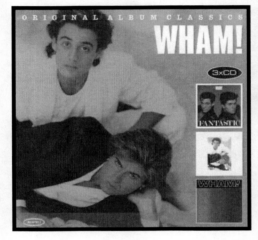

MUSIC FROM THE EDGE OF HEAVEN was released on iTunes in the UK for the first time in 2017.

5 ~ FAITH

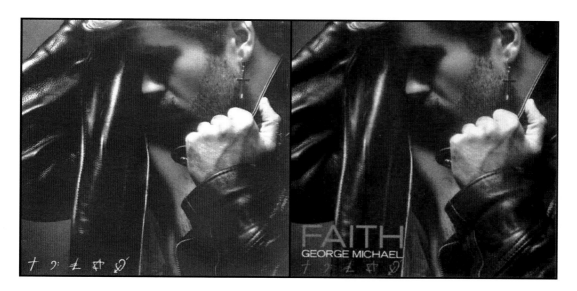

Faith/Father Figure/I Want Your Sex (Parts 1 & 2)/One More Try/Hard Day/Hand To Mouth/Look At Your Hands/Monkey/Kissing A Fool

CD & Cassette Bonus Tracks: *Hard Day (Shep Pettibone Remix)/A Last Request (I Want Your Sex Part 3)*

Produced by George Michael.

UK: Epic EPC 460000 (1987).

14.11.87: **1**-5-8-10-10-13-17-15-15-10-6-9-14-18-16-21-14-28-31-39-53-42-37-25-16-19-30-31-36-44-44-37-23-20-22-26-23-25-31-31-39-33-43-43-48-55-83-74-76-x-96

Pos	LW		Title, Artist		Peak Pos	WoC
1	New		**FAITH** GEORGE MICHAEL	EPIC	1	1
2	New		**ALL THE BEST** PAUL MCCARTNEY	PARLOPHONE	2	1
3	1 ↓		**TANGO IN THE NIGHT** FLEETWOOD MAC	WARNER BROTHERS	1	30

10.12.88: 93-86-86-78-71-55-48-55-71-50-63-46-48-51-57-56-63-65-64
15.09.90: 40-61-74

2.07.94: 99
22.04.95: 86-60-70-74-65-78
25.05.96: 74
12.02.11: 29-59
29.03.14: 80-81-77
5.01.17: 62-71-48-71-71
26.10.17: 88-58

Australia
23.11.87: peaked at no.**3**, charted for 48 weeks
15.01.17: 36

Austria
1.02.87: 29-6-4-4-8-**3**-6-8-16-14-14-11-12-13-15-17-25-21-18 (bi-weekly)

Belgium
5.02.11: 85-**33**-39-76

Canada
28.11.87: 62-23-9-5-3-3-3-2-**1-1**-2-3-3-4-3-2-2-4-4-7-8-8-12-10-10-9-12-11-9-5-4-5-4-4-
5-6-8-9-8-5-5-6-6-9-9-10-10-13-12-11-13-15-18-19-15-19-17-17-17-15-13-13-18-23-
24-27-30-38-39-56-65-74-89-97

25.02.17: 86-43-38-4-62-72-72-81-92

Finland
11.87: peaked at no.**5**, charted for 24 weeks

France
14.01.17: **52**-67-92

Italy
7.11.87: peaked at no.**2**, charted for 16 weeks

Germany
16.11.87: 41-14-**3**-**3**-8-9-16-18-16-20-18-16-18-14-14-14-13-12-16-14-29-24-33-29-35-
    33-33-29-29-23-26-23-21-26-36-46-44-40-46-38-44-39-44-47-54-56

Japan
21.11.87: peaked at no.**11**, charted for 29 weeks

Netherlands
14.11.87: 2-**1**-**1**-2-5-5-5-x-8-5-6-5-4-6-6-8-6-11-19-19-28-31-29-20-8-9-11-13-12-11-14-
    13-14-17-19-15-13-13-18-15-20-28-21-21-26

18.02.89: 56-59-61-62-72-80-94-85-89-85-100
5.02.11: 26-57

New Zealand
6.12.87: 7-5-**3**-3-4-4-6-6-7-7-6-4-**3**-8-12-14-21-17-31-25-34-34-x-42-42-31-23-39-31-38-
    34-33-38-40-34-36-37-44

Norway
14.11.87: 8-4-4-**3**-4-5-11-5-5-5-7-9-10-14-18

South Africa
5.12.87: peaked at no.**1** (1), charted for 20 weeks

Spain
30.11.87: peaked at no.**1** (1), charted for 49 weeks
31.07.05: 77-74-91

Sweden
11.11.87:11-**4**-8-14-12-10-17-26-34-42-41 (bi-weekly)
11.05.88: 27-42-31-49-40 (bi-weekly)
30.12.16: 42

Switzerland
15.11.87: 28-18-**4**-6-8-9-9-16-13-14-14-18-26-18-17-15-23-x-30
20.06.88: 9-12-12-17-13-24-21-14-22-20-23-30-25-20
8.01.17: 90

USA
21.11.87: 41-15-8-5-3-3-3-2-**1**-2-2-**1-1-1-1-1**-2-2-2-2-2-3-4-2-2-**1-1-1-1-1-1**-2-2-3-3-5-7-
    7-7-6-6-6-6-6-7-9-10-11-9-8-8-8-8-11-13-14-15-15-17-18-20-18-20-27-28-30-35-34-
    38-43-56-63-68-84-82-96

14.01.17: 18-45-x-64-65

Zimbabwe
7.02.88: peaked at no.**1** (1)

When he began writing songs for his first solo album, George took his inspiration from mega-successful black artists like Michael Jackson and Prince.

'I absolutely wanted to be in the same stratosphere,' he said. 'I'd gone from, a couple of years before, being perfectly happy with being on *Top Of The Pops*, to thinking, "I can do what Michael Jackson can do." I mean, he'd just done *THRILLER*, for f**ks sake! … I wanted to be in that vein but, mostly, I wanted to make music as good as theirs.'

George started working on the album that became *FAITH* in August and September 1986, when he recorded *I Want You Sex (Part 1)* and *Look At Your Hands* at London's

Sarm West studios. However, it wasn't until the following February that he started working on the album in earnest, choosing to do so at PUK Studios near Aarhus, Denmark ~ well away from any unwanted media attention.

George wrote and produced all the songs he recorded for *FAITH* himself, with the exception of *Look At Your Hands*, which he co-wrote with David Austin. George also played bass guitar, drums, keyboards and percussion on several of the recordings. He decided to title the album *FAITH* 'because I believe, today much more than during my adolescence, I believe that the forces of good and evil are real things.'

'Side one was all hits,' he said. 'From the point of view of the quality of the album, I expected it to do really well. When we were compiling it I was very, very pleased with it ~ I was surprised myself how well it had turned out.'

Seven of the tracks on *FAITH* were issued as singles:

- *I Want Your Sex*
- *Faith*
- *Hard Day*
- *Father Figure*
- *One More Try*
- *Monkey*
- *Kissing A Fool*

Six of the singles were big hits, the one exception being *Hard Day*, which was released exclusively in Australia and the United States ~ it failed to chart in either country, but it did peak at no.5 on Billboard's Hot Dance Club Songs chart.

Four singles ~ *Faith*, *Father Figure*, *One More Try* and *Monkey* ~ all went to no.1 on the Hot 100 in the United States, thus George became the first British male solo artist to achieve four chart topping singles from one album.

George promoted *FAITH* by embarking on his first solo tour, The Faith Tour, which opened with three dates in Tokyo, Japan, on the 19th, 20th and 21st February 1988. George played 47 dates in North America, 37 in Europe, 17 in Australasia and six in Asia, and wrapped up the tour in Barcelona, Spain, on 6th July 1989. Before taking the stage himself, George warmed up the crowd by opening each show by playing Janet Jackson's 1986 album, *CONTROL*.

FAITH made its chart debut in the UK at no.1, and the album topped the charts in Canada, the Netherlands, South Africa, Spain, the United States and Zimbabwe as well. In the United States, the album was no.1 for an impressive 12 non-consecutive weeks, and it became the first album by a white male solo artist to go to no.1 on Billboard's Top Black Albums chart, an achievement George was especially proud of.

'To me, that was a very big justification to what I was doing,' he said. 'I was much happier with it being the no.1 Black album than I was when it became the no.1 Pop album. There was much more of a sense of achievement. I knew this album would be a shock or a surprise to people in this country (America). The uptempo side of the new music is more overtly sexual, more black.'

Elsewhere, *FAITH* charted at no.2 in Italy, no.3 in Australia, Austria, Germany, New Zealand and Norway, no.4 in Sweden and Switzerland, no.5 in Finland and no.11 in Japan.

At the 1988 BRIT Awards, George won Best British Male Artist. The following year, at the 31st Grammy Awards, staged at the Shrine Auditorium, Los Angeles, on 22nd February 1989, *FAITH* won the prestigious Album of the Year award. George also picked up a nomination in the Best Vocal Performance, Male, category, but *Father Figure* didn't win the award.

FAITH was remastered and reissued in 2010-11 with a bonus CD:

- CD1 ~ Original track listing plus one bonus track: *A Last Request (I Want Your Sex, Part 3)*.

- CD2 ~ *Faith (Instrumental)/Fantasy/Hard Day (Shep Pettibone Mix)/I Believe When I Fall In Love/Kissing A Fool (Instrumental)/Love's In Need Of Love Today (Live at Wembley Arena, 1 April '87)/Monkey (7" Edit Version)/Monkey (A Cappella & Beats)/Monkey (Jam & Lewis Remix).*

Although not stated on the album's liner notes, *I Believe When I Fall In Love* was also a live recording.

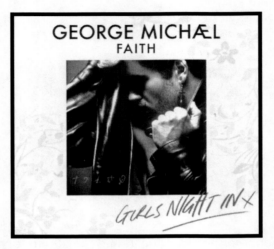

A special deluxe edition of *FAITH* was released around the same time, which included the two CDs, plus a remastered DVD that featured:

- George Michael and Jonathan Ross Have Words (1987)
- Music, Money, Love, Faith (February 1988)
- *I Want Your Sex (Music Video)*
- *I Want Your Sex (Music Video, Uncensored Version)*
- *Faith (Music Video)*
- *Father Figure (Music Video)*
- *One More Try (Music Video)*
- *Monkey (Music Video)*
- *Kissing A Fool (Music Video)*

FAITH is one of the best-selling albums of all-time, and has sold an estimated 25 million copies worldwide.

6 ~ LISTEN WITHOUT PREJUDICE VOL. 1

Praying For Time/Freedom! '90/They Won't Go When I Go/Something To Save/Cowboys And Angels/Waiting For That Day/Mother's Pride/Heal The Pain/Soul Free/Waiting (Reprise)

Produced by George Michael.

UK: Epic 467295 (1990).

15.09.90: **1**-2-2-3-4-4-7-7-9-14-16-19-19-19-14-10-10-9-9-11-17-16-13-3-3-3-10-11-7-7-13-19-16-20-24-26-36-39-47-51-59-54-57-59-57-53-59-60-61-56-62-72-70-74-72-68

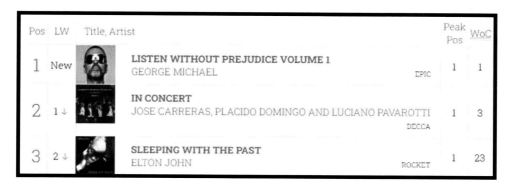

Pos	LW	Title, Artist		Peak Pos	WoC
1	New	**LISTEN WITHOUT PREJUDICE VOLUME 1** GEORGE MICHAEL — EPIC		1	1
2	1↓	**IN CONCERT** JOSE CARRERAS, PLACIDO DOMINGO AND LUCIANO PAVAROTTI — DECCA		1	3
3	2↓	**SLEEPING WITH THE PAST** ELTON JOHN — ROCKET		1	23

4.01.92: 75
28.08.93: 95

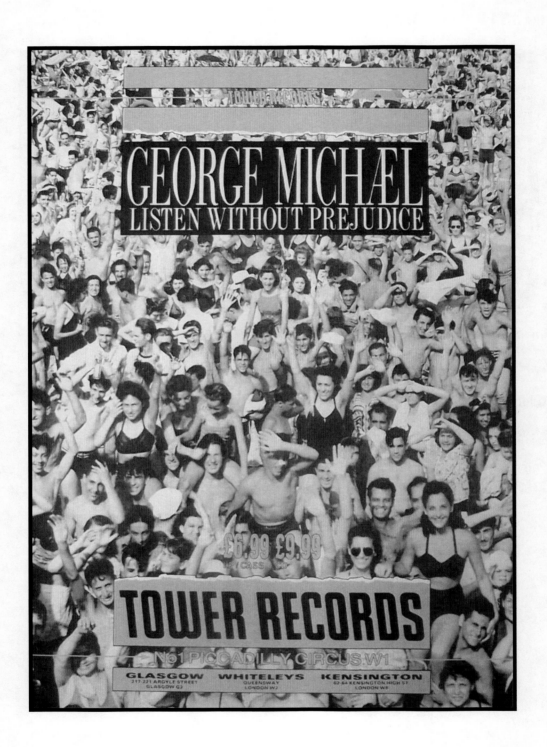

2.07.94: 89-x-84-96
25.05.96: 81
2.11.17: **1**-4-7-10-14-20-22-22-21-20-39-52-84 (MTV Unplugged)

Pos	LW	Title, Artist		Peak Pos	WoC
1	Re	**LISTEN WITHOUT PREJUDICE - VOL 1** GEORGE MICHAEL	SONY MUSIC CG	1	62
2	1↓	**BEAUTIFUL TRAUMA** PINK	RCA	1	2
3	New	**FLICKER** NIALL HORAN	CAPITOL	3	1

Australia
23.09.90: **2**-5-8-12-15-16-21-33-41-45
20.01.91: 41-38-24-33-31-35-39-33-31-34-35-37-32-39-37-26-15-15-10-12-6-14-13-19-
22-26-30-40-40-42-41
5.11.17: 5-10-28 (MTV Unplugged)

Austria
16.09.90: 28-20-6-**5-5**-9-13-11-17-12-18-20
3.11.17: 13-28-41 (MTV Unplugged)

Belgium
28.10.17: 9-**4**-10-14031028-38-42-33-16-24-32-47-60-88-x-84 (MTV Unplugged)

Canada
22.09.90: 44-18-9-8-8-7-**6**-7-7-7-13-16-14-18-18-18-17-14-16-19-17-17-17-13-13-24-25-
34-37-45-47-64-60-65-63-68-77-87-84-87-85-80-74-83-86-95-100
11.11.17: 34-84 (MTV Unplugged)

Finland
09.90: peaked at no.**10**, charted for 13 weeks

France
28.10.17: **20**-50-95 (MTV Unplugged)

Germany
17.09.90: 40-33-**7**-9-9-9-8-12-17-24-28-29-35-42-47-50-38-34-44-36-47-48-51-58-64-
73-84-82
27.10.17: 9-52 (MTV Unplugged)
29.12.17: 47-56 (MTV Unplugged)

Italy
8.09.90: peaked at no.**6**, charted for 14 weeks

Japan
3.09.90: peaked at no.**3**, charted for 10 weeks

Netherlands
15.09.90: 25-7-4-**2-2-2**-8-8-15-17-21-25-31-40-45-53-51-44-35-32-37-40-44-41-40-38-
43-47-52-63-68-61-43-30-20-20-18-18-17-14-14-15-18-24-32-37-44-66-88-94-99-100

28.10.17: 6-14-47-50-75-80-x-x-36-18-20-40-59-75-85 (MTV Unplugged)
8.08.20: 75 (MTV Unplugged)

New Zealand
30.09.90: 3-**2**-5-4-5-13-8-10-15-15-18-27-25-25-25-25-25-22-21-28-20-22-16-24-20-30-
38-41-x-x-41
30.10.17: 5-11-31 (MTV Unplugged)

Norway
8.09.90: 18-6-**4**-6-6-5-**4**-10-14

South Africa
27.09.90: peaked at no.**9**, charted for 12 weeks

Spain
10.09.90: peaked at no.**2**, charted for 25 weeks
29.10.17: 8-9-24-46-49-58-67-83 (MTV Unplugged)
31.12.17: 98-x-95
1.09.19: 92

Sweden
12.09.90: 11-4-**3**-9-20-34-36-23-22-28-30-41-48 (bi-weekly)

Switzerland
16.09.90: 8-9-**3**-4-8-11-12-16-22-28-34-x-40
29.10.17: 12-45-84-89 (MTV Unplugged)
31.12.17: 41-52-82 (MTV Unplugged)
21.07.19: 56

USA
29.09.90: 22-5-4-**2**-3-5-8-10-9-10-10-10-10-10-11-11-11-11-12-14-17-19-19-23-27-33-
  40-44-50-63-70-74-91-96

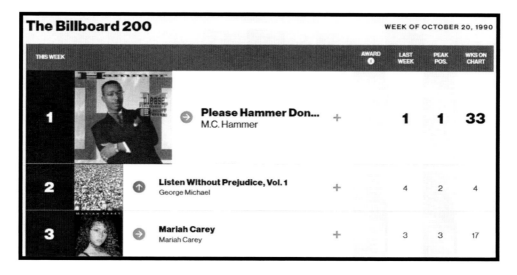

11.11.17: 41 (MTV Unplugged)

Zimbabwe
8.04.91: peaked at no.**10**

George recorded his second solo album, *LISTEN WITHOUT PREJUDICE VOL.1*, between December 1988 and July 1990 at two London studios, Metropolis and Sarm West.

'Everyone thought it meant "Listen to me without prejudice",' he said, explaining the album's title, 'which would have been so f**king wimpy and self-absorbed. It meant "I don't think you're prejudiced against me but if you are f**k off, you don't have to buy it".'

George wrote nine of the ten songs he recorded for *LISTEN WITHOUT PREJUDICE VOL.1*. One of them, *Waiting For That Day*, also credited Keith Richards and Mick Jagger, as the song's rhythm was similar to *You Can't Always Get What You Want*, which was a hit in 1969 for The Rolling Stones. The album also included one cover, *They Won't Go When I Go*, which was written by Stevie Wonder and Yvonne Wright, and was originally recorded by Stevie Wonder for his 1974 album, *FULFILLINGNESS' FIRST FINALE*.

Six singles were issued from *LISTEN WITHOUT PREJUDICE VOL.1* in various countries, as follows:

- *Praying For Time*
- *Waiting For That Day*
- *Freedom! '90*
- *Heal The Pain*
- *Cowboys And Angels*
- *Soul Free*

The first five singles all achieved Top 40 status in at least one country and, thanks to picking up airplay during the Gulf War, the B-side of *Waiting For That Day*, *Mothers Pride*, was a no.46 hit in the United States. *Soul Free* was released exclusively in Australia and Japan ~ it was a minor no.95 hit in Australia.

George's refusal to appear in any music videos for the singles released from *LISTEN WITHOUT PREJUDICE VOL.1* almost certainly had a detrimental effect on sales. *Praying For Time* was promoted with a fairly basic lyrics video, while the *Freedom! '90* promo featured supermodels lip-synching the song's lyrics. Had George himself appeared in the music videos, it's likely some of the singles would have charted higher, and in more countries, than they did.

LISTEN WITHOUT PREJUDICE VOL.1, like *FAITH* before it, made its chart debut in the UK at no.1, but the album didn't fare quite so well in other countries. The album achieved no.2 in Australia, the Netherlands, New Zealand, Spain and the United States, no.3 in Japan, Sweden and Switzerland, no.5 in Austria, no.6 in Canada, Italy and Norway, no.7 in Germany, no.9 in South Africa, and no.10 in Finland and Zimbabwe.

George was especially disappointed with sales of the album in the United States ~ so much so, he accused Sony Music of not fully supporting him as an artist, which resulted in him taking out a lawsuit against the company, to be set free from his recording contract.

George did plan on recording a follow-up album, *LISTEN WITHOUT PREJUDICE VOL.2*, which was pencilled in for a June 1991 release. However, for reasons that were never publically revealed, George decided to scrap the project. Four tracks he recorded for the project were subsequently released. Three ~ *Do You Really Want To Know*, *Happy* and *Too Funky* ~ featured on the 1992 charity compilation, *RED HOT + DANCE*, which was released to raise awareness of HIV/AIDS. *Too Funky* was also issued as a single, with the fourth new song *Crazy Man Dance* on the B-side.

MTV Unplugged Edition

LISTEN WITHOUT PREJUDICE VOL.1 was reissued in October 2017, as a 2CD standard edition and as a 3CD + DVD deluxe edition. The standard edition featured a remastered CD of the original album, plus a bonus CD featuring George's MTV Unplugged concert, which was recorded live at London's 3 Mills Studio on 11th October 1996. The deluxe edition featured a third CD of rarities, B-sides and remixes, while the DVD featured a documentary and music videos.

- CD1 ~ original album remastered.

- CD2 ~ MTV Unplugged: *Freedom! '90/Fastlove/I Can't Make You Love Me/ Father Figure/You Have Been Loved/Everything She Wants/The Strangest Thing/Older/Star People/Praying For Time*

  Bonus track: *Fantasy* ~ featuring Nile Rodgers

  Japan Bonus Track: *Don't Let The Sun Go Down On Me* ~ with Elton John

- CD3 (Deluxe Edition) ~ *Soul Free (Special Radio Edit)/Freedom! '90 (Back To Reality Mix)/Freedom! '90 (Back To Reality Mix Edit)/Fantasy/Freedom! '90 (Edit)/Cowboys And Angels (Edit)/If You Were My Woman (Live at Wembley Stadium, 11 June '88)/Too Funky (Single Edit)/Crazy Man Dance/Do You Really Want To Know/Happy/Too Funky (Extended)/Too Jazzy (Happy Mix)/Fantasy '98/Heal The Pain* (With Paul McCartney)/*Desafinado* (With Astrud Gilberto)

- DVD (Deluxe Edition) ~ *The Southbank Show 1990* (Documentary)/*Freedom! '90* (Music Video)/*Praying For Time* (Music Video)/*Freedom! '90* (MTV 10th Anniversary Performance)

The MTV Unplugged edition of *LISTEN WITHOUT PREJUDICE VOL.1* went straight to no.1 in the UK ~ 27 years after the original album had done the same. The reissue also achieved no.5 in Australia and New Zealand, no.6 in the Netherlands, no.8 in Spain, no.9 in Belgium and Germany, no.12 in Switzerland, no.13 in Austria, no.20 in France, no.34 in Canada and no.41 in the United States.

7 ~ FIVE LIVE

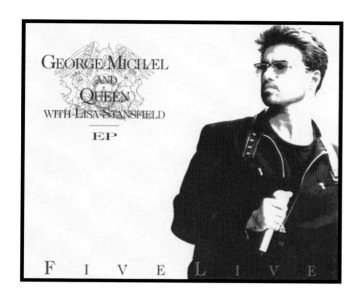

Somebody To Love ~ George Michael & Queen
Killer/Papa Was A Rollin' Stone ~ George Michael
These Are The Days Of Our Life ~ George Michael & Queen with Lisa Stansfield
Calling You ~ George Michael

Bonus Track (Outside UK): *Dear Friends* ~ Queen

Produced by George Michael, Queen & Roy Thomas Baker.

UK: Parlophone CDRS 6340 (1993).

1.05.93: **1-1-1**-2-4-6-16-22-27-56-72-x-74-x-x-97 (singles chart)

Pos	LW	Title, Artist		Peak Pos	WoC
1	New	**FIVE LIVE (EP)** GEORGE MICHAEL AND QUEEN WITH LISA STANSFIELD	PARLOPHONE	1	1
2	1 ↓	**YOUNG AT HEART {1993}** THE BLUEBELLS	LONDON	1	6
3	9 ↑	**I HAVE NOTHING** WHITNEY HOUSTON	ARISTA	3	2

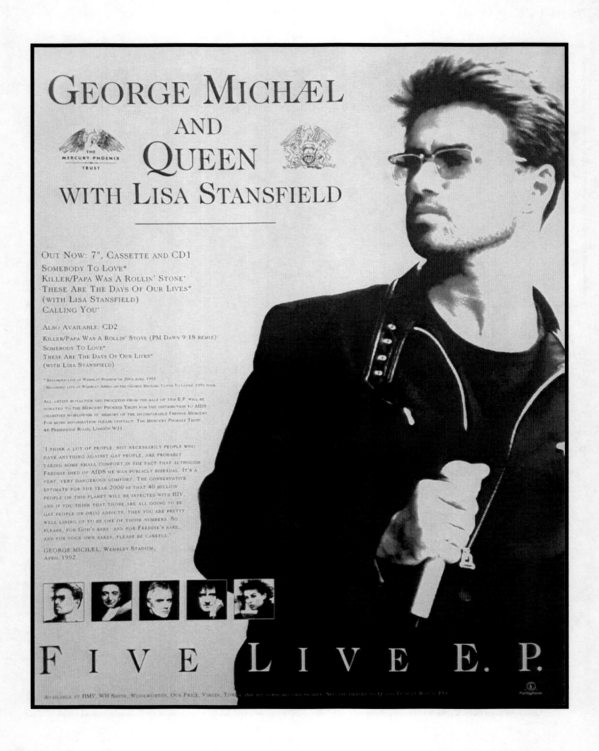

Australia
2.05.93: 38-24-24-**17-17**-19-23-30-38-45

Canada
8.05.93: 52-**32-32**-45-58-65-61-69-94

Austria
16.05.93: 32-9-7-5-3-8-7-7-**2**-8-4-6-17-15-17-15-16-25-16-18-36-34

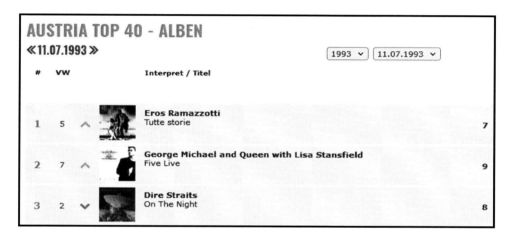

Finland
05.93: **38**

Netherlands
1.05.93: 65-7-**2-2**-4-4-7-7-9-10-15-19-24-24-25-23-23-34-37-30-32-36-52-62-98

Germany
10.05.93: 82-36-10-**8**-**8**-9-**8**-**8**-9-11-15-16-17-22-24-27-27-29-35-33-33-29-40-44-51-60-68-69-83-82

Ireland
25.04.93: 3-**1**-**1**-**1**-2-3-5-7-12-16-16-19-20-28 (singles chart)

Italy
24.04.93: peaked at no.**6**, charted for 9 weeks

Japan
2.06.93: peaked at no.**35**, charted for 4 weeks

New Zealand
23.05.93: 12-10-**9**-12-13-20-25-37

Norway
12.05.93: **19**

South Africa
26.06.93: **17**

Spain
24.05.93: peaked at no.**18**, charted for 5 weeks

Sweden
5.05.93: **45**-49-50 (bi-weekly)

Switzerland
2.05.93: 40-19-**6**-7-7-9-9-12-16-15-18-22-26-37-30-36-39-40

USA
8.05.93: **46**-47-50-60-61-71-80-90

Zimbabwe
9.08.93: peaked at no.**2**

The *FIVE LIVE* EP was treated as an album in most countries, but as a single in Ireland and the UK, where the bonus track *Dear Friends* by Queen was omitted.

George performed Queen's *Somebody To Love* and *These Are The Days Of Our Lives* at the Freddie Mercury Tribute concert, which was staged at Wembley Stadium on 20th April 1992. *Somebody To Love* was written by Freddie Mercury, and was originally recorded by Queen for their 1976 album, *A DAY AT THE RACES*. Queen took *Somebody To Love* to no.1 in the Netherlands, no.2 in Belgium and the UK, no.5 in Canada, no.6 in

Ireland, no.7 in South Africa, no.13 in the United States, no.15 in Australia, no.19 in Denmark and no.21 in Germany.

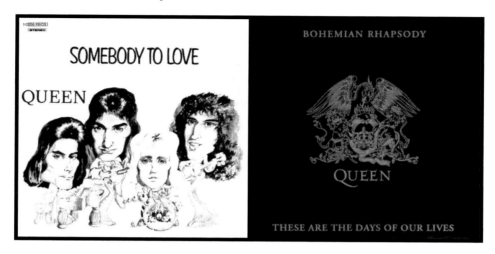

Queen's Roger Taylor wrote *These Are The Days Of Our Lives*, and Queen recorded the song for their 1991 album, *INNUENDO*. Following Freddie Mercury's passing, the track was issued as a double A-sided with *Bohemian Rhapsody*, and hit no.1 in Ireland and the UK. George's live version of *These Are The Days Of Our Lives* was effectively a duet with Lisa Stansfield, with the surviving members of Queen as their backing band.

The *Killer/Papa Was A Rollin' Stone* medley and *Calling You* were performed live by George at his concert staged at Wembley Arena on 22nd March 1991. *Killer* was written by Adamski and Seal, and was a hit in 1990 for Adamski, with Seal on lead vocals. *Papa Was A Rollin' Stone* was composed by Norman Whitfield and Barrett Strong, and is best known for the 1972-73 hit version by The Temptations.

Calling You was written by Bob Telson for the 1987 film, *Bagdad Café* ~ both he and Jevetta Steele recorded the song for the accompanying soundtrack album. Issued as a single, Jevetta Steele's version achieved no.8 in France and no.9 in Sweden.

In the UK, where it was classed as a single for chart purposes, the *Five Live* EP went straight to no.1, and stayed there for three weeks. The EP also topped the singles chart in Ireland.

In most countries, however, *FIVE LIVE* was seen as a mini-album, and so charted on the album charts. It achieved no.2 in Austria, the Netherlands and Zimbabwe, no.6 in Italy and Switzerland, no.8 in Germany, no.9 in New Zealand, no.17 in Australia and South Africa, no.18 in Spain, no.19 in Norway, no.32 in Canada, no.35 in Japan, no.38 in Finland, no.45 in Sweden and no.46 in the United States.

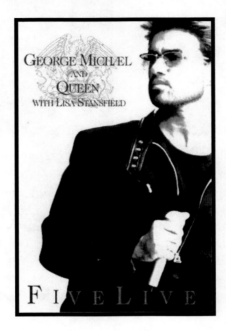

8 ~ OLDER

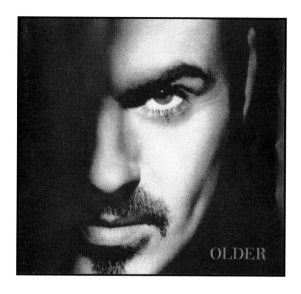

Jesus To A Child/Fastlove/Older/Spinning The Wheel/It Doesn't Really Matter/The Strangest Thing/To Be Forgiven/Move On/Star People/You Have Been Loved/Free

Produced by George Michael, Jon Douglas co-produced *Fastlove & Spinning The Wheel*.

UK: Virgin V 2802 (1996).

25.05.96: **1-1-1**-2-3-5-6-8-7-8-10-10-10-7-7-6-3-5-8-7-8-8-8-12-13-17-17-20-15-13-12-9-8-12-12- 9-9-7-11-10-21-8-9-13-16-18-21-22-25-25-21-14-10-7-13-14-19-25-31-36-42-39-37-28-24-31-33-46-24-14-7-9-16-23-30-35-35-45-54-60-65-36-43-44-38-30-32-32-39-52-69-63-99-93

Pos	LW	Title, Artist		Peak Pos	WoC
1	New	**OLDER** GEORGE MICHAEL	VIRGIN	1	1
2	2	**JAGGED LITTLE PILL** ALANIS MORISSETTE	MAVERICK	1	41
3	1 ↓	**1977** ASH	INFECTIOUS	1	2

9.05.98: 94-75-79-62-60-68-61-70-73-93-90-84-x-77-81-76-77-83-93-x-94-x-88-85-96
5.01.17: 84-x-63
26.10.17: 41-35-89

Australia

26.05.96: **1**-2-2-4-4-6-6-3-7-8-13-13-14-17-14-15-14-17-18-21-27-26-28-29-34-26-25-
21-20-15-16-23-31-38-33-33-36-49-x-x-38-44

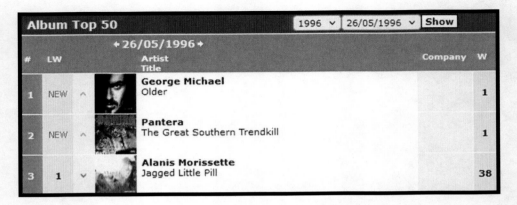

Austria

26.05.96: 4-**1**-2-4-3-4-11-15-14-16-13-13-15-17-22-19-22-22-20-20-16-25-26
26.01.97: 21-22-21-26-27-33-28-34-33-41

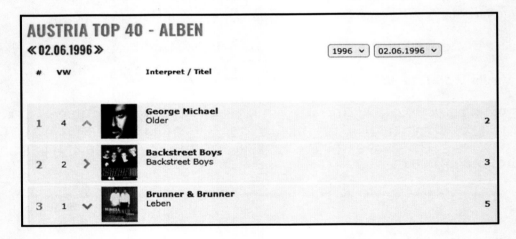

Belgium

25.05.96: 9-4-4-**3**-6-8-8-12-14-18-18-16-17-14-18-22-25-24-31-35-41-37-39
1.02.97: 41-x-44

Canada

27.05.96: **3**-4-**3**-7-6-8-6-8-9-13-15-16-18-23-25-26-30-46-45-45-50-47-52-59-69-75-79-
86-77-77

Finland

18.05.96: **3-3-3**-8-14-15-26-31-27-36-x-38-37

France
1.06.96: **2**-3-7-7-8-5-8

14.09.96: 15-21-23-x-x-x-28-37-45-49-x-x-x-47-27-x-25-24-31-38-x-50-x-x-50-35-36-40-43-43

Germany
20.05.96: 84-**3-3-3**-5-8-9-9-9-8-11-12-14-14-20-18-25-27-31-29-30-36-34-43-44-66-64-62-53-62-45-42-28-22-23-26-34-42-42-43-57-57-67-69-79-91-97-98
23.06.97: 70-62-66-80-77-78-86-93-98

Netherlands
25.05.96: 7-**1**-3-4-6-6-9-9-10-12-13-15-15-16-15-17-16-17-21-16-19-24-30-35-31-52-59-73-77-83-76-x-63-47-24-22-13-11-8-8-8-12-13-17-17-23-30-36-46-42-33-34-34-33-43-43-46-71-55-64-66-59-54-67-73-80-76-75-75-71-61-35-67-68-39-53-44-53-63-77-81-92-67-57-57-51-46-48-46-51-58-58-63-73-74-72-72-77-78-80-88-87-92-98-100

Italy
18.05.96: peaked at no.**2**, charted for 28 weeks

Japan
6.05.96: peaked at no.**3**, charted for 11 weeks

New Zealand
26.05.96: **1**-4-5-10-15-14-15-14-9-12-17-24-29-34-38-30-22-33-20-18-16-15-14-21-27-
25-31-19-30-34-28-28-28-28-28-23-27-34-45

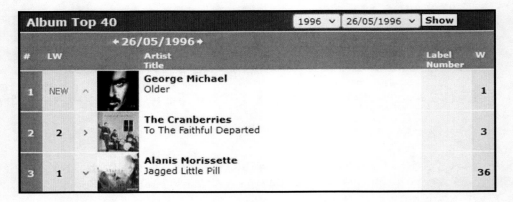

Norway
25.05.96: **1**-2-3-5-6-6-8-11-14-16-16-20-19-18-14-21-23-28-21-28-29

21.12.96: 24-26-20-15-16-20-24-20-24-33-32

Spain
13.05.96: peaked at no.**1** (6), charted for 33 weeks

Sweden

24.05.96: **1**-2-2-6-6-8-6-7-7-10-9-14-16-16-9-10-15-14-14-15-19-24-37-39-45-49-51-48-43-37-33-29-29-29-29-23-30-31-41

Switzerland

26.05.96: 4-3-**2**-5-5-8-9-10-11-10-10-11-10-10-10-11-14-19-18-15-22-21-33-46-x-46

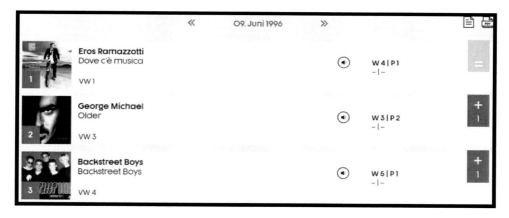

9.02.97: 48
8.01.17: 93
21.07.19: 80

USA

1.06.96: **6**-9-11-18-22-26-29-35-42-49-54-67-77-90

Zimbabwe

24.06.96: peaked at no.**3**

When his lover Anselmo Feleppa suddenly died in March 1993, George was devastated.

'I'm very proud of *LISTEN WITHOUT PREJUDICE*,' he said, 'but I think the whole experience of losing Anselmo, the period of grief, which was roughly two years that I didn't write a note of music. And then, the absolute knowledge that the next album I was going to write would be about grief and recovery. *OLDER* is my greatest moment, in my opinion, and as I've said before I don't ever want to be that inspired again.'

The five and a half year gap between albums was also the result of George's acrimonious legal battle with Sony Music, which he eventually lost but, having re-negotiated his contract, he signed with Virgin in the UK and internationally, and DreamWorks Records in North America. George recorded *OLDER* at London's Sarm West studios.

'I wrote *OLDER* within about I suppose eight months,' he said, 'and months I think I wrote the best, most healing piece of music that I've ever written in my life with that album.'

George wrote or co-wrote all eleven songs he recorded for *OLDER*, with Jon Douglas co-writing two tracks, *Fastlove* and *Spinning The Wheel*, and David Austin co-writing one, *You Have Been Loved*. George was also credited with playing bass guitar, drums, keyboards and percussion on the album.

Musically, George took much of his inspiration from the Brazilian composer, Antonio Carlos Jobim, who died in 1994, but his real inspiration for the sombre mood of the album was Anselmo Feleppa.

'There was a dedication to him (Anselmo) on the album,' he said, 'and fairly obvious male references. To my fans and the people that were really listening, I felt like I was trying to come out with them.'

At the time, George also changed his overall image, from the way he looked to the clothes he chose to wear.

'I had very short hair,' he said, 'I had really a kind of gay look in a way. I think I was trying to tell people I was okay with it, I just really didn't want to share it with journalists.'

Six singles were released from *OLDER* in most countries:

- *Jesus To A Child*
- *Fastlove*
- *Spinning The Wheel*
- *Older*
- *Star People '97*
- *You Have Been Loved*

Having refused to shoot any music videos to promote the singles from his *LISTEN WITHOUT PREJUDICE VOL.1* album, George did film promos for the first four singles from *OLDER*, and he made several live appearances on *Top Of The Pops* in the UK. Impressively, all six singles became Top 3 hits in the UK, making George the first artist to achieve this feat with six singles from one album.

Elsewhere, the singles generally fared much better than the singles from *LISTEN WITHOUT PREJUDICE VOL.1* had done, but after *Jesus To A Child* and *Fastlove*, the hits dried up in North America ~ a situation George blamed on his former record company, Sony Music, and a lack of airplay.

OLDER maintained George's impressive run of chart topping albums in the UK ~ it held the no.1 spot for three weeks. The album also hit no.1 in Australia, Austria, the Netherlands, New Zealand, Norway, Spain and Sweden, and peaked at no.2 in France, Italy and Switzerland, no.3 in Belgium, Canada, Finland, Germany, Japan and Zimbabwe, and a disappointing no.6 in the United States.

Just eighteen months after it was released, *OLDER* was reissued as a 2CD edition titled *OLDER & UPPER*. The bonus CD featured six songs and three music videos, plus various interactive links:

Fastlove (Part II)/Spinning The Wheel (Forthright Mix)/Star People '97 (Radio Version/The Strangest Thing '97 (Radio Version)/You Know That I Want To/Safe/ Jesus To A Child (Music Video)/Fastlove (Music Video)/Spinning The Wheel (Music Video)

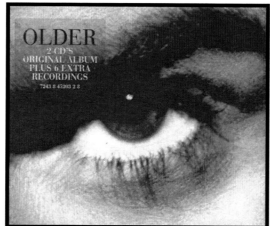

THE BEST OF

WHAM!

IF YOU WERE THERE . . .

featuring I'M YOUR MAN / CLUB TROPICANA / WAKE ME UP BEFORE YOU GO-GO
FREEDOM / THE EDGE OF HEAVEN / WHAM RAP! / YOUNG GUNS (GO FOR IT!)
LAST CHRISTMAS / WHERE DID YOUR HEART GO? plus EVERYTHING SHE WANTS '97
24/11/97 available on CD/MC/MD, also available The Best of Wham! - The Video

9 ~ THE BEST OF WHAM!

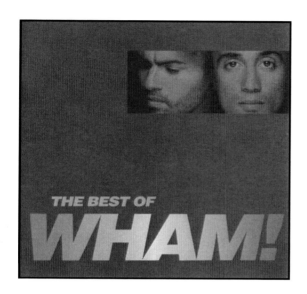

If You Were There/I'm Your Man/Everything She Wants/Club Tropicana/Wake Me Up Before You Go-Go/Like A Baby/Freedom/The Edge Of Heaven/Wham Rap!/Young Guns (Go For It!)/Last Christmas/Where Did Your Heart Go?/Everything She Wants '97/I'm Your Man '96

UK: Epic 489020 (1997).

6.12.97: **4-4-4-4-4**-6-10-11-19-28-32-32-36-42-48-46-45-55-65-69-78-83-81-80-78-88
8.08.98: 87-56-46-54-66-80-99
12.12.98: 95-94-94
2.01.99: 89-81

Australia
21.12.97: 43-47-41-35-32-**29**-36-39

Austria
21.12.97: 30-**23**-26-31-29-42-39-42-46-43-49

Belgium
29.11.97: 17-7-**5**-6-7-7-6-7-7-10-12-22-32-31-42-44-46

Finland
6.12.97: **35-35**

France
14.01.17: **97**-98

Germany
8.12.97: 93-68-83-80-99-x-45-43-49-47-**40**-54-62-98

Italy
13.12.97: peaked at no.**14**, charted for 7 weeks

Japan
12.12.97: peaked at no.**30**, charted for 9 weeks

Netherlands
29.11.97: 98-65-30-23-19-**18**-20-31-41-67-70-74-81

New Zealand
22.02.98: 39-**29**-34-47

Spain
29.12.97: peaked at no.**19**, charted for 19 weeks

Switzerland
11.01.98: 45-47-**28**-46-35-41-x-45

This was Wham!'s second greatest hits album, after 1986's *THE FINAL*, and was sub-titled 'If You Were There …'. One of the duo's hits, *Bad Boys*, was omitted from the compilation because George had grown to hate it.

Not surprisingly, *THE BEST OF WHAM!* charted highest in the UK, where it made its chart debut at no.4 ~ a position it held for five straight weeks, without ever rising any higher. The compilation also achieved no.5 in Belgium, no.14 in Italy, no.18 in the Netherlands, no.19 in Spain, no.23 in Austria, no.28 in Switzerland, no.29 in Australia, no.30 in Japan, no.35 in Finland and no.40 in Germany.

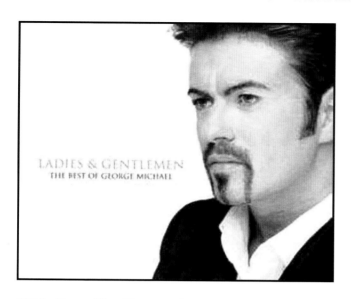

CD1: From The Heart ~ *Jesus To A Child/Father Figure/Careless Whisper (7" Version)/ Don't Let The Sun Go Down On Me/You Have Been Loved/Kissing A Fool/I Can't Make You Love Me/Heal The Pain/A Moment With You/Desafinado/Cowboys And Angels/ Praying For Time/One More Try/A Different Corner (New Mix)*

CD2: For The Feet ~ *Outside/As/Fastlove/Too Funky/Freedom! '90/Star People '97/Killer-Papa Was A Rollin' Stone/I Want Your Sex (Part II)/The Strangest Thing '97/Fantasy/Spinning The Wheel/Waiting For That Day/I Knew You Were Waiting (For Me)/Faith/Somebody To Love*

Cassette Bonus Track: *Waltz Away Dreaming*

CD2 (North America): *Outside/Fastlove/Too Funky/Freedom! '90/Star People '97/Killer-Papa Was A Rollin' Stone/I Want Your Sex (Part II)/Monkey/Spinning The Wheel/Waiting For That Day (You Can't Always Get What You Want)/I Knew You Were Waiting (For Me)/Hard Day/Faith/Somebody To Love*

CD2 (Japan): *Outside/As/Fastlove/Too Funky/Freedom! '90/Star People '97/Killer-Papa Was A Rollin' Stone/I Want Your Sex (Part II)/Monkey/Spinning The Wheel/Waiting For That Day/I Knew You Were Waiting (For Me)/Hard Day/Faith/Somebody To Love*

UK: Epic 491705 (1998).

21.11.98: **1-1-1-1-1-1-1-1**-2-4-4-6-6-5-10-14-14-6-14-14-13-15-18-15-14-14-16-20-21- 21-29-28-28-21-24-27-33-40-43-39-40-37-49-51-58-75-55-49-50-64-65-79-98-x-x-

100-89-80-67-x-96

Pos	LW	Title, Artist		Peak Pos	WoC
1	New	**LADIES & GENTLEMEN - THE BEST OF** GEORGE MICHAEL	EPIC	1	1
2	1↓	**THE BEST OF 1980-1990 & B-SIDES** U2	ISLAND	1	2
3	2↓	**THE MASTERPLAN** OASIS	CREATION	2	2

8.04.00: 63-52-60-75-86
8.07.00: 100-78-98-x-x-63-57-61-72
29.03.03: 74-73-100-x-x-69-87
20.03.04: 67-52-68-83-x-x-x-x-98
8.01.05: 47-49-48-55-78
5.01.17: 8-11-4-4-8-9-14-13-11-8-20-22-17-21-34-37-35-58-58-70-75-89-93
26.10.17: 9-15-26-46-39-65-77-75-76-82-89

Australia
22.11.98: **2-2**-5-6-6-8-5-5-5-7-9-10-12-12-18-23-25-25-26-21-28-29-34-33-28-27-30-38-
39-49

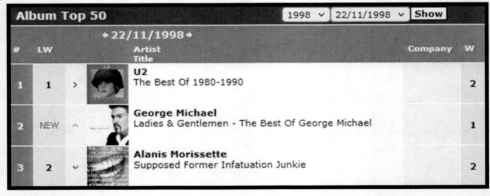

8.08.99: 34-13-9-13-9-12-11-20-17-25-47
2.01.00: 49-24-33-46
14.03.10: 21-32
8.01.17: 14-8-11-17-15-29-39-40-34-45
5.11.17: 42-29

Canada
16.11.98: 85-86-**15**-32-37-37-37-37-32-32-26-43-51-56-58-56-68-70-91

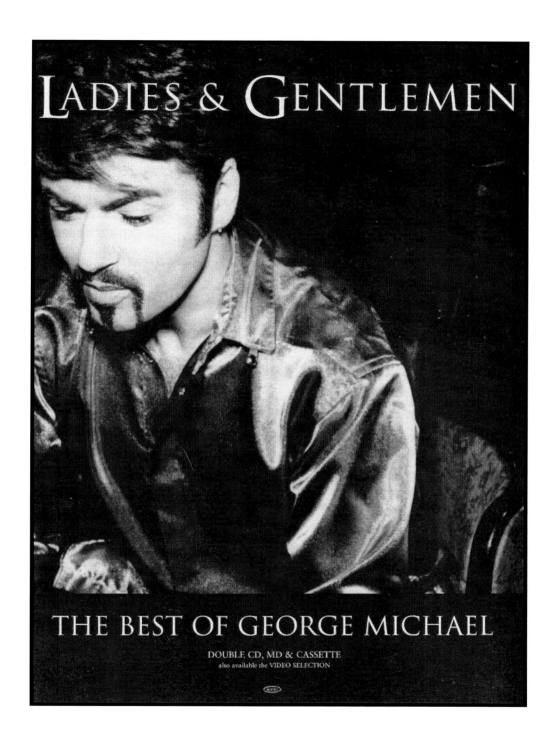

Austria
22.11.98: 4-3-4-8-9-6-5-7-**2**-5-6-13-21-19-30-29

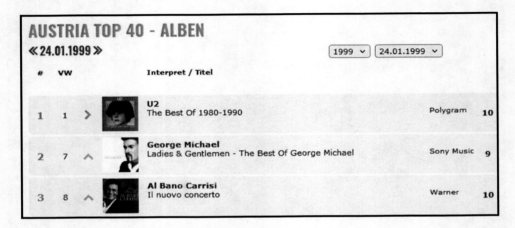

23.05.99: 28-30-23-29-35-41-44-44-35-42-42-33
11.04.04: 50-56-60-67-65
13.01.17: 31-20

Belgium
14.11.98: 14-6-4-3-3-**2**-3-3-4-7-5-4-5-4-4-7-15-16-17-17-19-23-25-21-25-28-30-32-39-
42-36-35-37-42

Finland
14.11.98: 12-12-10-13-17-14-11-**5**-7-11-13-19-26-20-28

France
31.12.16: 76-58-**39**-45-51-63-83

Germany
23.11.98: **3-3-3**-6-11-9-3-6-3-6-11-11-11-13-22-29-12-14-11-9-6-9-20-21-17-21-39-37-
37-42-32-31-31-36-35-46-44-45-48-51-65-65-76-79-100
27.12.99: 57-41-51-58-59-68-78-88-81-99
30.12.16: 50-43-28-77
29.12.17: 82
19.07.19: 93

Italy
14.11.98: peaked at no.**2**, charted for 26 weeks

Japan
6.11.98: peaked at no.**23**, charted for 4 weeks

Netherlands

14.11.98: 18-5-4-4-**2-2-2-2-2**-3-5-5-9-8-7-6-9-16-13-3-4-4-6-7-7-5-5-7-9-12-11-11-13-
19-22-23-23-23-27-26-32-33-34-38-36-44-51-28-29-28-35-45-62-69-70-64-63-55-60-
67-72-80-86-96

23.02.02: 85-90
31.08.02: 97
8.08.20: 77
9.01.21: 95

New Zealand

29.11.98: 7-6-6-8-6-10-6-11-**3**-7-8-9-12-21-16-17-34-43-23-17-23-28-28-26-29-35-41-
31-20-26-26-25-28-22-35-36-43-43-34-36-24-25-32-35-40-29-19-22-44-40-43-50
2.01.17: 30-16-26

Norway

21.11.98: 3-2-3-6-5-4-**1-1**-5-5-7-10-18-22-28-29-33

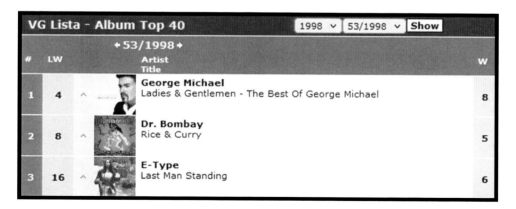

31.12.16: 29

Spain
16.11.98: peaked at no.**4**, charted for 30 weeks

Sweden
19.11.98: 5-**2**-5-9-14-12-14-10-16-26-25-33-33-44-59-47-59-56-x-x-28-14-14-13-14-20-
   25-35-41-44-50-42-36-31-41-54-58
30.12.16: 33

Switzerland
22.11.98: **5-5**-6-7-8-8-8-7-6-6-7-8-16-15-16-23-27-31-27-29-25-22-25-22-27-28-31-36-
   x-49
27.09.15: 92
1.01.17: 11-14-15-48-51
7.01.18: 91
21.07.19: 70-x-98

USA
28.11.98: **24**-39-58-59-79-88-91-77-74-79-82-84-89-91-96
14.01.17: 84-x-41

As part of his settlement with Sony Music, George was contractually obliged to release a greatest hits album, and *LADIES & GENTLEMEN – THE BEST OF GEORGE MICHAEL* was the result.

The compilation took in his solo career to date, and was issued as a double album, with the first disc mostly ballads ~ 'From The Heart' ~ and the second disc more uptempo, dance recordings ~ 'For The Feet'.

LADIES & GENTLEMEN featured three duets not previously issued on one of George's albums, namely *I Knew You Were Waiting (For Me)* with Aretha Franklin, *Don't Let The Sun Go Down On Me* with Elton John and *Desafinado* with Astrud Gilberto. The cassette edition also included George's collaboration with Toby Bourke, *Waltz Away Dreaming*, as a bonus track.

Most of the hits featured on the album were the original album versions, but the single version of *Careless Whisper* was used, and *A Different Corner* was remixed especially for the album. The album also featured two new songs, both of which were issued as singles and became hits:

- *Outside*
- *As*

As was a cover of a Stevie Wonder song, which George recorded as a duet with Mary J. Blige ~ however, its release, both as a single and on *LADIES & GENTLEMEN*, was blocked in the United States by Mary J. Blige's record company, following George's arrest in a public restroom at Will Rogers Memorial Park in Beverly Hills, California, on 7th April 1998, for engaging in a lewd act.

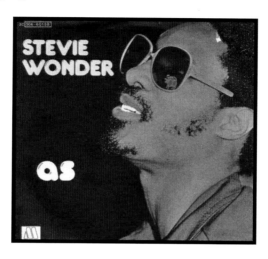

George, despite his falling out with Sony Music, wanted *LADIES & GENTLEMEN* to do well.

'It clearly shows the two sides of my appeal,' he said, 'f**k off pop songs people can't resist and songs that make you feel, and they (Sony Music) are putting it out at a reasonable price, which I'm pleased about.'

LADIES & GENTLEMEN went straight to no.1 in the UK, and held the top spot for an impressive eight weeks. The compilation also hit no.1 in Norway, and achieved no.2 in Australia, Austria, Belgium, Italy, the Netherlands and Sweden, no.3 in Germany and New Zealand, no.4 in Spain, no.5 in Finland and Switzerland, no.15 in Canada, no.23 in Japan and no.24 in the United States.

A similarly titled home DVD, featuring 23 of George's music videos, was released in 1999.

One of George's closest friends in the music business was the former Spice Girl, Geri Halliwell. It wasn't until after his passing that Geri revealed George had generously donated all his British proceeds from *LADIES & GENTLEMEN* to the UK's leading HIV/AIDS and sexual health charity, The Terence Higgins Trust.

11 ~ SONGS FROM THE LAST CENTURY

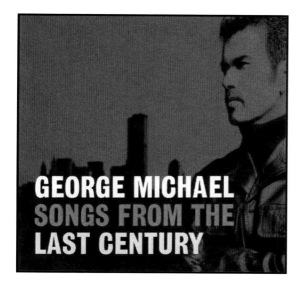

Brother, Can You Spare A Dime/Roxanne/You've Changed/My Baby Just Cares For Me/The First Time Ever I Saw Your Face/Miss Sarajevo/I Remember You/Secret Love/Wild Is The Wind/Where Or When/It's All Right With Me (Instrumental)

Produced by George Michael & Phil Ramone.

UK: Virgin CDV 2920 (1999).

18.12.99: **2**-3-3-17-14-16-18-25-33-39-43-52-72-76-27-25-26-70

Pos	LW	Title, Artist		Peak Pos	WoC
1	1	**COME ON OVER** SHANIA TWAIN	MERCURY	1	88
2	New	**SONGS FROM THE LAST CENTURY** GEORGE MICHAEL	VIRGIN	2	1
3	4 ↑	**THE MAN WHO** TRAVIS	INDEPENDIENTE	1	29

29.07.00: 83-81-84-93-89-91
28.10.00: 84-89

Australia
19.12.99: **12**-19-17-33-39-42-48

Austria
19.12.99: 13-19-**12**-19-**12**-23-31-38-47

Belgium
18.12.99: 28-16-18-17-18-17-**11**-15-17-21-22-27-38-49

Canada
20.12.99: **33-33**-35-**33**-54-64-72-67-67-79-78-96

France
11.12.99: 17-16-16-14-**7**-9-15-18-22-30-43-55-64-70

Germany
20.12.99: **4**-7-5-8-7-8-15-21-28-35-45-60-61-66-82-92

Italy
6.01.00: peaked at no.**4**, charted for 10 weeks

Japan
6.12.99: peaked at no.**59**, charted for 3 weeks

Netherlands
18.12.99: 13-**6**-8-10-15-14-18-23-28-37-49-61-72-79-98-93

New Zealand
26.12.99: **8-8-8-8-8**-46-37

Norway
18.12.99: 15-16-**13**-27-27-37-35-x-37-x-39

Spain
6.12.99: peaked at no.**11**, charted for 10 weeks

Sweden
16.12.99: **16**-28-32-32-27-30-31-46-x-x-58

Switzerland
19.12.99: 8-**6-6**-12-14-13-21-23-28-44-46-65-80-88

SONGS FROM THE LAST CENTURY was very different from George's previous albums, in that it was an album of cover versions ~ songs from the last century, that is, songs from the 20th century. The songs George chose to cover were mostly old jazz standards and his own interpretations of more recent songs.

George's version of The Police's 1978 hit *Roxanne*, which was written by Sting, was released as a promo CD single in the UK, select European countries and Japan, ahead of *SONGS FROM THE LAST CENTURY*, but it wasn't given a full release and it wasn't a hit anywhere.

George admitted *Roxanne* wasn't one of his favourite Police songs, but the two British songwriters who impressed him most during his career were Sting and U2's Bono, so he really wanted to cover one of their songs on the album.

'So really it was a matter of what Sting song can I do?' he explained. 'And, to be honest, I really like to cover songs that, not that I think that could not necessarily be better, but that I don't think were perfect in the first place. I've never really liked *Roxanne* that much, but it's a great song. I don't like the original record that much.'

SONGS FROM THE LAST CENTURY made its chart debut in the UK at no.2, kept off the top spot by Shania Twain's *COME ON OVER* ~ it was the first, and what proved to be the only, solo album released by George during his lifetime that failed to go to no.1.

Outside the UK, *SONGS FROM THE LAST CENTURY* achieved no.4 in Germany and Italy, no.6 in the Netherlands and Switzerland, no.7 in France, no.8 in New Zealand, no.11 in Belgium and Spain, no.12 in Australia and Austria, no.13 in Norway, no.16 in Sweden, no.33 in Canada and no.59 in Japan.

SONGS FROM THE LAST CENTURY failed to enter the Top 100 of the Billboard 200 in the United States, where the album peaked at a lowly no.157.

12 ~ PATIENCE

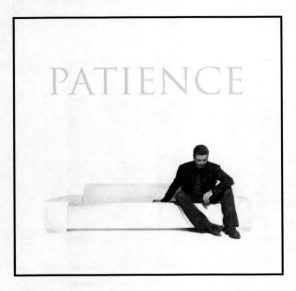

Patience/Amazing/John And Elvis Are Dead/Cars And Trains/Round Here/Shoot The Dog/ My Mother Had A Brother/Flawless (Go To The City)/American Angel/Precious Box/ Please Send Me Someone (Anselmo's Song)/Freeek '04/Through/Patience (Pt.2)

North America: *Patience/Amazing/John And Elvis Are Dead/Cars And Trains/Round Here/My Mother Had A Brother/Flawless (Go To The City)/American Angel/Precious Box/Please Send Me Someone (Anselmo's Song)/Freeek! '04/Through*

Japan Bonus Track: *Please Send Me Someone (Anselmo's Song) (Alternative Version)*

Produced by George Michael.

UK: Aegean / Sony Music 515402 2 (2004).

27.03.04: **1**-2-4-8-11-16-21-24-35-49-52-51-60-49-43-43-21-29-45-52-61-64-71-86

Pos	LW	Title, Artist			Peak Pos	WoC
1	New	**PATIENCE** GEORGE MICHAEL		AEGEAN	1	1
2	New	**GREATEST HITS** GUNS N' ROSES		GEFFEN	2	1
3	1 ↓	**CALL OFF THE SEARCH** KATIE MELUA		DRAMATICO	1	20

13.11.04: 82-96-x-x-79-82-100-92

Australia
28.03.04: **2**-3-5-8-11-17-17-10-21-16-26-33-33-35-39-48-41-36-19-17-15-6-12-21-27-34-42-36

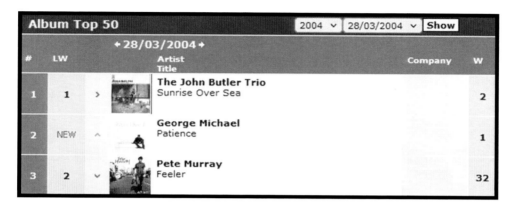

Austria
28.03.04: **3-3**-5-4-9-11-16-17-24-23-39-39-63-68

Belgium
20.03.04: 25-**5-5**-6-9-8-13-12-16-24-31-35-41-41-56-63-63-67-78-75-62-67-87

Finland
20.03.04: **3**-7-12-14-16-24-x-34

Germany
29.03.04: **1**-4-5-5-10-10-15-20-26-37-39-60-81-76-85-94-84-90-90

Japan
7.03.04: peaked at no.**26**, charted for 8 weeks

Italy
18.03.04: peaked at no.**1** (1), charted for 27 weeks

Netherlands
20.03.04: 5-2-**1**-3-3-4-6-10-8-13-18-31-34-34-41-26-31-34-32-42-36-37-43-43-45-37-
   39-74

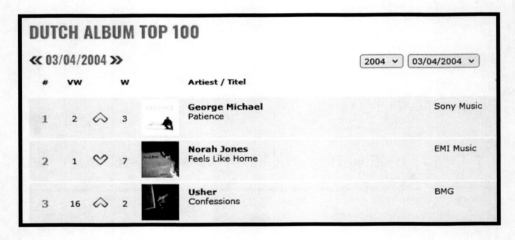

New Zealand
28.03.04: **2**-5-4-4-14-17-23-24-35-40

Norway
27.03.04: **11**-15-23-27-30

Switzerland
28.03.04: **2**-5-6-8-7-10-12-14-20-31-37-44-61-62-87-83-75-80-x-84-86

Sweden
26.03.04: **1**-6-9-10-14-12-15-18-32-41

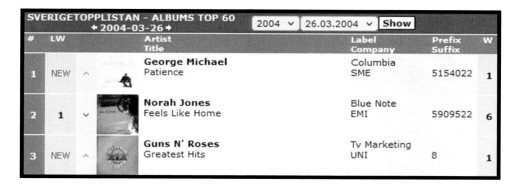

USA
5.06.04: 29-**12**-25-49-35-63-94-x-x-x-52-100

George re-signed with Sony Music on 17th November 2003, and early the following year he released his first album of original songs for eight years, since *OLDER* in 1996.

'I struggled for a long time to come up with a title,' he admitted. 'Quite often, the title emerges from the last few tracks you record for an album. My best work tends to be towards the end of the album because most of the anxiety is gone … I couldn't think of anything.'

Then, when George hit upon *PATIENCE*, it made sense to him for two reasons.

'One, because of the time and energy I had spent on the Iraq situation and the secular versus religious world situation,' he said. 'To me, we are being introduced via satellite in a very rude manner. On top of that, we have war, which almost all of us believe is about oil. I believe the only thing that will save us from total destruction is patience.'

The back of the album's sleeve saw two boys ~ one white, one Asian ~ pictured, which George said are supposed to represent the fact that it is our children who will decide whether or not we get through this.

'Second, of course, my fans,' said George. 'The most patient fans in pop history as far as I am concerned, who had to wait eight years since my last collection of songs. No fan should have to wait that long.'

Six singles were released from *PATIENCE* in various countries:

- *Freeek!*
- *Shoot The Dog*
- *Amazing*
- *Flawless (Go To The City)*
- *Round Here*
- *John And Elvis Are Dead*

The first five singles all achieved Top 40 status in at least one country. The sixth, *John And Elvis Are Dead* ~ John Lennon and Elvis Presley, that is ~ was only issued as a digital download single, and wasn't a hit anywhere.

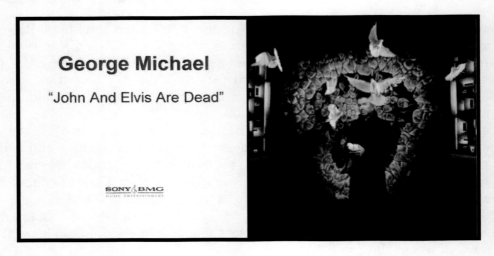

As well as the UK, *PATIENCE* hit no.1 in Germany, Italy, the Netherlands and Sweden, and charted at no.2 in Australia, New Zealand and Switzerland, no.3 in Austria and Finland, no.5 in Belgium, no.11 in Norway, no.12 in the United States and no.26 in Japan.

Following its release, George announced *PATIENCE* would be his last physical album, and he said that any future music would be made freely available for download only, with fans encouraged to make a donation to one of his favourite charities. This would also relieve the pressure on him to release a new album every few years, and afford him more privacy.

'I've been very well remunerated for my talents over the years,' he said, 'so I really don't need the public's money. I'd like to have something on the internet which is a charitable download site where anyone can download my music for free. I'll have my favourite charities up there and people will hopefully donate to that.'

13 ~ TWENTY FIVE

CD1: For Living ~ *Everything She Wants (12" Remix)/Wake Me Up Before You Go-Go/Freedom/Faith/Too Funky (Single Version)/Fastlove/Freedom! '90/Spinning The Wheel/Outside/As/Freeek!/Shoot The Dog/Amazing/Flawless (Go To The City) (Radio Edit)/An Easier Affair*

Japan Bonus Track: *Kissing A Fool*

CD2: For Loving ~ *Careless Whisper (Single Edit)/Last Christmas (Single Edit)/A Different Corner (Single Edit)/Father Figure/One More Try/Praying For Time/Heal The Pain/Don't Let The Sun Go Down On Me/Jesus To A Child/Older/Round Here/You Have Been Loved/John And Elvis Are Dead/This Is Not Real Love*

Japan Bonus Track: *Club Tropicana*

CD3: For The Loyal (Limited Edition) ~ *Understand/Precious Box/Roxanne/Fantasy/Cars And Trains/Patience/You Know That I Want To/My Mother Had A Brother/If You Were There/Safe/American Angel/My Baby Just Cares For Me/Brother, Can You Spare A Dime/Please Send Me Someone (Anselmo's Song)/Through*

Digital Download Bonus Tracks: *I'm Your Man/Edith & The Kingpin/I'm Your Man (Video)/John And Elvis Are Dead (Video)/An Easier Affair (Video)/Father Figure (Video)*

CD1: For Living (North America) ~ *Everything She Wants (12" Remix)/Wake Me Up Before You Go-Go/Feeling Good/Faith/Too Funky/Fastlove/Freedom! '90/Spinning The*

Wheel/Outside/As/Freeek!/Shoot The Dog/Amazing/Flawless (Go To The City)/An Easier Affair

CD2: For Loving (North America) ~ *Careless Whisper/Last Christmas/A Different Corner/Father Figure/One More Try/Praying For Time/Heal The Pain/Don't Let The Sun Go Down On Me/Jesus To A Child/Older/The First Time Ever I Saw Your Face/You Have Been Loved/John And Elvis Are Dead/This Is Not Real Love*

CD3: For The Loyal (North America Best Buy Exclusive) ~ *Understand/Precious Box/ Roxanne/Fantasy/Cars And Trains/Patience/You Know That I Want To/My Mother Had A Brother/If You Were There/Safe/American Angel/My Baby Just Cares For Me/ Brother, Can You Spare A Dime/Please Send Me Someone (Anselmo's Song)/Through*

UK: Aegean / Sony Music 88697009002 (2006).

25.11.06: **1**-5-8-8-9-5-10-21-26-32-40-57-68-67

Pos	LW	Title, Artist		Peak Pos	WoC
1	New	**TWENTY FIVE** GEORGE MICHAEL	AEGEAN	1	1
2	1 ↓	**HIGH TIMES - SINGLES 1992-2006** JAMIROQUAI	COLUMBIA	1	2
3	New	**OVERLOADED - THE SINGLES COLLECTION** SUGABABES	ISLAND	3	1

24.03.07: 98
23.06.07: 69-55-75-88
19.12.09: 100-50-68-88-95
5.04.14: 78-72
5.01.17: 47-45-19-35-55-37-59-75-72-45-81-x-x-82
26.10.17: 61-21-40-29-21-36-24-19-15-11-15-18-23-29-32-46-49-43-51-54-67-61-72-82-
72-94-95-x-x-87-x-85-99-x-x-x-69-83-76-82-77-85-71-86-89-88-99-95-x-100-x-96-83-
94-99-85-93-89-98-x-x-x-98-74-78-71-94-94-98-73-85-87-94-87-82-91-95-92-x-x-64-
x-90-78-82-78-79-80-83-62-58-56-59-49-48-49-47-50-44-55-61-52-65-58-50-53-60-
70-76-66-60-58-61-66-59-53-33-46-55-62-62-66-62-71-70-69-73-82-62-47-42-35-68-
54-51-41-48-43-46-62-60-55-66-66-55-61-61-52-38-54-50-55-57-50-59-58-65-60-57-
53-60-59-66-77-70-80-75-67-30-35-51-58-55-57-63-57-58-62-62-58-55-60-47-52-45-
45-59-58-56-60-42-45-47-44-50-49-46-31-55-56-53-54-58-52-53-74-64-66-68-59-61-
62-53-51-58-69-77-78-71-62-32-19-50-54-62-62-65-65- (still charting)

Australia
26.11.06: 25-23-31-42-47-40-48
28.02.10: 49-24-**9**-16-28
8.01.17: 11-13-41-23-27-39
5.11.17: 28-33

Austria
24.11.06: **19-19**-27-45-52-72
27.07.07: 52
3.02.17: 51-72-58-66

Belgium
18.11.06: 48-4-**2**-8-10-10-10-11-14-20-28-51-55-56-69-75-93

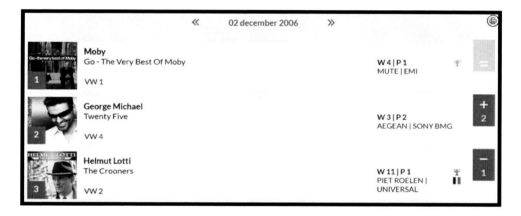

30.06.07: 86-65-66-75-97

Canada
14.01.17: **10**-18-34-37-76-35-63-58-98

Finland
7.07.07: **39**

France
7.01.17: 80-**45**-61-74-100

Germany
24.11.06: **13**-45-43-57-66-68-60-79-90
2.01.14: 69-67

Italy
16.11.06: peaked at no.**2**, charted for 34 weeks

Netherlands
18.11.06: **2**-9-10-17-17-18-20-28-25-27-30-41-45-51-60-65-80-82-91

30.06.07: 13-11-29-53-50-52-43-49-85-75-81
20.10.07: 76-96
24.05.08: 91-91
6.09.08: 90
2.01.21: 75

New Zealand
20.11.06: **18**-25-36
2.01.17: 29

Switzerland
26.11.06: **2**-8-15-22-30-33-43-42-49-76-90

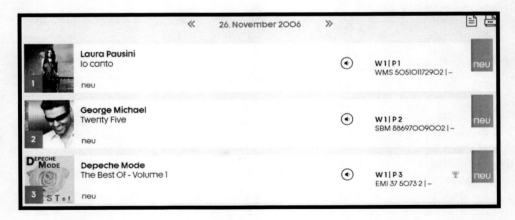

1.01.17: 45-15-38

Norway
25.11.06: **10**-13-16-23-26-31-37-37-40-28-37
20.06.09: 40
1.10.11: 32

Spain
19.11.06: 11-**10**-18-27-33-33-45-46-52-60-93

Sweden
23.11.06: **3**-11-16-29-34-25-33-48-53-28-40-x-55

USA
19.04.08: 25
14.01.17: **12**-35

George's second greatest hits album, appropriately titled *TWENTY FIVE*, marked his 25th anniversary in the music business.

The compilation was released in two formats, a standard 2CD edition and a limited deluxe edition of 3CDs + DVD. Unlike George's previous greatest hits package, *LADIES & GENTLEMEN*, *TWENTY FIVE* also featured several songs he recorded with Wham! The track listing of the second CD was slightly different from the international edition in North America, as was the Japanese release.

TWENTY FIVE featured two new songs and a duet version of a previously released song: *An Easier Affair, This Is Not Real Love* and *Heal The Pain. This Is Not Real Love* was a duet with Mutya Buena of Sugababes fame, while George re-recorded *Heal The Pain* as a duet with Paul McCartney. *An Easier Affair* and *This Is Not Real Love* were both issued as singles, and achieved Top 40 status in one or more countries.

The bonus CD of the deluxe edition featured some lesser known songs, and came with a 36 page colour booklet, which included song lyrics and screen shots from music videos. The digital download version came with a further two bonus tracks, plus four music videos.

TWENTY FIVE gave George another no.1 album in the UK, and elsewhere the album achieved no.2 in Belgium, Italy, the Netherlands and Switzerland, no.3 in Sweden, no.10 in Canada, Spain and Norway, no.13 in Germany, no.18 in New Zealand, no.19 in Austria, no.23 in Australia, no.25 in the United States, no.39 in Finland and no.45 in France.

Following George's passing in December 2016, *TWENTY FIVE* re-entered the Billboard 200 in the United States, and rose to a new peak of no.12.

Australian Tour Edition 2010

George played three concerts in Australia in early 2010: Perth on 20th February, Sydney on 26th February and Melbourne on 3rd March.

To coincide with these dates, a tour edition of *TWENTY FIVE* was issued in Australia only, with a bonus CD that featured the following tracks:

Kissing A Fool/Feeling Good/My Baby Just Cares For Me/Roxanne/Club Tropicana/ I'm Your Man (Extended Stimulation)

The tour edition rose to no.9, fourteen places higher than the album achieved when it was originally released.

14 ~ SYMPHONICA

Through/My Baby Just Cares For Me/A Different Corner/Praying For Time/Let Her Down Easy/The First Time Ever I Saw Your Face/Feeling Good/John And Elvis Are Dead/ One More Try/Cowboys And Angels/Idol/Brother, Can You Spare A Dime/Wild Is The Wind/You've Changed

Digital Bonus Track: *I Remember You*

Deluxe Edition: *Through/My Baby Just Cares For Me/A Different Corner/Praying For Time/Let Her Down Easy/The First Time Ever I Saw Your Face/Feeling Good/John And Elvis Are Dead/Roxanne/One More Try/Going To A Town/Cowboys And Angels/Idol/ Brother, Can You Spare A Dime/You Have Been Loved/Wild Is The Wind/You've Changed*

Digital Bonus Track: *I Remember You*

Produced by George Michael & Phil Ramone.

UK: Aegean / Virgin EMI 3769932 (2014).

29.03.14: **1**-2-3-4-6-10-13-25-26-19-31-47-58-80-x-x-x-63-62-63-65-78
5.01.17: 73-x-46-91
2.11.17: 96

Pos	LW	Title, Artist			Peak Pos	WoC
1	New	**SYMPHONICA** GEORGE MICHAEL		EMI	1	1
2	New	**KISS ME ONCE** KYLIE MINOGUE		PARLOPHONE	2	1
3	3	**GIRL** PHARRELL WILLIAMS		COLUMBIA	1	3

Australia
30.03.14: **11**-12-16-26

Austria
28.03.14: **7**-16-19-32-56-70
13.01.17: 52-27

Belgium
29.03.14: **3-3**-8-9-20-22-23-29-40-52-59-59-46-57-x-89-x-x-48-63-79-85

Germany
28.03.14: **6**-17-42-50-57-68
13.01.17: 92

Netherlands
22.03.14: **2**-6-4-11-23-36-18-33-35-69-57-83

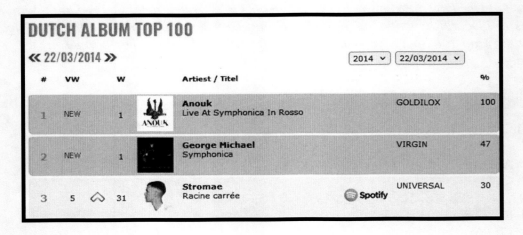

2.08.14: 51-71-68-76

France
29.03.14: **15**-48-71-98

Italy
27.03.14: peaked at no.**2**, charted for 15 weeks

New Zealand
24.03.14: **14**-17-18-22-33-x-29-24-28

Norway
29.03.14: **33**

Spain
23.03.14: **16**-24-33-40-43-56-67-90-78-95

Switzerland
23.03.14: **6**-11-18-31-68-80-63-95
1.01.17: 73-x-52

USA
5.04.14: **60**

SYMPHONICA was George's first full length live album ~ it also proved to be the last album he released during his lifetime.

George's Symphonica: The Orchestral Tour kicked off on 22nd August 2011 in Prague, Czech Republic. He played a total of 67 dates, all of them within Europe, and rounded off the tour with three concerts at London's Earls Court on the 13th, 14th and 17th October 2012.

SYMPHONICA was a mix of George's own songs and cover versions, recorded live during George's four dates at London's Royal Albert Hall in October 2011 and September 20212. The string arrangements were recorded at two different studios, London's AIR Studios and Legacy Studios in New York City. The album was produced by George with Phil Ramone ~ sadly, it also proved to be Phil Ramone's final project, as he lost his life on 30th March 2013, due to complications following heart surgery.

Three singles were released from *SYMPHONICA*:

- *Let Her Down Easy*
- *Going To A Town*
- *Feeling Good*

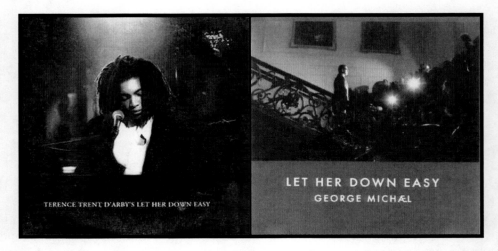

Let Her Down Easy, which was written and originally recorded by Terence Trent D'Arby, was a minor no.53 hit in the UK, but both *Going To A Town* and *Feeling Good* failed to chart anywhere.

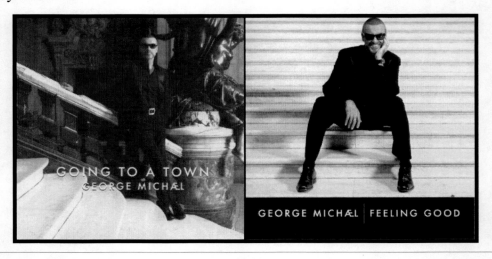

Two versions of *SYMPHONICA* were released, a standard one CD edition and a 2CD deluxe edition. The week the album was issued, a further live recording ~ *Patience* ~ was made available as a free download on amazon.com, for one week only.

SYMPHONICA gave George his seventh and final solo no.1 album in the UK, from just eight releases ~ the only album that failed to top the chart was *SONGS FROM THE LAST CENTURY*, which peaked at no.2.

Around the world, *SYMPHONICA* charted at no.2 in the Netherlands and Italy, no.3 in Belgium, no.6 in Germany and Switzerland, no.7 in Austria, no.11 in Australia, no.14 in New Zealand, no.15 in France, no.16 in Spain, no.33 in Norway and a lowly no.60 in the United States.

15 ~ LAST CHRISTMAS

Last Christmas/Too Funky (Single Edit)/Fantasy/Praying For Time (Remastered)/Faith (Remastered)/Waiting For That Day (Remastered)/Heal The Pain (Remastered)/One More Try (Remastered)/Fastlove (Part 1)/Everything She Wants (Edit)/Wake Me Up Before You Go-Go (Edit)/Move On/Freedom! '90 (Remastered)/Praying For Time (MTV Unplugged Version)/This Is How (We Want You To Get High)

Japan Bonus Track: *Last Christmas (Pudding Mix)*

UK: Sony Music 19075978832 (2019).

21.11.19: 11-**9**-15-13-15-16-18-30-58

Australia
24.11.19: **7**-10-15-17-22-21-22-40

Austria
29.11.19: 61-**60**

Belgium
16.11.19: **74**

Canada
23.11.19: 52-54-58-48-52-50-30
28.11.20: 79-49-40-32-36-**19**-30
4.12.21: 77-45-40-39-30-27

Germany
22.11.19: **85**

Italy
14.11.19: peaked at no.**70**, charted for 2 weeks

Netherlands
16.11.19: 81
5.12.20: 46-34-28-32-**13**
1.01.22: 61

Spain
17.11.19: **37**-41-77-86-69-90

USA
23.11.19: 55-85-60-64-59
12.12.20: 79-65-67-50-95
11.12.21: 86-80-64-**48**-54

LAST CHRISTMAS served as the soundtrack album to the similarly titled romantic comedy, which premiered in November 2019 and starred Emilia Clarke, Henry Golding and Emma Thompson. Towards the end of the film, Andrew Ridgeley made a brief, uncredited cameo in the film, when he was seen in the audience. The film was directed by Paul Feig.

    LAST CHRISTMAS was the first album to be credited to both George solo and Wham!, although only three Wham! hits featured on the soundtrack: *Last Christmas*, *Everything She Wants* and *Wake Me Up Before You Go-Go*. The soundtrack also included one previously unreleased song, *This Is How (We Want You To Get High)*, which George had completed in 2015.

    In the UK, *LAST CHRISTMAS* peaked at no.9 in its second weeks on the chart, and made its debut at no.1 on the Soundtracks chart.

Pos	LW	Title, Artist		Peak Pos	WoC
1	New	**LAST CHRISTMAS - OST** GEORGE MICHAEL & WHAM	SONY MUSIC CG	1	1
2	New	**PEAKY BLINDERS** ORIGINAL SOUNDTRACK	UMC	2	1
3	2 ↓	**THE GREATEST SHOWMAN** MOTION PICTURE CAST RECORDING	ATLANTIC	1	91

LAST CHRISTMAS achieved no.7 in Australia, no.13 in the Netherlands, no.19 in Canada, no.37 in Spain and no.48 in the United States. The soundtrack album was also a minor hit in Austria, Belgium, Germany and Italy.

GEORGE'S TOP 10 ALBUMS

This Top 10 has been compiled using the same points system as for the Top 40 Singles listing.

Rank/Album/Points

1   *FAITH* ~ 2462 points

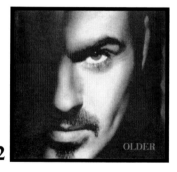

2   *OLDER* ~ 2407 points

3   *LISTEN WITHOUT PREJUDICE VOL.1*

                 ~ 2185 points

4   *MAKE IT BIG* ~ 2156 points

5   *LADIES & GENTLEMEN* ~ 2143 points

6 *TWENTY FIVE* ~ 1663 points
7 *THE FINAL* ~ 1657 points
8 *PATIENCE* ~ 1458 points
9 *SONGS FROM THE LAST CENTURY* ~ 1215 points
10 *FANTASTIC* ~ 1172 points

George's debut solo album *FAITH* is his most successful album, narrowly ahead of *OLDER*. In third place is *LISTEN WITHOUT PREJUDICE VOL.1*, with Wham!'s *MAKE IT BIG* and the compilation *LADIES & GENTLEMEN* not far behind.

George's most recent album to make the Top 10 is another compilation, *TWENTY FIVE*, which is ranked at no.6.

ALBUMS TRIVIA

To date, George has achieved 15 Top 40 albums in one or more of the countries featured in this book, including five with Wham! and one credited to George Michael & Wham!

There follows a country-by-country look at his most successful albums, starting with George's homeland.

Note: The *Five Live* EP was classed as an album in most countries, so is included here where relevant.

GEORGE IN THE UK

George has achieved 13 hit albums in the UK, which spent 1040 weeks on the chart.

No.1 Albums

1983	*FANTASTIC*
1984	*MAKE IT BIG*
1987	*FAITH*
1990	*LISTEN WITHOUT PREJUDICE VOL.1*
1996	*OLDER*
1998	*LADIES & GENTLEMEN*
2004	*PATIENCE*
2006	*TWENTY FIVE*
2014	*SYMPHONICA*

Most weeks at No.1

8 weeks	*LADIES & GENTLEMEN*
3 weeks	*THE FINAL*
3 weeks	*OLDER*
2 weeks	*FANTASTIC*
2 weeks	*MAKE IT BIG*

Albums with the most weeks

252 weeks	*TWENTY FIVE*
121 weeks	*OLDER*
119 weeks	*LADIES & GENTLEMEN*
116 weeks	*FANTASTIC*

92 weeks	*FAITH*
75 weeks	*LISTEN WITHOUT PREJUDICE VOL.1*
72 weeks	*MAKE IT BIG*
67 weeks	*THE FINAL*
38 weeks	*THE BEST OF WHAM!*
30 weeks	*PATIENCE*

The Brit Certified/BPI (British Phonographic Industry) Awards

The BPI began certifying albums in 1973, and between April 1973 and December 1978, awards related to a monetary value and not a unit value. When this system was abolished, the awards that were set remain in place today:

- Silver = 60,000, Gold = 100,000, Platinum = 300,000.

Multi-Platinum awards were introduced in February 1987.

In July 2013 the BPI automated awards, and awards from this date are based on actual sales (including streaming 'sales') since February 1994, not shipments.

9 x Platinum	*LADIES & GENTLEMEN* (January 2019) = 2.7 million
6 x Platinum	*OLDER* (December 1997) = 1.8 million
4 x Platinum	*MAKE IT BIG* (March 1987) = 1.2 million
4 x Platinum	*LISTEN WITHOUT PREJUDICE VOL.1* (February 1992) = 1.2 million
4 x Platinum	*FAITH* (September 1993) = 1.2 million
4 x Platinum	*TWENTY FIVE* (November 2019) = 1.2 million
3 x Platinum	*FANTASTIC* (February 1987) = 900,000
2 x Platinum	*THE BEST OF WHAM!* (January 1998) = 600,000
2 x Platinum	*SONGS FROM THE LAST CENTURY* (December 1999) = 600,000
2 x Platinum	*PATIENCE* (March 2004) = 600,000
Platinum	*THE FINAL* (December 1986) = 300,000
Gold	*SYMPHONICA* (April 2014) = 100,000
Silver	*LAST CHRISTMAS* (January 2020) = 60,000

GEORGE IN AUSTRALIA

George has achieved 14 hit albums in Australia, which spent 361 weeks on the chart.

No.1 Albums

1985	*MAKE IT BIG*
1996	*OLDER*

MAKE IT BIG topped the chart for two weeks, and *OLDER* for one week.

Albums with the most weeks

59 weeks	*LADIES & GENTLEMEN*
49 weeks	*FAITH*
44 weeks	*LISTEN WITHOUT PREJUDICE VOL.1*
40 weeks	*OLDER*
28 weeks	*FANTASTIC*
28 weeks	*MAKE IT BIG*
28 weeks	*THE FINAL*
28 weeks	*PATIENCE*
20 weeks	*TWENTY FIVE*

ARIA (Australian Recording Industry Association) Awards

Platinum = 70,000, Gold = 35,000

7 x Platinum	*LADIES & GENTLEMEN* = 490,000
5 x Platinum	*FAITH* = 350,000
2 x Platinum	*LISTEN WITHOUT PREJUDICE VOL.1* = 140,000
2 x Platinum	*OLDER* = 140,000
2 x Platinum	*THE BEST OF WHAM!* = 140,000
2 x Platinum	*TWENTY FIVE* = 140.000
Platinum	*PATIENCE* = 70,000
Gold	*SONGS FROM THE LAST CENTURY* = 35,000

GEORGE IN AUSTRIA

George has achieved 13 hit albums in Austria, which spent 232 weeks on the chart.

No.1 Albums

1996	*OLDER*

OLDER topped the chart for one week.

Albums with the most weeks

38 weeks	*FAITH*
35 weeks	*LADIES & GENTLEMEN*
33 weeks	*OLDER*
22 weeks	*FIVE LIVE* EP

20 weeks	*MAKE IT BIG*
15 weeks	*LISTEN WITHOUT PREJUDICE VOL.1*
14 weeks	*THE FINAL*
14 weeks	*PATIENCE*
11 weeks	*THE BEST OF WHAM!*
11 weeks	*TWENTY FIVE*

GEORGE IN BELGIUM (Flanders)

Since 1995, when the album chart was launched, George has achieved 10 hit albums in Belgium (Flanders), which spent 177 weeks on the chart.

No.2 Albums

| 1998 | *LADIES & GENTLEMEN* |
| 2006 | *TWENTY FIVE* |

Both albums spent one week at no.2.

Albums with the most weeks

34 weeks	*LADIES & GENTLEMEN*
27 weeks	*OLDER*
23 weeks	*PATIENCE*
22 weeks	*TWENTY FIVE*
19 weeks	*SYMPHONICA*
17 weeks	*THE BEST OF WHAM!*
16 weeks	*LISTEN WITHOUT PREJUDICE VOL.1*
14 weeks	*SONGS FROM THE LAST CENTURY*

GEORGE IN CANADA

George has achieved 10 hit albums in Canada, which spent 321 weeks on the chart.

No.1 Albums

| 1985 | *MAKE IT BIG* |
| 1988 | *FAITH* |

Most weeks at No.1

5 weeks	*MAKE IT BIG*
2 weeks	*FAITH*

Albums with the most weeks

84 weeks	*FAITH*
72 weeks	*MAKE IT BIG*
47 weeks	*LISTEN WITHOUT PREJUDICE VOL.1*
30 weeks	*OLDER*
20 weeks	*LAST CHRISTMAS*
19 weeks	*MUSIC FROM THE EDGE OF HEAVEN*
19 weeks	*LADIES & GENTLEMEN*
12 weeks	*SONGS FROM THE LAST CENTURY*

GEORGE IN FINLAND

George has achieved 11 hit albums in Finland, which spent 127 weeks on the chart.

No.1 Albums

1984	*MAKE IT BIG*

MAKE IT BIG topped the chart for four weeks.

Albums with the most weeks

24 weeks	*FAITH*
22 weeks	*MAKE IT BIG*
15 weeks	*FANTASTIC*
15 weeks	*THE FINAL*
15 weeks	*LADIES & GENTLEMEN*
13 weeks	*LISTEN WITHOUT PREJUDICE VOL.1*
12 weeks	*OLDER*
7 weeks	*PATIENCE*

GEORGE IN FRANCE

George has achieved nine hit albums in France, which spent 66 weeks on the chart.

His highest charting album is *OLDER*, which peaked at no.2.

Albums with the most weeks

27 weeks   *OLDER*
14 weeks   *SONGS FROM THE LAST CENTURY*
7 weeks   *LADIES & GENTLEMEN*

GEORGE IN GERMANY

George has achieved 14 hit albums in Germany, which spent 364 weeks on the chart.

No.1 Albums

2004   *PATIENCE*

PATIENCE topped the chart for one week.

Albums with the most weeks

62 weeks   *LADIES & GENTLEMEN*
57 weeks   *OLDER*
46 weeks   *FAITH*
33 weeks   *LISTEN WITHOUT PREJUDICE VOL.1*
30 weeks   *FIVE LIVE* EP
25 weeks   *MAKE IT BIG*
22 weeks   *FANTASTIC*
22 weeks   *THE FINAL*
19 weeks   *PATIENCE*
16 weeks   *SONGS FROM THE LAST CENTURY*

GEORGE IN ITALY

George has achieved 13 hit albums in Italy, which spent 229 weeks on the chart.

No.1 Albums

1984   *MAKE IT BIG*
2004   *PATEINCE*

Most weeks at No.1

7 weeks   *MAKE IT BIG*

PATIENCE topped the chart for one week.

Albums with the most weeks

34 weeks	*TWENTY FIVE*
28 weeks	*OLDER*
27 weeks	*PATIENCE*
26 weeks	*LADIES & GENTLEMEN*
25 weeks	*MAKE IT BIG*
21 weeks	*THE FINAL*
16 weeks	*FAITH*
15 weeks	*SYMPHONICA*
14 weeks	*LISTEN WITHOUT PREJUDICE VOL.1*
10 weeks	*SONGS FROM THE LAST CENTURY*

GEORGE IN JAPAN

George had achieved 13 hit albums in Japan, which spent 178 weeks on the chart.

No.1 Albums

1984	*MAKE IT BIG*

Albums with the most weeks

44 weeks	*FANTASTIC*
29 weeks	*FAITH*
26 weeks	*MAKE IT BIG*
15 weeks	*THE FINAL*
11 weeks	*OLDER*
10 weeks	*LISTEN WITHOUT PREJUDICE VOL.1*

GEORGE IN THE NETHERLANDS

George has achieved 15 hit albums in the Netherlands, which spent 619 weeks on the chart.

No.1 Albums

1984	*MAKE IT BIG*
1986	*THE FINAL*
1987	*FAITH*

1996	*OLDER*
2004	*PATIENCE*

Most weeks at No.1

5 weeks	*MAKE IT BIG*
3 weeks	*THE FINAL*
2 weeks	*FAITH*

Albums with the most weeks

105 weeks	*OLDER*
74 weeks	*THE FINAL*
71 weeks	*LADIES & GENTLEMEN*
68 weeks	*FAITH*
66 weeks	*LISTEN WITHOUT PREJUDICE VOL.1*
48 weeks	*FANTASTIC*
45 weeks	*MAKE IT BIG*
36 weeks	*TWENTY FIVE*
28 weeks	*PATIENCE*
25 weeks	*FIVE LIVE* EP

GEORGE IN NEW ZEALAND

George has achieved 13 hit albums in New Zealand, which spent 301 weeks on the chart.

No.1 Albums

1983	*FANTASTIC*
1984	*MAKE IT BIG*
1986	*THE FINAL*
1996	*OLDER*

Most weeks at No.1

7 weeks	*THE FINAL*
3 weeks	*FANTASTIC*

Albums with the most weeks

58 weeks	*LADIES & GENTLEMEN*
40 weeks	*THE FINAL*
40 weeks	*FAITH*

39 weeks	*OLDER*
32 weeks	*LISTEN WITHOUT PREJUDICE VOL.1*
26 weeks	*FANTASTIC*
25 weeks	*MAKE IT BIG*
10 weeks	*PATIENCE*

GEORGE IN NORWAY

George has achieved 12 hit albums in Norway, which spent 147 weeks on the chart.

No.1 Albums

1984	*MAKE IT BIG*
1996	*OLDER*
1999	*LADIES & GENTLEMEN*

Most weeks at No.1

| 5 weeks | *MAKE IT BIG* |
| 2 weeks | *LADIES & GENTLEMEN* |

Albums with the most weeks

32 weeks	*OLDER*
19 weeks	*MAKE IT BIG*
17 weeks	*THE FINAL*
17 weeks	*LADIES & GENTLEMEN*
15 weeks	*FAITH*
13 weeks	*TWENTY FIVE*
9 weeks	*FANTASTIC*
9 weeks	*LISTEN WITHOUT PREJUDICE VOL.1*
9 weeks	*SONGS FROM THE LAST CENTURY*

GEORGE IN SOUTH AFRICA

George has achieved six hit albums in South Africa, which spent 111 weeks on the chart.

No.1 Albums

1984	*MAKE IT BIG*
1986	*THE FINAL*
1987	*FAITH*

Most weeks at No.1

| 10 weeks | *MAKE IT BIG* |
| 6 weeks | *THE FINAL* |

Albums with the most weeks

33 weeks	*THE FINAL*
24 weeks	*MAKE IT BIG*
21 weeks	*FANTASTIC*
20 weeks	*FAITH*
12 weeks	*LISTEN WITHOUT PREJUDICE VOL.1*

GEORGE IN SPAIN

George has achieved 11 hit albums in Spain, which spent 248 weeks on the chart.

No.1 Albums

| 1988 | *FAITH* |
| 1996 | *OLDER* |

OLDER topped the chart for six weeks, and *FAITH* for one week.

Albums with the most weeks

52 weeks	*FAITH*
36 weeks	*THE FINAL*
36 weeks	*LISTEN WITHOUT PREJUDICE VOL.1*
33 weeks	*OLDER*
30 weeks	*LADIES & GENTLEMEN*
19 weeks	*THE BEST OF WHAM!*
11 weeks	*TWENTY FIVE*
10 weeks	*SONGS FROM THE LAST CENTURY*
10 weeks	*SYMPHONICA*

GEORGE IN SWEDEN

George has achieved 11 hit albums in Sweden, which spent 211 weeks on the chart.

No.1 Albums

1996   *OLDER*
2004   *PATIENCE*

Both albums topped the chart for one week.

Albums with the most weeks

40 weeks   *OLDER*
37 weeks   *LADIES & GENTLEMEN*
33 weeks   *FAITH*
26 weeks   *LISTEN WITHOUT PREJUDICE VOL.1*
22 weeks   *MAKE IT BIG*
12 weeks   *TWENTY FIVE*
10 weeks   *PATIENCE*

GEORGE IN SWITZERLAND

George has achieved 13 hit albums in Switzerland, which spent 226 weeks on the chart.

No.1 Albums

1984   *MAKE IT BIG*

MAKE IT BIG topped the chart for one week.

Albums with the most weeks

38 weeks   *LADIES & GENTLEMEN*
33 weeks   *FAITH*
28 weeks   *OLDER*
23 weeks   *MAKE IT BIG*
20 weeks   *LISTEN WITHOUT PREJUDICE VOL.1*
20 weeks   *PATIENCE*
18 weeks   *FIVE LIVE* EP
14 weeks   *THE FINAL*
14 weeks   *SONGS FROM THE LAST CENTURY*
14 weeks   *TWENTY FIVE*

GEORGE IN THE USA

George has achieved 12 hit albums in the United States, which spent 275 weeks on the Top 100 of the Billboard 200.

No.1 Albums

1985   *MAKE IT BIG*
1988   *FAITH*

Most weeks at No.1

12 weeks   *FAITH*
 3 weeks   *MAKE IT BIG*

Albums with the most weeks

81 weeks   *FAITH*
73 weeks   *MAKE IT BIG*
34 weeks   *LISTEN WITHOUT PREJUDICE VOL.1*
17 weeks   *MUSIC FROM THE EDGE OF HEAVEN*
17 weeks   *LADIES & GENTLEMEN*
15 weeks   *LAST CHRISTMAS*
14 weeks   *OLDER*
 9 weeks   *PATIENCE*

RIAA (Recording Industry Association of America) Awards

The RIAA began certifying Gold albums in 1958, Platinum albums in 1976, and multi-Platinum albums in 1984. Gold = 500,000, Platinum = 1 million. Awards are based on shipments, not sales, and each disc is counted individually (so, for example, a double album has to ship 500,000 to be eligible for Platinum).

10 x Platinum   *FAITH* (December 1996) = 10 million
6 x Platinum   *MAKE IT BIG* (October 1994) = 6 million
2 x Platinum   *LISTEN WITHOUT PREJUDICE VOL.1* (September 1994) = 2 million
2 x Platinum   *LADIES & GENTLEMEN* (October 2000) = 2 million
Platinum   *MUSIC FROM THE EDGE OF HEAVEN* (October 1986) = 1 million
Platinum   *OLDER* (August 1996) = 1 million
Gold   *FANTASTIC* (August 1989) = 500,000

GEORGE IN ZIMBABWE

George has achieved seven hit albums in Zimbabwe.

No.1 Albums

1988   *FAITH*

FAITH topped the chart for one week.

Note: The number of weeks each album spent on the chart is not known.

Made in United States
North Haven, CT
21 October 2023

43028432R00170